FOURTH REVISED
AND EXPANDED EDITION

THROUGH JAPANESE EYES

RICHARD H. MINEAR

A CITE BOOK

New York

Copyright ©2008 by Richard H. Minear. Fourth Revised Edition

CITE books are distributed by The Apex Press,
777 United Nations Plaza, Suite 3C, New York, NY 10017
Phone: 1/800-316-2739
Fax: 1/800-316-2739
E-mail: cipany@igc.org
Web address: www.eyesbooks.org

CITE (Center for International Training and Education)
is a program of the Council on International and Public Affairs. The Apex
Press is an imprint of the Council.

Library of Congress Cataloging-in-Publication Data

Minear, Richard H.
Through Japanese eyes / by Richard H. Minear. -- 4th rev. and expanded ed.
p. cm.
Includes bibliographical references and index.
ISBN 0-938960-53-9 (pbk.) -- ISBN 0-938960-54-7 (hardcover)
1. Japan. I. Title.

DS806.M537 2008
952--dc22

                                    2007052177

Cover and interior design by Mary Ellen McCourt.
Printed in the United States of America.

For Kathy Masalski,

her colleagues in Asian Studies Outreach around the country,

and the K-12 teachers who have taken their programs.

My contacts with them over the past thirty years

have affected my own teaching of Japan

and the successive editions of this book.

ABOUT THE AUTHOR

Richard H. Minear is Professor of History at the University of Massachusetts Amherst. He received his B.A. from Yale in 1960 and his Ph.D. in History and East Asian Languages from Harvard in 1968. He lived in Japan from 1964 to 1966, from 1970 to 1971, and from 1992 to 1993; he made briefer visits in 1975, 1983, and 1994. He is author of *Japanese Tradition and Western Law* (1970); *Victors' Justice: The Tokyo War Crimes Trial* (1971), and *Dr. Seuss Goes to War* (1999). He is editor and translator of *Requiem for Battleship Yamato* (1985), *Hiroshima: Three Witnesses* (1990), *Black Eggs* (1994), the autobiography of Japanese historian Ienaga Saburō (2001), and *The Scars of War: Tokyo During World War II* (2007).

CONTENTS

INTRODUCTION

FOR MOST OF US living in the United States today, Japan means very specific things: cars, VCRs, camcorders. For sports fans, Japan means Ichiro Suzuki (really Suzuki Ichirō) and Hideki Matsui (really Matsui Hideki) and "Dice-K" Matsuzaka (really Matsuzaka Daisuke). To artists, Japan means ink painting, woodblock prints, flower arrangement, rock gardens, pottery. To others, especially to those older than fifty, Japan means World War II and/or economic threat.

As vivid as these images may be, they do not constitute a complete or balanced picture of Japan. Is Japan today an economic success? Why? What has modern life done to Japan and the Japanese? Do the Japanese control their technology, or does it control them?

Japanese today enjoy a prosperity that only the world's advanced nations know: more TV sets than people, heavy internet usage, MacDonald's hamburgers and Dunkin' Donuts and MTV. And the Japanese impact in the United States is enormous. Toyota is the world's largest manufacturer of cars. *Sushi* is increasingly a mainstream American food. Animé (cartoon films—the word comes from the loan-word in Japanese, *a-ni-mee-shon* [animation]) have U.S. fans in the millions. Growing numbers of Americans try each day to solve *sudoku* puzzles.

And yet Japanese are very different from Americans. Or are they? Indeed, is there a "typical" Japanese? If so, who is it? Is there a "typical" American? If so, who? And what do we do in searching for a "typical" person of any nationality?

In at least one sense, all humans are alike. Japanese, Americans, Chinese, Indians—all are confronted with the human condition: we are all born, we live, we die. But similarities between Japanese and Americans do not stop there. Both societies are highly industrialized; both find themselves asking what material prosperity means. So in reading about Japan we will find ourselves reflecting on the United States and on our own lives.

This volume has ten sections. It starts with a look at Japan's economic achievement since 1945 and some views of life in Japan today. It moves then

(Sections II through V) through a chronological treatment of Japanese history: before 1850, 1850-1940, World War II, the U.S. Occupation and since. Then follow sections on textbooks, on ecology, on gender, and on several current issues. The final section treats the experience in the U.S. of immigrants from Japan and their descendants.

Throughout, we focus on those issues that are most useful in helping U.S. students gain insight into their own lives, their own society, their own schools. *Through Japanese Eyes* achieves its purpose only if it meets this dual goal: to offer great readings about Japan that also stimulate thinking about the United States.

The first edition of *Through Japanese Eyes* appeared in 1974, nearly thirty-five years ago. The inspiration was *Through African Eyes*, the reader edited by Leon E. Clark. Lee Clark died in 2003 and has played no concrete part in the preparation of this fourth edition. But his influence lives on. Here, in tribute to Lee and his approach, is an excerpt from his "Foreword" to the third edition (1994):

> People—and nations—have a tendency to look at the outside world from their own perspectives. This is natural and perhaps necessary, for we are all prisoners of a particular space and time. But how limited and biased our information would be if we listened only to ourselves!
>
> The main goal of *Through Japanese Eyes* is to broaden our perspective by presenting a Japanese view of Japan and the world. Most of the material in this book has been written by Japanese, and it comes from a variety of sources: autobiographies, fiction, poetry, newspaper and magazine articles, letters, diaries, and historical documents....
>
> Human beings, no matter where they live, face the same basic needs: to eat, to work, to love, to play, to get along with their fellow men. Learning how the Japanese respond to these needs may teach us something useful for our own lives.
>
> More important, getting to know the Japanese as people—sharing in their thoughts and feelings, their beliefs and aspirations—should help us to develop a sense of empathy, a feeling of identity, with human beings everywhere. In the end, we should know more about ourselves— indeed, we should have an expanded definition of who we are—because we will know more about the common humanity that all people share. Self-knowledge is the ultimate justification for studying about others.

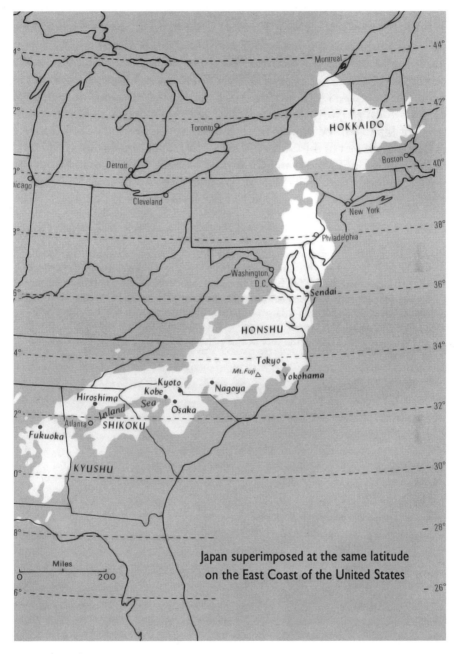

Japan superimposed at the same latitude
on the East Coast of the United States

Source: E. O. Reischauer, *Japan: The Story of a Nation,* New York: Alfred A.
Knopf, 1970.

I
JAPAN TODAY

TEN COMPARISONS BETWEEN JAPAN AND THE UNITED STATES

Editor's Introduction: Economists and political scientists often rely on statistics to compare countries. If—it's a big if—the statistics are commensurate (that is, if they measure the same things in the two countries by the same yardstick), they can be useful.

The following essay offers ten statistical comparisons. Which of these comparisons is the most important? The least important? What factors resist statistical treatment? How do we measure culture? Love? Happiness? [1]

Area. Japan's land area—the four main islands of Honshu, Shikoku, Kyushu, and Hokkaido, plus the many smaller islands—measures nearly 378,000 square kilometers. The U.S. land area is 9,828,000 square kilometers. If you prefer to work with square miles, one square kilometer is 0.38608 square mile.

What is the ratio? Can you find individual U.S. states as large as Japan? Are there other nations closer to Japan's size? Germany? The United Kingdom?

Population. In 2004, Japan's population was 128,000,000. The U.S. population that year was 294,000,000. What other countries are close to Japan in population?

Knowing land area and population, we can calculate population density (people per square kilometer). Compare Japan's figure with the U.S. figure. Other nations include the United Kingdom (246) and Germany (231). What is the population of New York state? Of your own state? How many states have populations as dense as Japan?

Age distribution. Does it matter how many people in a given population are young or old? Why? What are some of the effects of having a large proportion of the population under ten or over sixty-five?

The following two graphics come from U.N. sources:

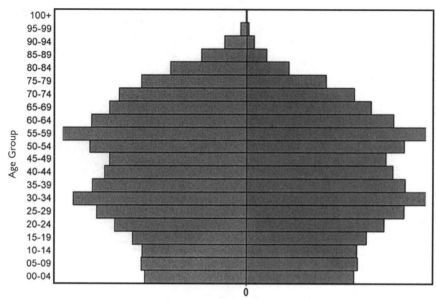

Japan Age Distribution

Age Group	Males	Females
00-04	3,014,676	2,856,789
05-09	3,109,536	2,947,679
10-14	3,072,970	2,927,847
15-19	3,362,557	3,205,908
20-24	3,854,557	3,687,760

The chart allows a maximum cohort size (male or female) of almost 5,500,000.
Source: UN Statistics Division.

Japan today has the largest population over sixty-five of any major power. Japan's figure is 20.1 percent. Compare that with these figures: Italy 19.7 percent, Germany 18.8 percent, United States 12.3 percent.

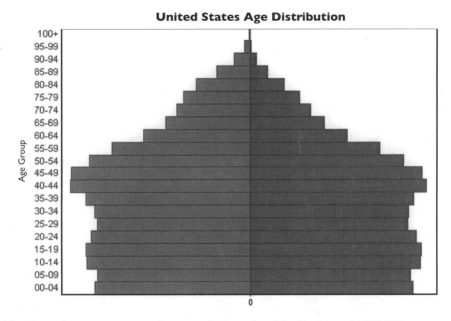

United States Age Distribution

The chart allows a maximum cohort size (male or female) of just over 12,000,000.
Source: UN Statistics Division.

World's Ten Largest Cities, 2005

Note: this tabulation is for "urban agglomerations." The phrase "urban agglomeration" refers to a metropolitan area as a whole. So New York City includes Newark, New Jersey. How many of these cities can you locate?

Tokyo	35,200,000
Mexico City	19,400,000
New York	18,700,000
Sao Paulo	18,300,000
Mumbai	18,200,000
Delhi	15,000,000
Shanghai	14,500,000
Calcutta	14,300,000
Jakarta	13,200,000
Buenos Aires	12,600,000

Source: Infoplease.com/ipa/A0884418.html.

The following graphic comes from Japanese government statisticians. It compares the Japanese population of 1930 with that of 2000 and includes a projection for 2030, by which time nearly 40 percent of the Japanese population will be over sixty-five.

Changes Over Time

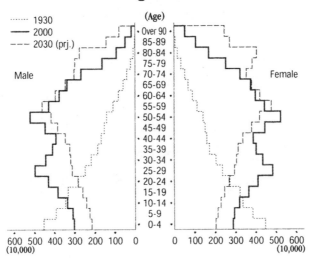

Source: Japan Statistical Yearbook.

In this pyramid, what explanation can you suggest for the low numbers in 1930 of people over seventy? Why are there more such women than men? How would you begin to calculate the life expectancy for someone born in 1935?

What might explain the sudden shrinking (2000) of the population of the ages over 54? Approximately how many million boys and girls were between fifteen and twenty in 1950? How many millions of men and women were between sixty-five and seventy in 2005? Where does the gender "balance" become most "unbalanced"?

The UN's *World Population Prospects* (2004) estimates that in 2050 the population over 65 will form these percentages of the total population: China 23.6 percent; Germany 28.4 percent; India 14.8 percent; Italy 35.5 percent; Japan 35.9 percent; United Kingdom 23.2 percent; U.S. 20.6 percent.

Japan in World Rankings, I

Land area (square miles)		Population		Density
1. Russia	6,600,000	1. China	1,250,000,000	29. Japan
2. Canada	3,850,000	2. India	1,000,000,000	33. India
3. China	3,700,000	3. U.S.	275,000,000	70. China
4. U.S.	3,700,000	4. Indonesia	210,000,000	86. Indonesia
60. Japan	145,850	9. Japan	130,000,000	161. U. S.

Source; *The Illustrated Book of World Rankings*, ed. G. T. Kurian, New York: Sharpe, 2001.

Life expectancy. As of 2004, life expectancy in Japan was 79 for men and 86 for women. In the U.S. that year the figures were 75 (men) and 80 (women). Why do women live longer than men? What factors beside gender might affect life expectancy?

Health expenditures per capita. In 2002, Japan spent $2,476 per person on health; the U.S. figure was $5,274. The world average was $524. What does that figure say about both Japan and the U.S.?

Households headed by women. In Japan in 1990, 17 percent of households were headed by women; in the U.S. (1994) that figure was 35.9 percent. What factors might affect those percentages? (Japanese speak of marriages that took place "after a child was conceived.")

Gross domestic product. A nation's gross domestic product (GDP) is the sum total of the goods and services that that nation produced on its own soil. In 2004, Japan's GDP was $4.7 trillion. That is $4,669,322,000,000. The U.S. figure that year was $11.7 trillion. What was the per capita figure for each country? Why are the per-capita figures so much closer? Other figures for 2004 per capita GDP include the U.K.—$35,700; Germany—$33,200; France—$32,000.

Energy consumption per capita. Japan's 2003 per capita energy consumption (in kilograms of oil) was 4,053; the U.S. figure was 7,843. The world average was 1,734.

PCs per 100 people. In 2004, Japan had 54 personal computers per 100 people; twenty years earlier that figure was 1.7. In the U.S. in 2004, there were 76 computers per 100 people; twenty years earlier that figure was 11.

What additional statistics might help us understand what these figures mean? Household size? Office computers vs. home computers? Age distribution? Ease of internet access?

Internet users. In 2004 in Japan 50 percent of the population used the internet; in 1990 that figure was zero percent. The comparable figures for the U.S. are 63 percent (2004) and 1 percent (1990).

What other comparative figures would be helpful? Defense budget? Number of military bases in foreign countries? Number of military bases of foreign countries? Rate of economic growth? Rate of population growth? Infant mortality? Average weight? Educational achievement? Winners of Nobel Prizes? Caliber of professional or non-professional athletes? Internationally known artists and musicians?

Are some of those other figures more important than the ten we've discussed here? Which ones? Why? What factors resist quantification? How important are they?

Japan in World Rankings, II

Fertility Rate		Population over 65	
1. Albania	20.4	1. Monaco	28.7
163. U.S.	2.0	6. Japan	20.9
171. China	1.8	29. U.S.	16.8
209. Japan	1.4	73. China	8.6

Source: *The Illustrated Book of World Rankings*, ed. G. T. Kurian, New York: Sharpe, 2001.

BIG BOSS OF
THE THUNDER HERD

Editor's Introduction: The majority of Japanese today are reaping the benefits and confronting the problems of affluence. Their role in Japan's economic boom has been central, for industry cannot get far without willing and able workers.

But there must also be vision at the top.

Here is a description of the man behind the success of the Honda Motor Company, Honda Sōichirō. (Throughout this book we will follow Japanese order and give family name first, given name second; Honda is his family name, Sōichirō his "first" name.) Until his death in 1991, Mr. Honda was an everpresent reminder of Japan's post-World War II economic success. [2]

"I THINK BEST when I have a wrench in my hands," says Honda Sōichirō, head of Honda Motor Co. Ltd., which has made motorcyclists out of over nine million people throughout the world and will soon invade the United States with a snappy midget sedan and a racy sports car. Honda has an awesome office overlooking Tokyo, as befits the boss of a $330 million empire, but he has been there only twice in the past two years and rarely attends his own monthly directors' meetings. Instead, the man Japanese call "Big Boss of the Thunder Herd" enmeshes himself in the grease and clatter of his research lab, dressed in white overalls and green-and-white baseball cap. He runs eagerly about, fiddling with carburetors, stopping for a bowl of noodles in the workers' cafeteria, his playful face often exploding with laughter. Instead of bowing and calling him "Honorable President," the workers call him "Pop." But when his famous temper explodes they call him the *kaminari* (thunderbolt). He seems blissfully oblivious to such things as sales and marketing. "If you make a superior product," he says, "people will buy it."

Honda Sōichirō goes over design plans in his research lab. Photo from American Honda Motor Co., Inc.

Honda Sōichirō, who is 60, was eight when he saw his first motorcar. It was a Model T Ford, one of the first cars to come to Japan, and it clattered its way through the small town of Hamamatsu, 120 miles south of Tokyo, where Honda's father was the village blacksmith. Honda ran excitedly after the car. "It leaked oil," he recalls, "and I got down on my hands and knees to smell it. It was like perfume."

It was the beginning of a love affair. In school, Honda would sit in the back of the room, whittling wooden blocks into things that looked like engines. His favorite toy was a pair of his father's pliers, which he had taken to bed with him ever since he was a small boy. When he was 18, he moved to Tokyo to become an apprentice at an auto repair shop, but to prove himself worthy he had to spend six months babysitting for the boss's three children.

When he was 22, he opened his own repair shop. In his spare time, he built racers: one vehicle powered by a converted airplane engine roared along at 70 mph. He next souped up an old Ford and set a new all-Japan record of 75 mph before cracking up the machine in a spectacular crash that tossed him 15 feet into the air and broke his arm and shoulder.

During the war he manufactured piston rings and propellers for Zero fighters, but Allied bombing soon reduced his small shop to ruins. After the war, which left Japan almost bereft of motorized vehicles, Honda foresaw a great need for cheap transportation. In 1948, he scrounged 500 engines discarded by the Imperial Army, attached them to bicycles, and began turning out motorbikes.

MR. THUNDER'S BIG BASH

It was a great night for Honda Sōichirō , 82, founder of the company that bears his name. Before an audience of 800 autoindustry elite in Detroit last week, Honda was the first Japanese carmaker to be inducted into the Automotive Hall of Fame, where his name will join those of Henry Ford and Walter P. Chrysler. "As I stand here, it feels as if I am standing on a cloud," said Kaminari-san, or Mr. Thunder, as he is known to his workers. His company has put 1.4 million American-made Hondas on the road and sold 5.1 million imports since 1970. Said he: "I found doing business here much easier than in Japan. Our company in Ohio has been so well accepted that I believe it is an American company in substance."

Source: *Time,* October 23, 1989.

Since gas was then severely rationed, he fueled them with an extract made from crushed pine roots. Despite the fact that the first models took 20 minutes of pumping to get them started, the bikes sold quickly. He improved the engines, and in five years sales reached $6 to $7 million. But, says Honda, "I wanted to be Number One in the world, not just in Japan."

To overcome prewar Japan's reputation for shoddy, bamboo-and-beer-can merchandise, Honda entered his cycles in Europe's Grand Prix races. European racers scoffed: "We didn't think the Japanese made anything except rickshaws," said one. The first year, Honda's entries ran dead last.

For weeks, Honda followed the racing circuit about Europe, spending days and nights redesigning and rebuilding. The work paid off. Within two years, Honda's cycles swept seven of the top ten races, amazing European manufacturers. "It's time the British firms copied Japanese know-how," blustered the *London Daily Mirror*. One British expert took one of Honda's bikes apart piece by piece, then exclaimed in awe, "The bloody thing is made like a watch." ...

Besides motorcycles and cars, Honda has pushed his company into making farm machinery, lawn mowers, generators, and a variety of industrial engines. But he has avoided the wide-ranging diversification of many Japanese firms. "If it doesn't have a motor," he says, "I don't want to build it."

Quotations from Mr. Honda

"When I drive, I almost feel like a god. It is always difficult for me to comprehend that half the world is not yet even in the bicycle stage and most of the other half is just entering the motorcycle stage."

DIED, Honda Sōichirō, 84, pioneering Japanese manufacturer who built his motorcycle company into a global automotive giant; in Tokyo. A hands-on mechanic as well as a visionary, Honda scored his first success in postwar Japan by selling bicycles powered by military-surplus engines. By the early 1960s his firm was the world's largest motorcycle maker. Defying Japanese government bureaucrats who tried to limit the nation's auto industry to a few dominant firms, Honda began making cars in 1963. In 1982 Honda became the first Japanese automaker to build cars in the U.S.

Source: Time, August 19, 1991.

"My biggest thrill is when I plan something and it fails. My mind is then filled with ideas on how I can improve it. There is nothing for me in my life but my work. I think so much about it I sometimes have to take a sleeping pill if I have something important to do the next day so I can be well rested."

"I don't require my engineers to have diplomas. When I was going to school before the war, the principal told me I had failed because even though I was Number One in the class, I hadn't taken the final. I told him, 'I don't give a damn for the diploma. What I want is the knowledge.'"

   In many ways, Honda was typical of Japan's top business executives. Most of them are hard workers, dedicated to the success of their enterprise. Says Takenaka Renichi, president of Japan's largest construction company, 'Japanese corporate executives are really very simple men who live simple lives and have one simple aim: We want our companies and hopefully our country to be the very best possible. We leave the 'high life' to other people—and other places."

   The simple life is characteristic of these tycoons. Says Yoshiyama Hirokichi, president of a top company manufacturing electrical equipment, "It is not the Japanese way to flaunt one's wealth. My wife and I live in a five-room apartment here in Tokyo and it is quite sufficient for us. In my opinion, luxuries only complicate life."

JAPAN, INC.:
THE COMIC

Editor's Introduction: Japan today is a paradise for comic-book lovers. There are comics that deal with adventure, science fiction, sports, romance, sex, the Gulf War—even economics. And there is little sense that comics are juvenile; even bankers on their way to work on mass transit read comics without embarrassment.

The following excerpt comes from a book-length treatment of the economic realities behind trade friction between Japan and the U.S. The comic features the company president of Toyosan (a combination of *Toyo*ta and Nis*san*), a white-collar employee of Mitsutomo (a combination of *Mitsu*bishi and Sumi*tomo*) trading company, and a union leader in the Toyosan factory. The American side features President Ironcoke (after Iacocca) of Chrysky (Chrysler) Motors.

Phonetic symbols represent sounds like "whack," "twock," etc. All the material here—including the data in the notes—is from the original cartoon. [3]

After the second oil crisis, sales of gas-saving Japanese cars took off in the U.S. In 1980 there was a recorded growth of 17.6% over 1979, and automobile friction rose.

The U.S. trade balance took a turn for the worse in the middle of the 1960s. Beginning in the 1970s, the deficit came to stay; the gap Increased every year, reaching $148.4 billion in 1985.

The U.S. trade deficit with Japan was less than $2 billion in the early 1970s. In the late 1970s, it increased to nearly $10 billion; in 1985, to nearly $50 billion.

ADVANCED MECHANIZATION IN A JAPANESE AUTOMOBILE FACTORY, WHERE THERE IS GREAT INDUSTRIAL ROBOT ACTIVITY

The U.S. produced about 11,480,000 cars in 1979. In 1982 production fell below 7,000,000. Japan became the world's top manufacturer of cars in 1980, and the U.S. had to be content with second place.

Analysts say that the U.S. lost its place as king of the car makers because it failed to update its equipment and because it has not put its efforts into production.

The U.S. plays up the claim that 500,000 workers are unemployed because of Japanese car imports. Others have suggested, however, that if the U.S. mechanized and rationalized like Japan, that change would produce about 400,000 unemployed workers (Omae Ken'ichi, *The World Appears, Japan Appears*).

CONTEMPORARY JAPAN: THREE NOVELS

Editor's Introduction: Statistics give us one picture of a society. It is a relatively bloodless picture. Novels give us another picture. In this reading, three novelists alive today give three different takes on contemporary Japan. The first novel appeared in 1987; the second, in 1992; the third, in 2002. As you read, ask yourself this question: If you were a psychologist or an anthropologist and had only these words as evidence, what picture could you paint of the authors, their values, and their society? And this: What other evidence would you like to have before painting your picture?

1. *Kitchen*, by Yoshimoto Banana. The author Yoshimoto Banana was born in 1964, daughter of a prominent cultural critic. She published *Kitchen*, her first prize-winning work, in 1987, at the age of twenty-three; the Japanese title, *Kitchin*, is a phonetic representation of the English word. These three excerpts are from the beginning and end of Chapter 1. [4]

THE PLACE I LIKE BEST in this world is the kitchen. No matter where it is, no matter what kind, if it's a kitchen, if it's a place where they make food, it's fine with me. Ideally it should be well broken in. Lots of tea towels, dry and immaculate. White tile catching the light.

I love even incredibly dirty kitchens to distraction—vegetable droppings all over the floor, so dirty your slippers turn black on the bottom. Strangely, it's better if this kind of kitchen is large. I lean up against the silver door of a towering, giant refrigerator stocked with enough food to get through a winter. When I raise my eyes from the oil-spattered gas burner and the rusty kitchen knife, outside the window stars are glittering, lonely.

Now only the kitchen and I are left. It's just a little nicer than being all alone.

When I'm dead worn out, in a reverie, I often think that when it comes time to die, I want to breathe my last in a kitchen. Whether it's cold and I'm all alone, or somebody's there and it's warm, I'll stare death fearlessly in the eye. If it's a kitchen, I'll think, "How good."

[The narrator visits a friend's apartment.]

I looked up at the towering apartment building and thought, their apartment on the tenth floor is so high, the view must be beautiful at night....

Getting off the elevator, I was alarmed by the sound of my own footsteps in the hall. I rang the bell, and abruptly Yūichi opened the door. "Come in."

"Thanks." I stepped inside. The room was truly strange.

First thing, as I looked toward the kitchen, my gaze landed with a thud on the enormous sofa in the living room. Against the backdrop of the large kitchen with its shelves of pots and pans—no table, no carpet, just "it." Covered in beige fabric, it looked like something out of a commercial. An entire family could watch TV on it. A dog too big to keep in Japan could stretch out across it—sideways. It was really a marvelous sofa....

"Take a look around if you'd like. Should I give you the tour? Or pick a room, then I'll know what kind of person you are," said Yūichi, making tea.

"What kind?..." I seated myself on the deep, comfy sofa.

"I mean, what you want to know about a house and the people who live there, their tastes. A lot of people would say you learn a lot from the toilet," he said, smiling, unconcerned. He had a very relaxed way of talking.

"The kitchen," I said.

"Well, here it is. Look at whatever you want."

While he made tea, I explored the kitchen. I took everything in: the good quality of the mat on the wood floor and of Yūichi's slippers; a practical minimum of well-worn kitchen things, precisely arranged. A Silverstone frying pan and a delightful German-made vegetable peeler—a peeler to make even the laziest grandmother enjoy slip-slipping those skins off.

Movie Attendance		
	Annual total	**Per person**
France (1999)	155,400,000	2.63
India (1998)	2,860,000,000	2.91
Japan (1999)	145,000,000	1.14
United States (1999)	1,465,000,000	5.20

Source: *Japan Statistical Yearbook.*

Lit by a small fluorescent lamp, all kinds of plates silently awaited their turns; glasses sparkled. It was clear that in spite of the disorder everything was of the finest quality. There were things with special uses, like...porcelain bowls, cheese dishes, gigantic platters, two beer steins. Somehow it was all very satisfying. I even opened the small refrigerator (Yūichi said it was okay)—everything was neatly organized, nothing just "left."

I looked around, nodding and murmuring approvingly, "Mmm, mmm." It was a good kitchen. I fell in love with it at first sight.

[The narrator moves in with her friend and his mother, and Chapter 1 ends with this:]

Dream kitchens.

I will have countless ones, in my heart or in reality. Or in my travels. Alone, with a crowd of people, with one other person—in all the many places I will live. I know that there will be so many more.

Newspapers and Books

	Books published	Daily Newspapers	Circulation
China	n.a.	85,470 (2002)	.09 per person
Japan	56,221 (1996)	70,339	.65 per person
United Kingdom	110,965 (1998)	18,591	.39 per person
United States	68,175 (1996)	55,185	.26 per person

Source: *Japan Statistical Yearbook.*

2. *All She Was Worth*, by Miyabe Miyuki. Miyabe Miyuki was born in 1960 and published her first short story in 1987. *All She Was Worth* (*Kasha* is the Japanese title) appeared in 1992 and won a major prize in 1993. Miyabe has written many books in many genres: mystery fiction (like *All She Was Worth*), science fiction, historical fiction, and juvenile fiction.

In this passage, a lawyer named Mizoguchi and a detective are discussing how people get deeply into debt. With the exchange rate at roughly 120 yen to the dollar, thirty million yen is about $250,000. [5]

"About a year ago, I handled a personal bankruptcy case. An office worker, twenty-eight years old. He had thirty-three different credit cards. His total debt ran to more than thirty million *yen*, and he had no property to speak of. What do you make of that?"

Thirty million *yen*—that was more than a lowly public servant like Homma could ever hope to see, even as severance pay.

"Now, how do you suppose a person who pulls in a mere two hundred thousand a month could ever manage to borrow thirty million *yen*? Who's going to lend him that much? Why would they? This is what I mean by overextended credit."

He reached for his glass of water, but found it empty and set it back down.

"The typical scenario for getting deep into debt goes like this. First a person gets himself a credit card. He finds it handy for shopping, for taking trips. It's nice and simple, and one card does the trick quite well. Then pretty soon, without thinking about it much, he gets himself a couple more. Assuming that he's a regular company employee, he shouldn't have any problem with the screening procedures. The department stores, banks and supermarkets will all encourage him to take out cards. 'Become a cardholder and you'll get all these discounts and member benefits,' they'll say. 'Special deals galore.' So he adds a few more cards to his hand.

"Soon enough, he's using them not just for shopping but for cash as well, again because they're so convenient. Now he's made that imperceptible shift from *using* credit cards to *borrowing* against them. This happens almost before a person realizes it. With bank-issued cards, cash machines will deduct money straight from depositors' accounts. But with non-bank and retailer-affiliated cards, somewhere in or around the store you'll find one of those cheerful-looking machines that look like bank cash machines. You just stick the card in, punch in your PIN number, and it's as easy as taking money out of your bank account. A very simple way to run up debts."

The waitress came to clear away the dishes and refill their glasses. Mizoguchi thanked her with a wave of his hand.

Mobile Phones Fast Becoming Pocket-sized Computers

Cell Phone companies are competing to add functions to their phones. Built-in cameras have gone from 300,000 pixels to 1,000,000 pixels. Some now have infrared remote control capability (to operate TV sets), fingerprint recognition, MP3 players. More than 60% of the population already own a mobile phone.

Source: *Japan Now*, July 2003.

"That's what you might call an archetypal example. You wouldn't believe how many clients tell me they got started borrowing cash by mistake."

"By mistake?"

"Yes. The client wants just to withdraw money from his bank account, but somehow sticks his credit card into the cash machine instead of his bank card. Since he's chosen the same PIN number for all his cards, money comes out anyway. He may think it a bit odd that the transaction slip doesn't show any balance, only the amount withdrawn, or he may not really notice. Often it's not until the end of the month, when his credit card bill comes, that he realizes his mistake."

"Must be a jolt. Especially being charged interest on top of that."

"Probably. But it may also get him thinking, 'Hey, borrowing cash is easy.' The interest, at that point, doesn't strike him as particularly high—a mere three thousand *yen* per hundred thousand borrowed. So every now and then, he dips in." Mizoguchi gulped down half his water and continued. "He uses his card habitually, for shopping, for cash, for sheer convenience. He doesn't draw out huge chunks all at once, but just a little at a time, so he never feels he's doing anything risky. Still, loans are loans. When they come due, you have to pay up.

"Imagine a young businessman just starting out. Suppose his take-home pay is, say, a hundred and fifty thousand *yen*. He can afford to pay maybe twenty or thirty thousand a month in purchases on the card. Forty to fifty thousand would be tight. If he's not careful, though, pretty soon he's up there anyway. So that's when he starts borrowing cash with the card. In order to meet his payments to company A, he draws cash on company B's card. And once he does that, the whole thing snowballs to the point where he can't keep up by borrowing on the card any more. So what do you think he does?"

"Goes to a loan shark?"

"Exactly," the attorney said, nodding. "And with the loan sharks he repeats the same cycle. Before long, he's borrowing from company B to make payments on money from company A. Then it's gone and he goes on to C, D and E. Some unscrupulous consumer finance companies even introduce clients to other companies. Only to lower-profile firms, of course, the ones with less capital clout, who are especially lax in their screening. They need whatever business they can get, so they don't set a ceiling on total debt. That's what drives up the interest. And that's how the system works.

"The customers, all they can think about is when their next payment is going to come due. If there's another loan to be had, they'll go for it—that's just part of the vicious circle."

Self portrait of Japanese teens. Photo by Yoshiara Mayu, from *Japan Forum*; used with permission.

3. Cell, by Okuda Hideo. This is the beginning of *Cell*, a short story by Okuda Hideo. Okuda was born in 1959 and wrote this story in 2002. It appeared in a volume titled *In the Pool*; the Japanese original is phonetic, *In za pu-ru*. The exchange rate was about 120 yen to the dollar, so six hundred yen was about five dollars. [6]

He was sending out more than two hundred text messages a day from his cell phone.

It cost him three *yen* per text, which added up to a total of six hundred *yen* a day. Since he sent this many every day, his monthly bill—including both the basic charge and the usage fees—easily topped twenty thousand *yen*.

Tsuda Yūta was in his second year of high school. He got twenty thousand *yen* a month in pocket money from his parents. "You're an only child. So you're lucky," his friends would tease him. But since he had to use the money to buy his lunch, for all practical purposes it turned out to be a lot less.

His mom would always say, "That's quite enough for you to buy yourself clothes or CDs."

She was totally clueless. High school kids these days could barely keep up with their cell phone bills.

Self portrait of Japanese teens. Photo by Hongo Jin, from *Japan Forum*; used with permission.

Yūta was more or less managing, thanks to his part-time job at a fast-food joint. He earned nearly fifty thousand a month, with his five three-hour stints a week. That just about brought him up to a level where he really could buy some clothes and CDs.

"Put the two together and that's seventy thousand *yen*! How much do you think your damn mother doles out to me from my own damn salary each month?"

His father had said that last month, getting angry and going all red in the face. He might earn the money, but Yūta's mom was the one who managed it.

His mother liked to lecture him regularly, once in the morning and once in the evening. "When are you going to get down to some serious studying?" she would say. "You'll be graduating next year, you know."

But as time went on, his parents toned down their criticism. It was because of the spasms Yūta had started getting in his left hand.

It was dinnertime, but Yūta just kept on typing into his phone. "You'd better cut that out, or I'll give you a good slap," his father had threatened.

Yūta paid no attention and continued staring at the little screen of the phone, so his father made good on his promise and slapped him in the head.

"Hey! What are you—" Yūta said.

But his father grabbed his cell phone and flung it onto the living room couch. The atmosphere around the table became tense and oppressive. And it was several minutes later that Yūta's left hand had begun to tremble uncontrollably.

The trembling started in his fingertips and then moved up to his elbow, until finally the whole arm started to jerk up and down, as if he were strumming a banjo.

He made a frantic dash to retrieve his phone. Once he had it firmly in his grasp, the spasm died away.

His mother and father had both gone pale. They swallowed nervously and did not say a word.

"Take the boy to the doctor," said his father curtly....

Yūta didn't think it was a big deal. One of his friends had been typing too much on his cell and had got tendonitis. Whatever he had was probably like that. The friend had started using his right hand to type, and since then everything had been okay.

"It scares me, you know, the way you're always holding onto that phone of yours as if your life depended on it."

His mother looked permanently upset. She had remembered that for a while Yūta had briefly refused to go to school, back in junior high.

"I'm too busy with my job. I don't have the time to go see some stupid doctor," he said, hinting at the need for financial compensation. His mother came right back, offering him ten thousand *yen* on condition that he go see a doctor....

Fantastic! And he'd be able to skip some classes.

But he drew the line at letting his mom go with him. He was seventeen, and to go with his mother would be terminally uncool. She told him that she had made an appointment at the neurology department. Yūta was not all that worried. His experience with hospitals was zilch: he knew that internal medicine and surgery were two different things—that was about it.

Young Japanese who don't like the Big Mac may prefer Dunkin' Donuts or Kentucky Fried Chicken. All three chains have had operations in Japan for decades. Photo by Doug Hurst.

II
JAPAN BEFORE
1850

A CLOSED SOCIETY:
1600-1853

Editor's Introduction: Japan today is a cosmopolitan nation. It is one of the economic and technological giants of the world. It is deeply involved in international trade. Indeed, Japan depends on trade for its economic success.

But only 150 years ago, Japan was a very different place. Its economy was largely agricultural. Its technology was "backward." Its foreign trade was almost nonexistent. For all practical purposes, Japan was cut off from the rest of the world.

The geography of Asia—the fact that Japan is separated from the mainland by 120 miles of water—made isolation possible, but it was a decision of the Japanese government that made isolation a reality.

From 1600 to 1868, Japan deliberately and systematically avoided contact with other people. Here are five articles from an exclusion edict issued by the Japanese government in 1636:

1. *No Japanese ships may leave for foreign countries.*

2. *No Japanese may go abroad secretly. If anyone tries to do this, he will be killed, and the ship and owner(s) will be placed under arrest while higher authority is informed.*

3. *Any Japanese now living abroad who tries to return to Japan will be put to death.*

4. *No offspring of Southern Barbarians [Europeans] will be allowed to remain. Anyone violating this order will be killed and all his relatives punished according to the gravity of the offense.*

5. *If any deportees should try to return or to communicate with Japan by letter or otherwise, they will of course be killed if they are caught.*

At this time, only a very few Dutch, Chinese, and Korean traders were allowed into Japan. All others learned to stay away. If they didn't, they paid a high price.

In 1640 a Portuguese expedition—one ship with 74 men—sought to reopen trade with Japan. The Japanese authorities arrested the men and executed 61 of them. The remaining 13 were spared so that they could carry the word back to the outside world. At the burial ground, where the heads of the executed sailors were displayed on wooden poles, the Japanese authorities erected a sign with this message:

> A similar penalty will be suffered by all those who henceforward come to these shores from Portugal, whether they be ambassadors or whether they be sailors, whether they come by error or whether they be driven hither by storm. Even more, if the King of Portugal, or Buddha, or even the God of the Christians were to come, they would all pay the very same penalty.

Why did the Japanese pursue this policy of exclusion? What kind of society would want to isolate itself from the rest of the world? There are no easy answers to these questions, but the following selection, based on the recollections of a number of Japanese born and brought up in the early nineteenth century, supplies some insight into the nature of Japanese society during the long period of isolation. [5]

Vending Machines

Vending machines now dispense beverages, bread, candy, cigarettes, newspapers and magazines, noodles, box lunches. Computerized terminals sell theater and concert tickets, boarding passes for airplanes and fast trains, and alcoholic beverages (these machines can read drivers' licenses). For about $2.00 machines dispense capsules that contain a personal introduction; buyers can write a response and send it to the company, which forwards it to the individual. There are even vending-machine supermarkets, where all items are dispensed through machines: customers make selections by machine and pay for the selections at the check-out counter.

Source: *Japan Now*, November/December 2000.

Suzuki Tarō was born in 1832 in a town 150 miles west of present-day Tokyo (then called Edo). By then, the government of the *shogun,* or military governor based in Tokyo, had been in power for more than 200 years. It was shogunal policy to minimize change, to freeze Japanese society into a rigid social class structure. For this reason, little in Japan in 1832 was unpredictable. In 1832, any of Tarō's fellow Japanese, knowing a few basic facts about Tarō's background, could have predicted just how he would be brought up and just how he would spend his life.

Tarō was born a samurai, a warrior. His father had been a samurai. His sons would be samurai. It was far better to be born a samurai than to be born a farmer or a merchant. Only about one person in twenty was a samurai, and only samurai could bear swords or hold administrative office. The vast majority of the population, 80 percent or more, were farmers. The others were artisans and merchants, except for a tiny group of Buddhist and Shinto priests and monks and a tiny group of outcasts—people who did such unclean tasks as tanning hides.

Swords were part of Tarō's life from a very early age. His parents were so happy their new child was a boy that they had trouble restraining themselves from giving him a sword almost at birth. But restrain themselves they did, and Tarō had only wooden swords to play with until he was five. It was indeed a time for celebration when Tarō's father presented him with his first real sword. Tarō continued often to wear a wooden sword instead of the real thing, but he had taken a major step on the road to samurai manhood. Outside his home, he was never without a sword, real or wooden, and people who saw him on the street knew immediately that he was a samurai.

From the age of 15 on, Tarō carried two swords: a long sword and a short one. To carry these instruments of death at all times made Tarō deeply aware of his mission in life, the mission of all samurai: to serve his lord bravely and loyally, and to set an example for others. Should any situation arise in which dishonor seemed likely, Tarō would use the short sword to end his own life, displaying in his ritual suicide his selflessness and devotion to his lord.

To grow up as a samurai meant learning the military arts, so Tarō spent many hours wrestling and fencing and riding and studying archery. But Japan had enjoyed nearly 200 years of peace, and in peacetime one needed other skills as well. So Tarō studied reading and writing and, as he grew older, began to read the Chinese classics.

Tarō's training was strict, for becoming a worthy samurai was not an easy task. At the age of six, Tarō began to memorize the Chinese classics. At the time, the words meant very little to him and he memorized only the sounds. But his teachers were sure that gradually the wisdom of the sages would penetrate his young

The castle of Tarō's lord was not so grand as this one, the house of one of the most important lords of northern Japan. Photo from the Japan National Tourist Organization.

mind, that what he had at first merely memorized would eventually take on real meaning. To his dying day, Tarō was able to recite long passages from the classics.

Tarō met his teacher all during the year. Fall and spring were no problem, but the heat of the summer sometimes made him so weak he thought he would faint. The winter cold brought a different kind of suffering. His clothing was not heavy, and the room was unheated. To use a fire simply to warm himself was considered the way of a weakling. When his hands became too cold to hold his writing brush, his teacher would say, "Dip them in that bucket of water." The water in the bucket was ice cold. When his bare feet became numb, his teacher would say, "Go run around in the snow."

There were many things Tarō was not allowed to do simply because he was a samurai. For instance, at home he never saw a *samisen,* perhaps the most important musical instrument of his day. Why not? Because the music of the *samisen* was unworthy for samurai to hear. Townsmen, maybe, but not samurai.

For the same reason, Tarō never saw a *kabuki* play. When the *kabuki* players came around, Tarō's lord would issue orders reminding the samurai not to attend. The temptation was strong, for *kabuki* offered songs and dances and fine actors and exciting plots, and Tarō wished more than once that he could see what went on inside the theater.

Samurai were supposed to be above such matters as money and commerce. Ideally, a samurai never handled money. But Tarō, like most samurai, had no servants, and so he often wound up going to the market himself. To hide his embarrassment, he usually went out after dark.

Tarō's family and almost all the other samurai families lived near the castle of the lord. The castle sat high on a hill with a moat, thick walls, and a tall tower. The lord himself and his two most trusted advisers lived in the castle. The rest of the samurai lived in the houses spread out around the lower slopes of the hill. The most important samurai families lived closest to the castle walls. Tarō's family was not very important (Tarō's father could never become a high official or have a personal interview with the lord) and therefore lived down the hill, closer to the temples and stores of the town.

A few temples and a moat separated Tarō's neighborhood from the quarter set aside for the townsmen—artisans and merchants. No artisan or merchant could live near Tarō, nor was Tarō permitted to live in their quarter.

Even though townsmen and samurai lived within a stone's throw of each other, their lives were worlds apart. A townsman of Tarō's age could not go to the official school. He could not wear a sword or fine clothes. He could not ride in that day's version of a taxi—a small compartment suspended from a pole carried on the shoulders of two bearers. Townsmen could not build three-story buildings or use gold and silver leaf in decorating their houses. Tarō's house occupied a fair-sized lot with a broad front on the street, but the houses of townsmen were built on smaller lots with only narrow fronts.

As a samurai, Tarō was free to walk through the townsmen's quarter, and he did so often: past the street of the armorers, closest to the samurai quarter, and then past the street of the rice dealers, the fish market, and the street of the *tatami* [straw floor mats] makers. But townsmen were not so free to wander. They had to stay out of the samurai quarter, except when they had a specific reason for entering. Still, the regulations were not so strict in Tarō's town as in some other towns, where townsmen were required to remove their wooden clogs before entering the samurai district.

As Tarō walked on past the *tatami* makers, he came to a border area between town and country. Here he saw temples and shrines and cemeteries, along with an irrigation ditch, which could serve as a first line of defense. Beyond the bor-

Samurai ride again—this time in one of Japan's many historical pageants. Photo from the Japan National Tourist Organization.

der area lay the countryside, a checkerboard of small rice paddies with a tiny farm village every mile or so.

On a fine June day, Tarō would find the fields full of farmers—men, women, and children—knee-deep in mud, transplanting rice seedlings to be harvested in November. The stench was almost overpowering, for the farmers collected human excrement from the town to fertilize their fields. Tarō thanked his stars that he was a samurai when he saw how these farmers labored. Bending from the waist to push the seedlings into the mud with their bare fingers, the rice planters, mainly women, sometimes sang for relief from their brutal drudgery.

Tarō's father served his lord in the capacity of overseer of four farm villages, so Tarō had heard considerable discussion at home of the farmers and their problems. In theory, the farmers were a prized class: after all, they produced the rice crop that fed Japan and supported the government of the samurai. But Tarō knew that reality was something different. Taxes on the farmers were very high. And last year had been a bad crop year: heavy rains had come just before the harvest and much of the crop had rotted in the fields.

Indeed, Tarō remembered his father's anxiety during the winter, when one group of farmers had seemed on the point of lodging formal protest with the lord. In a year of bad crops, they wanted the tax rate lowered. Tarō's father had met with them and assuaged their anger, and the formal protest had not been made. That was certainly a good thing for Tarō's father, and perhaps also for the farmers.

Had the protest been made, Tarō's father might well have lost his job, been disgraced, and perhaps even driven to commit suicide in atonement. The lord expected his officials to control all matters within their jurisdiction. The fact that a group of farmers took political action—whatever the merits of their case— was enough to indicate that the official in charge was not fulfilling his duty. The farmers leading the protest might have been executed or deported, even if the lord determined that their protest was justified, for such unauthorized political action was a challenge to the stability of the social order. Farmers, after all, were farmers. They grew rice, paid taxes, and obeyed the directions of their natural superiors. Samurai were samurai. Samurai ruled. There could be no mixing of the two functions.

Tarō had never ventured more than five miles away from home. From the top of the hill near his house he could see the ocean, but he had never been in a boat. Nor was it likely that he would travel at all until he was 18 or 20. Then his lord might well order him to Edo to serve there as a guard. This would mean a trip of 150 miles on foot that would take Taro a good 10 days.

Should he get to Edo, he would meet for the first time samurai from other parts of the land and would begin to sense the immense size of this land called Japan. He might even—perhaps—begin to think first of his duty to Japan and only second of his duty to his lord. Only the future would tell.

THE OLD VALUES

Editor's Introduction: The samurai class had its origin in warfare, but for 250 years there was peace in Japan. What was the peacetime role of the samurai class? Here is one answer, given by a high-ranking samurai of the seventeenth century:

> From ancient times the people have been divided into four classes: samurai, farmer, artisan, and merchant. Each class has its own vocation. The farmers devote themselves to agriculture, the artisans promote industry, and the merchants are engaged in trade. All three of these classes contribute to the good of society.
>
> What, then, is the use of the samurai class? Its only vocation is to preserve righteousness. The people of other classes deal with visible things, while the samurai deal with invisible, colorless, and intangible things.
>
> Since visible and invisible things are so different from each other, some may think that the members of the samurai class are entirely unnecessary. But if there were no samurai, righteousness would disappear from human society, the sense of shame would be lost, and wrong and injustice would prevail. In that case, you would seldom find a faithful subject, a dutiful son, or a trustworthy friend; and such shameful acts as cheating and stealing would be daily occurrences. In short, in the absence of the samurai the whole country would be thrown into great confusion. This is the chief reason why they are placed above other people. It is also why other people are pleased to pay them great respect, in spite of the fact that the samurai appear to have no visible occupation. [8]

The samurai saw themselves as the protectors of public virtue, the guardians of traditional values. Today many Japanese see a marked similarity between the samurai of long ago and the Japanese salaried man of today. Like the samurai, the salaried man is the ideal type of his society. Just as the samurai served his lord, the salaried man serves his company. The samurai had his sword; the salaried man has his briefcase.

We may never fully understand how Japan was able to transform itself into a highly industrialized society, but surely part of the explanation lies in the realm of values, in the attitudes toward self and society that the Japanese brought with them into the modern world.

The following selection attempts to examine these traditional values by presenting evidence about the lifestyles of the two most important classes, samurai and farmer. [9]

Recollections of a
Seventeenth-Century Samurai

When I was about 16 I had a tendency toward corpulence. I had noticed a lack of agility in other fleshy persons and thought a heavy man would not make a first-class samurai. So I tried every means to keep myself agile and lean. I slept with my girdle drawn tight and stopped eating rice. I took no wine and abstained from sexual intercourse for the next ten years. While on duty at Edo, there were no hills or fields at hand where I could hunt and climb, so I exercised with spear and sword. When I was on the night watch at my master's residence in Edo, I kept a wooden sword and a pair of straw sandals in my bamboo hamper, and with these I used to put myself through military drill in the darkened court after everyone was asleep. I also practiced running about over the roofs of the outbuildings far removed from the sleeping rooms. This I did so as to be able to handle myself nimbly if a fire should break out.

There were a few who noticed me at these exercises and they were reported to have said that I was probably possessed by a hobgoblin. This was before I was 20 years old. After that I hardened myself by going into the fields on hot summer days and shooting skylarks with a gun, since I did not own a falcon for hawking. In the winter months I often spent several days in the mountains, taking no night clothes or bed quilt with me and wearing only a lined jacket of cotton over a thin cotton shirt. My little hamper was almost filled by my inkstand, paper, books, and two wadded silk kimonos. I stayed overnight in any house I came across in my rambles.

In this way I disciplined myself until I was 37 or 38 years old and avoided becoming fleshy. I was fully aware of my want of talent and believed I could never hope to be of any great service to my country, so I was all the more resolved to do my best as a common samurai [one who could not aspire to high office].

Employed persons by industy

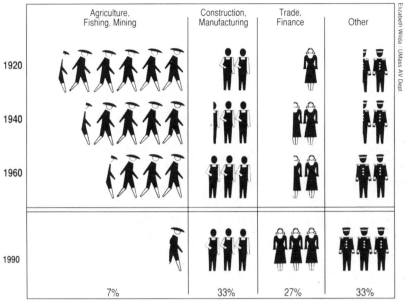

Each complete symbol represents 10% of the employed population.
Other includes transportation, communication, services, and government.

From Eighteenth-Century
Handbooks for Samurai

Every morning make up your mind how to die. Every evening freshen your mind in the thought of death. And do this without ceasing. Thus your mind will be prepared. When your mind is set always on death, your way through life will always be straight and simple....

When you realize how for generations your family has served the house of your lord; when you remember how those who have gone before you served that house, and how those who will come after you will serve it—then you will be moved to a deep sense of gratitude. For you, there should be no thought but of service to the one master who has a claim on your grateful heart....

When you leave a festive place, depart while you still want to stay. When you feel you are satisfied and ready to leave, you have already had too much. Enough is too much. [10]

Being on guard over oneself when one is alone means that the self-control which we exercise over our conduct when we are within the observation and hearing of other people should ... be kept up when there is nobody else looking

Rice technology has changed remarkably little in the past 200 years, except that yields, which were high in Tarō's day, have become even higher. Here, farm women transplant rice seedlings. Photo from the Japan National Tourist Organization.

on or within hearing of us. No matter whether other people are ... able to see or hear us, each one should ... be careful how he behaves. Bad actions are easily found out. "An evil deed runs a thousand miles," as the proverb says....[11]

From a Nineteenth-Century Handbook for Farmers

Wealth and poverty are not far apart; the disparity between the two is only slight. Whether one attains wealth or is reduced to poverty depends upon the degree of his preparedness. A poor man works today or during the current year to dispose of the task he should have done yesterday or during last year. Accordingly, he struggles all through his life to no avail.

On the other hand, a wealthy man works today or during the current year to prepare himself for the needs of tomorrow or next year, so that he is at ease and free and succeeds in whatever thing he undertakes. Many people who have no rice wine to drink or rice to eat today will borrow money or rice. This is the cause that drives them into poverty.

If you gather wood today to boil rice with tomorrow morning, or if you make rope tonight for tying fences the next day, then you can be at your ease. But the poor man wants to boil rice tonight with wood he may gather the next day, or tie fences today with rope he may make tomorrow. Consequently, struggle as he may, he will not succeed.

Therefore, I often say that unpreparedness is the cause of poverty.... It is not by accident that one becomes rich or poor.

Wealth comes from adequate causes, as does poverty. It is wrong to think, as people generally do, that wealth finds its way to those who are wealthy. As a matter of fact, it goes to those who are thrifty and industrious. [12]

TRADITION
AND ITS USES

Editor's Introduction: What people celebrate about a national past is never value-free; it always serves a purpose. Why "Remember the Alamo"? Why "Remember Pearl Harbor"? As the title—The Invention of Tradition—of a pioneering work indicates, traditions serve purposes. When we celebrate Sturbridge Village or Colonial Jamestown and their recreation of colonial life, when we re-enact a Civil War battle, when we visit the site of the Battle of Little Bighorn, when we commemorate September 11, 2001, we do so for a reason, and the celebration or commemoration serves purposes, purposes that we or someone in a position of authority have decided are important.

One such example in Japan is Zen Buddhism. Zen arose in Japan in the medieval period (it spread to Japan from India through China about the year 1400 A.D.), and it seemed to match the needs of one group: Japan's samurai (warriors). Zen is one sect of Buddhism, and though most Japanese today identify themselves as Buddhist, Zen adherents are a tiny minority. But from the late nineteenth century on, Japanese traditionalists (and many Western students of Japan) have claimed that Zen is somehow "typically Japanese."

Here are two photographs and a cartoon. What usefulness does Zen have today?

Most Japanese today visit Zen Buddhist gardens for the same reason American tourists do—to see something out of the past.

Japanese tourists visit the most famous Zen rock-sand-moss garden in Kyoto. Photo from the Japan National Tourist Organization.

This is a recent cartoon by an American cartoonist in Japan

Used by permission of cartoonist Roger Dahl.

Workers in a Japanese construction firm spend the first three days of their employment living as Zen Buddhist monks, on the theory that the training will improve their concentration at work. The monk uses a kyōsaku (stick) to hit the trainees if they become drowsy from the long hours of motionless meditating. Photo from United Press International.

FUJI-ICHI, THE TYCOON

Editor's Introduction: After the samurai and the farmers, the third important class in traditional Japanese society was the townsmen—the artisans and merchants. In theory, the artisans were superior to the merchants because they actually produced goods, whereas the merchants only sold goods that others had produced. But in reality, the artisans and merchants fused into one class. In theory, farmers outranked townsmen, but in reality townsmen were often much better off.

What values did these townsmen hold? How do these values compare with those of the samurai and the farmers? The following short story, published first in 1688, describes the activities of a miserly merchant. It does not tell the whole story of the townsman's life, of course, but it provides insight into the commercial values of the times. [13]

FUJI-ICHI WAS A CLEVER MAN, and his substantial fortune was amassed in his own lifetime. But first and foremost he was a man who knew his own mind, and this was the basis of his success. In addition to carrying on his regular business, he kept a separate ledger, bound from odd scraps of paper, in which, as he sat all day in his shop, pen in hand, he entered a variety of chance information. As the clerks from the money exchanges passed by, he noted down the market ratio of copper and gold; he inquired about the current quotations of the rice brokers; he sought information from druggists' and haberdashers' assistants on the state of the market at Nagasaki; for the latest news on the prices of ginned cotton, salt, and sake, he noted the various days on which the Kyoto dealers received dispatches from the Edo branch shops. Every day a thousand things were entered in his book, and people came to Fuji-ichi if they were ever in doubt. He became a valuable asset to the citizens of Kyoto.

Invariably his dress consisted of an unlined vest next to his skin, and on top of that a cotton kimono, stuffed on occasion with three times the usual amount of padding. He never put on more than one layer of kimono. It was he

Many traditional art forms are practiced in Japan today, pottery in particular. Japanese pottery is famous throughout the world. One of these pots may well command a price of up to $100,000. Photo from the Japan National Tourist Organization.

who first started the wearing of detachable cuffs on the sleeves—a device both fashionable and economical. His socks were of deerskin and his clogs were fitted with high leather soles, but even so he was careful not to walk too quickly along the hard main roads. Throughout life his only silk garments were of pongee, dyed plain dark blue. There was one, it is true, which he had dyed a persistently undisguisable seaweed brown, but this was a youthful error of judgment, and he was to regret it for the next twenty years. For his ceremonial dress he had no settled [family] crests, being content with a three-barred circle or a small conventional whirl, but even during the summer airing time he was careful to keep them from direct contact with the floor. His pantaloons were of hemp, and his starched jacket of an even tougher variety of the same cloth, so that they remained correctly creased no matter how many times he wore them.

When there was a funeral procession which his whole ward was obliged to join, he followed it perforce to the cemetery, but coming back he hung behind the others and, on the path across the moor at Rokuhara, he and his apprentices pulled up sour herbs by the roots.

"Dried in the shade," he explained, "they make excellent stomach medicine."

He never passed by anything that might be of use. Even if he stumbled he used the opportunity to pick up stones for firelighters and tucked them in his sleeve. The head of a household, if he is to keep the smoke rising steadily from his kitchen, must pay attention to a thousand things like this.

Fuji-ichi was not a miser by nature. It was merely his ambition to serve as a model for others in the management of everyday affairs. Even in the days before he made his money he never had the New Year rice cakes prepared in his own lodgings. He considered that to bother over the various utensils, and to hire a man to pound the rice, was too much trouble at such a busy time of the year; so he placed an order with the rice-cake dealer in front of the Great Buddha. However, with his intuitive grasp of good business, he insisted on paying by weight—so much per pound. Early one morning, two days before the New Year, a porter from the cake-maker, hurrying about his rounds, arrived before Fuji-ichi's shop and, setting down his load, shouted for someone to receive the order. The newly pounded cakes, invitingly arrayed, were as fresh and warm as spring itself. The master, pretending not to hear, continued his calculations on the abacus, and the cake-man, who begrudged every moment at this busy time of the year, shouted again and again. At length a young clerk, anxious to demonstrate his businesslike approach, checked the weight of the cakes on the large scales with a show of great precision, and sent the man away.

About two hours later Fuji-ichi said: "Has anyone taken in the cakes which arrived just now?"

"The man gave them to me and left long ago," said the clerk.

"Useless fellow!" cried Fuji-ichi. "I expect people in my service to have more sense! Don't you realize that you took them in before they had cooled off?"

He weighed them again, and to everyone's astonishment their weight had decreased. Not one of the cakes had been eaten, and the clerk stood gazing at them in open-mouthed amazement....

In an empty space in his grounds he planted an assortment of useful trees and flowers such as willow, holly, laurel, peach, iris, and bead-beans. This he did as an education for his only daughter. Morning-glories started to grow of their own accord along the reed fence, but Fuji-ichi said that if it was a question of beauty such shortlived things were a loss, and in their place he planted runner-beans, whose flowers he thought an equally fine sight.

Nothing delighted him more than watching over his daughter. When the young girl grew into womanhood he had a marriage screen constructed for her, and since he considered that one decorated with views of Kyoto would make her restless to visit the places she had not yet seen, and that illustrations of "The Tale of Genji" or "The Tales of Ise" might engender frivolous thoughts, he had the screen painted with busy scenes of the silver and copper mines at Tada. He composed Instructional Verses on the subject of economy and made his daughter recite them aloud. Instead of sending her to a girls' temple school, he taught her how to write himself, and by the time he had reached the end of his syllabus, he had made her the most finished and accomplished girl in Kyoto.

Imitating her father in his thrifty ways, after the age of eight she spilt no more ink on her sleeves, played no longer with dolls at the Dolls Festival, nor joined in the dancing at Bon [a summer festival]. Every day she combed her own hair and bound it in a simple bun. She never sought others' help in her private affairs. She mastered the art of stretching silk padding and learned to fit it perfectly to the length and breadth of each garment. Since young girls can do all this if properly disciplined, it is a mistake to leave them to do as they please.

Once, on the evening of the seventh day of the New Year, some neighbors asked leave to send their sons to Fuji-ichi's house to seek advice on how to become millionaires. Lighting the lamp in the sitting room, Fuji-ichi set his daughter to wait, bidding her let him know when she heard a noise at the private door from the street. The young girl, doing as she was told with charming grace, first

HIGH SCHOOL STUDENTS: SPEND OR SAVE?

To commemorate Sony America Corporation's 30th anniversary, Sony Corporation invited 48 American high school students to spend two weeks in Japan. During the visit, Sony asked the students what they would do with $1,000. The most common answer from the Americans was "save it." The most common answer from a comparable group of 48 Japanese high school students was "spend it." In reality, adults in Japan save at double the rate of Americans.

Source: *JETRO Monitor*, September 1990.

carefully lowered the wick in the lamp. Then, when she heard the voices of the visitors, she raised the wick again and retired to the scullery. By the time the three guests had seated themselves the grinding of an earthenware mortar could be heard from the kitchen, and the sound fell with pleasant promise on their ears. They speculated on what was in store for them. "Pickled whaleskin soup?" hazarded the first. "No. As this is our first visit of the year, it ought to be rice-cake gruel," said the second.

The third listened carefully for some time, and then confidently announced that it was noodle soup. Visitors always go through this amusing performance. Fuji-ichi then entered and talked to the three of them on the requisites for success....

"As a general rule," concluded Fuji-ichi, "give the closest attention to even the smallest details. Well now, you have kindly talked with me from early evening, and it is high time that refreshments were served. But not to provide refreshments is one way of becoming a millionaire. The noise of the mortar which you heard when you first arrived was the pounding of starch for the covers of the Account Book."

ETHNOCENTRISM, JAPANESE STYLE

Editor's Introduction: Sealed off from the outside world and proud of their own tradition, the Japanese all too naturally looked with scorn at those unfortunates scattered around the world who had not been born Japanese.

Hirata Atsutane was a conservative thinker and writer of the early nineteenth century. Unlike most of his contemporaries, Hirata had read a good deal about the West. He knew something of Western medicine, astronomy, even theology. But he put his knowledge to some strange uses. For example, he read in the Christian Bible of a great flood, which was not mentioned in Japanese myths and legends. It followed, he concluded, that Japan, even though it was an island country, was higher above sea level than all those lands that were flooded in Biblical times. By "higher," of course, he also meant culturally superior.

In the first part of this reading, Hirata affirms Japan's status as the "Land of the Gods." In the second part, he attempts to misinform his readers about Dutch people. For more than 200 years, from 1640 to 1853, the Dutch were the only Westerners allowed to trade with Japan. In slandering the Dutch, Hirata is actually demeaning all Westerners.

PEOPLE ALL OVER THE WORLD refer to Japan as the Land of the Gods and call us the descendants of the gods. Indeed, it is exactly as they say: our country, as a special mark of favor from the heavenly gods, was begotten by them, and there is thus so immense a difference between Japan and all the other countries of the world as to defy comparison.

Ours is a splendid and blessed country, the Land of the Gods beyond any doubt, and we, down to the most humble man and woman, are the descendants of the gods. Nevertheless, there are unhappily many people who do not understand why Japan is the land of the gods and we their descendants....

Is this not a lamentable state of affairs? Japanese differ completely from and are superior to the peoples of China, India, Russia, Holland, Siam, Cambodia, and all other countries of the world, and for us to have called our country the Land of the Gods was not mere vainglory. It was the gods who formed all the lands of the world at the Creation, and these gods were without exception born in Japan.

Japan is thus the homeland of the gods, and that is why we call it the Land of the Gods. This is a matter of universal belief, and is quite beyond dispute. Even in countries where our ancient traditions have not been transmitted, the peoples recognize Japan as a divine land because of the majestic effulgence that of itself emanates from our country.

In olden days, when Korea was divided into three kingdoms, reports were heard there of how splendid, miraculous, and blessed a land Japan is, and, because Japan lies to the east of Korea, they said in awe and reverence, "to the East is a divine land, called the Land of the Rising Sun."

Word of this eventually spread all over the world, and now people everywhere refer to Japan as the Land of the Gods, irrespective of whether or not they know why this is true. [14]

Until the twentieth century, the only professional women in Japan were entertainers. These entertainers of today wear the elaborate costumes and coiffures of their predecessors. Photo from the Japan National Tourist Organization.

As everybody knows who has seen one, the Dutch are taller than other people, have fair complexions, big noses, and white stars in their eyes. By nature they are very light-hearted and often laugh. They are seldom angry, a fact which does not accord with their appearance and is a seeming sign of weakness. They shave their beards, cut their nails, and are not dirty like the Chinese. Their clothing is extremely beautiful and ornamented with gold and silver.

Their eyes are really just like those of a dog. They are long from the waist downward, and the slenderness of their legs also makes them resemble animals. When they urinate they lift one leg, the way dogs do. Moreover, apparently because the backs of their feet do not reach to the ground, they fasten wooden heels to their shoes, which makes them look all the more like dogs. This may explain also why a Dutchman's penis appears to be cut short at the end, just like a dog's. This may sound like a joke, but it is quite true, not only of Dutchmen but of Russians too.... This may be the reason why the Dutch are as lascivious as dogs and spend their entire nights at erotic practices.... Because they are thus addicted to sexual excesses and to drink, none of them lives very long. For a Dutchman to reach 50 years is as rare as for a Japanese to live to be over 100. [15]

Self-portrait of Japanese teens. Photo by Hongo Jin, from *Japan Forum* used by permission.

Japan and China, 2006

Japan and China have long historical links. Japan and China today have active links. These include travelers from China to Japan (nearly one million in 2006) and travelers from Japan to China (nearly four million). Over half a million Chinese citizens reside in Japan; more than one hundred thousand Japanese reside in China. This pie chart shows foreign students in Japan as of May 2006.

Nearly 7,000,000 foreigners entered Japan in 2004. More than one million each came from Korea and Taiwan; just less than one million from China; eight hundred thousand from all of Europe; almost eight hundred thousand from the United States; one hundred thousand from all of South America; under twenty-five thousand from all of Africa.

Source: Japan Statistical Yearbook.

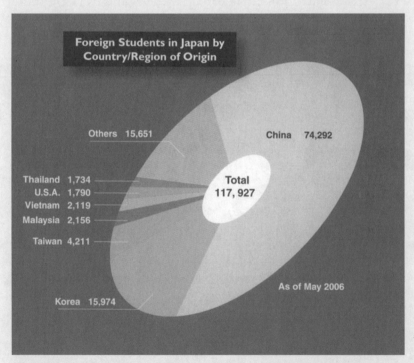

Foreign Students in Japan by Country/Region of Origin

Others 15,651

China 74,292

Thailand 1,734
U.S.A. 1,790
Vietnam 2,119
Malaysia 2,156

Total
117, 927

Taiwan 4,211

As of May 2006

Korea 15,974

Japan-China Relations Enter a New Era, Ministry of Foreign Affairs, Japan.

Editor's Postscript: Hirata wanted his countrymen to think of the Dutch as animals. But many Japanese were immune to his urgings. Indeed, in the late eighteenth century, an older scholar, named Ōtsuki, had written the following dialogue:

Q. There is a rumor that Dutchmen are short-lived. Is it true?
A. I cannot imagine where such a report originated. The length of human life is bestowed by Heaven and does not appear to differ in any country in the world ... just as in Japan, the life-span of the Dutch is not the same for all. Some men live to be 100 years while others die when a bare ten or twenty years of age.

Q. People say that the Dutch are born without heels, or that their eyes are like animals', or that they are giants. Is it true? A. Where, I wonder, do such false reports originate? Is it because their eyes differ somewhat in shape from ours that they are slandered as being animal-like? Perhaps because of the difference in continents, Europeans do differ somewhat from us Asiatics in appearance. But there is no difference whatever in the organs which they possess or their functions.... Even among fellow Japanese there are differences in the appearance of the eyes of people from different quarters of the country which can be recognized. In each instance the eyes thus differ a little in appearance, but the use made of them is always identical. If Japanese differ, how much more is it to be expected that people living over 20,000 miles away on a different continent should differ somewhat! Although we are all products of the same Nature, it is only to be expected that there should be regional differences in looks. As for the heels, they are the base on which the entire body rests—how could anyone get along without them? It is a subject unworthy of discussion. And as for the Dutch being giants, to judge by the height of the three men I have seen ... it is just as in the case of age I mentioned—some are tall and some short.... Moreover, stories to the effect that when Dutchmen urinate they lift one leg like dogs, or that they have many erotic arts, or that they use all kinds of aphrodisiacs are all base canards undeserving of consideration. [16]

III
1850 TO 1940

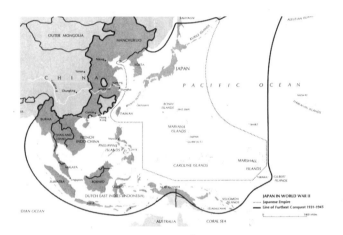

AN END TO
THE CLOSED SOCIETY

Editor's Introduction: In the nineteenth century, various Western governments attempted to bring Japan's policy of isolation to an end. It was the American government and its agent, Admiral Matthew C. Perry, that succeeded.

Perry arrived off the Japanese coast in 1853. He had only four ships; but even this small force was more than the Japanese could handle. The prohibition against Japanese leaving Japan and the years of seclusion had left Japan at a great disadvantage militarily.

During his first visit, Perry delivered a letter from President Millard Fillmore and explained that he would return a year later for the answer. With great reluctance, the Japanese authorities accepted Perry's documents and considered abandoning their policy of seclusion.

The following selections are taken from Perry's letter of instructions from the U.S. government and a letter of advice to the shogun from one Japanese leader. [17]

Instructions to Commodore Perry
Washington, November 5, 1852

AS THE SQUADRON destined for Japan will shortly be prepared to sail, I am directed by the President to explain the objects of the expedition, and to give some general directions as to the mode by which those objects are to be accomplished.

Since the islands of Japan were first visited by European nations, efforts have constantly been made by the various maritime powers to establish commercial intercourse with a country whose large population and reputed wealth hold out great temptations to mercantile enterprise. Portugal was the first to make the attempt, and her example was followed by Holland, England, Spain, and Russia; and finally by the United States. All these attempts, however, have thus far been

During Japan's long period of seclusion, it was illegal to build ships capable of crossing the ocean to China. Today, Japan is far and away the largest shipbuilding nation in the world. Photo from the Japan National Tourist Organization.

unsuccessful; the permission enjoyed for a short period by the Portuguese to trade with the islands, and that granted to Holland to send annually a single vessel to the port of Nagasaki, hardly deserving to be considered exceptions to this remark.

China is the only country which carries on any considerable trade with these islands.

So rigorously is this system of exclusion carried out, that foreign vessels are not permitted to enter their ports in distress, or even to do an act of kindness to their own people....

When vessels are wrecked or driven ashore on the islands their crews are subjected to the most cruel treatment. Two instances of this have recently occurred....

That the civilized nations of the world should for ages have submitted to such treatment by a weak and semibarbarous people, can only be accounted for on the supposition that, from the remoteness of the country, instances of such treatment were of rare occurrence, and the difficulty of chastising it very great. It can hardly be doubted that if Japan were situated as near the continent of Europe or of America as it is to that of Asia, its government would long since have been either treated as barbarians, or been compelled to respect those usages of civilized states of which it receives the protection....

Recent events—the navigation of the ocean by steam, the acquisition and rapid settlement by this country of a vast territory on the Pacific, the discovery of gold in that region, the rapid communication established across the isthmus which separates the two oceans—have practically brought the countries of the east in closer proximity to our own; although the consequences of these events have scarcely begun to be felt, the intercourse between them has already greatly increased, and no limits can be assigned to its future extension....

The objects sought by this government are:

1. To effect some permanent arrangement for the protection of American seamen and property wrecked on these islands, or driven into their ports by stress of weather.

2. The permission to American vessels to enter one or more of their ports in order to obtain supplies of provisions, water, fuel, etc., or, in case of disasters, to refit so as to enable them to prosecute their voyage. It is very desirable to have permission to establish a depot for coal, if not on one of the principal islands, at least on some small uninhabited one, of which, it is said, there are several in their vicinity.

3. The permission to our vessels to enter one or more of their ports for the purpose of disposing of their cargoes by sale or barter....

The next question is, how are the above-mentioned objects to be attained?

It is manifest, from past experience, that arguments or persuasion addressed to this people, unless they be seconded by some imposing manifestation of power, will be utterly unavailing.

You will, therefore, be pleased to direct the commander of the squadron to proceed, with his whole force, to such point on the coast of Japan as he may deem most advisable, and there endeavor to open a communication with the government, and, if possible, to see the emperor in person, and deliver to him the letter of introduction from the President with which he is charged....

If, after having exhausted every argument and every means of persuasion, the commodore should fail to obtain from the government any relaxation of their system of exclusion, or even any assurance of humane treatment of our shipwrecked seamen, he will then change his tone, and inform them in the most unequivocal terms that it is the determination of this government to insist, that hereafter all citizens or vessels of the United States that may be wrecked on their coasts, or driven by stress of weather into their harbors shall, so long as they are compelled to remain there, be treated with humanity; and that if any acts of cruelty should hereafter be practiced upon citizens of this country, whether by the government or by the inhabitants of Japan, they will be severely chastised. In case he should succeed in obtaining concessions on any of the points above mentioned, it is desirable that they should be reduced into the form of a treaty, for negotiating which he will be furnished with the requisite powers.

Carbon Dioxide Emissions, 2004

World Total (in million metric tons)	7,376
China	1,284
Germany	235
India	304
Japan	344
Russia	460
United Kingdom	158
United States	1,612

Source: *Statistical Abstract of the United States: 2007.*
Note: One metric ton is 2,205 pounds. How many pounds are there in 7,376,000,000 tons? How much is one pound of CO_2 emission?

A Japanese Leader to the Shogunate
14 August 1853

It is my belief that the first and most urgent of our tasks is for the Shogunate to make its choice between peace and war....

I propose to give here in outline the ... reasons why in my view we must never choose the policy of peace.

1. Although our country's territory is not extensive, foreigners both fear and respect us. That, after all, is because our resoluteness and military prowess have been clearly demonstrated to the world outside.... Despite this, the Americans who arrived recently, though fully aware of the Shogunate's prohibition, entered Uraga displaying a white flag as a symbol of peace and insisted on presenting their written requests. Moreover they entered Edo Bay, fired heavy guns in salute and even went so far as to conduct surveys without permission. They were arrogant and discourteous, their actions an outrage. Indeed, this was the greatest disgrace we have suffered since the dawn of our history. The saying is that if the enemy dictates terms in one's own capital one's country is disgraced. The foreigners having thus ignored our prohibition and penetrated our waters even to the vicinity of the capital, threatening us and making demands upon us, should it happen not only that the Shogunate fails to expel them but also that it concludes an agreement in accordance with their requests, then I fear it would be impossible to maintain our national prestige. That is the first reason why we must never choose the policy of Peace....

2. To exchange our valuable articles like gold, silver, copper, and iron for useless foreign goods like woolens and satin is to incur great loss while acquiring not the smallest benefit. The best course of all would be for the Shogunate to put a stop to the trade with Holland. By contrast, to open such valueless trade with others besides the Dutch would, I believe, inflict the greatest possible harm on our country. That is [another] reason why we must never choose the policy of peace.

3. For some years Russia, England, and others have sought trade with us, but the Shogunate has not permitted it. Should permission be granted to the Americans, on what grounds would it be possible to refuse if Russia and the others [again] request it? ...

4. I hear that all, even though they be commoners, who have witnessed the recent actions of the foreigners, think them abominable; and if the Shogunate does not expel these insolent foreigners root and branch there may be some

who will complain in secret, asking to what purpose have been all the preparations of gun-emplacements. It is inevitable that men should think in this way when they have seen how arrogantly the foreigners acted at Uraga. That, I believe, is because even the humblest are conscious of the debt they owe their country, and it is indeed a promising sign. Since even ignorant commoners are talking in this way, I fear that if the Shogunate does not decide to carry out expulsion, if its handling of the matter shows nothing but excess of leniency and appeasement of the foreigners, then the lower orders may fail to understand its ideas and hence opposition might arise from evil men who had lost their respect for Shogunal authority. It might even be that Shogunal control of the great lords would itself be endangered....

I have tried to explain above in general terms the relative advantages and disadvantages of the war and peace policies. However, this [policy I recommend] is something that it is easy to understand but difficult to carry out. In these feeble days men tend to cling to peace; they are not fond of defending their country by war. They slander those of us who are determined to fight, calling us lovers of war, men who enjoy conflict. If matters become desperate they might, in their enormous folly, try to overthrow those of us who are determined to fight, offering excuses to the enemy and concluding a peace agreement with him. They would thus in the end bring total destruction upon us. In view of our country's tradition of military courage, however, it is probable that once the Shogunate has taken a firm decision we shall find no such cowards among us. But good advice is as hard to accept as good medicine is unpleasing to the palate. A temporizing and time-serving policy is the one easiest for men to adopt. It is therefore my belief that in this question of coast defense it is of the first importance that the Shogunate pay due heed [to these matters] and that having once reached a decision it should never waver from it thereafter.

THE BEGINNINGS
OF CHANGE

Editor's Introduction: Admiral Perry returned to Japan the following year, 1854. This time he had eight ships, a tiny force today but one-fourth of the U.S. Navy in 1854! Perry's show of force did the trick, and he got his treaty. Japanese seclusion had come to an end.

Japan's renewed contact with the West sparked upheaval in Japanese government and society. Discontented politicians blamed the government in power for Japan's military weakness. This was understandable, for that government had ruled for more than 250 years. Indeed, it had brought about Japan's isolation in the first place.

In 1868 a very different government came to power. Because in theory the new government restored power to the emperor, this change of government is called the Meiji Restoration. (Meiji means enlightened rule.) In fact, however, the new government simply ruled in the name of the emperor, for in 1868 the emperor was only 15 years old.

Beginning in 1868, the government brought about important changes in Japan's economy, politics, and society. It fostered the development of new industries, as well as trade with the West. It promised a new form of government, which would consult those outside the government. Perhaps most important, it abolished the old system of class divisions, making samurai, farmers, and townsmen legal equals. Samurai could now engage in commerce, and townsmen and farmers could enter Japan's new army.

Throughout the reforms of the Meiji government ran a new spirit, summed up best in one of its pledges of 1868: "Knowledge shall be sought throughout the world so as to strengthen the foundations of imperial rule." This openness to new ways on the part of government leaders made possible the emergence of a group of intellectuals who advocated the adoption of important aspects of Western culture.

Fukuzawa Yukichi (1835-1902) was the most famous of these "Westernizers."

Prior to 1868, education beyond basic reading and writing had been open only to a few. One reason was Japan's class society. Samurai might benefit from book learning, but it was a waste of time for others—so people thought. In the first two paragraphs that follow, written in 1871, Fukuzawa discusses human equality and education. In the later passage, Fukuzawa extends his discussion from the level of individuals to the level of nations. [18]

HEAVEN DOES NOT SET one man above another, nor does heaven set one man below another, so it is said. If this is so, then when Heaven gives birth to men, all men are equal. At birth there is no distinction between noble and ig-

The universal education Fukuzawa called for is today a reality. Japan's literacy rate is among the world's highest despite the great complexity of written Japanese. Photo from the Consulate General of Japan, N.Y.

noble, high and low.... Nevertheless, when one looks broadly at this human society of ours today, there are wise people and there are stupid ones; there are poor and there are rich; there are men of high birth and there are men of low birth. Their respective conditions are as far apart as the clouds and the mud. Why is this? The answer is very clear. [It] is a matter of whether or not they have received an education.⟩

In pursuing an education, it is essential to know one's limitations. At birth man has no natural restrictions. Boys are boys and girls, girls. They are free and unrestricted; but if they think only of their own freedom and lack of restriction and do not know their limitations, many will become selfish and dissolute. That is, their limitation is that they should advance their own freedom based on natural principle and in accord with human nature, without creating harm for other people. The boundary which separates freedom from selfishness is that between harming and not harming other people....

Moreover, the matter of freedom and independence is not merely a personal matter. It applies also to nations. Our Japan is an island country to the east of the Asian continent. Since antiquity, it has had no relations with foreign countries. It has clothed and fed itself solely with its own produce. Nor did it feel any insufficiency.

But since the arrival of the Americans in the 1850s, foreign trade has begun, and things have developed to their present condition. Even after the opening of the various ports, there was much dissension. There were those who clamored for closing the country off and expelling the barbarians, but their perspective was extremely narrow. They were like the proverbial frog in the well, and their assertions did not merit adoption.

The peoples of Japan and the Western nations exist in the same world, are warmed by the same sun, look up at the same moon, share the seas and share the air, and have the same human emotions. This being the case, we should hand over our surplus to them, and we should take their surplus. Without shame and without pride, we should both teach each other, both learn from each other. We should assist each other and pray for each other's good fortune. We should establish ties with each other in accord with the principles of heaven and the way of man.

Think Globally...

Five questions that will open the eyes of all concerned to the vastness of the Pacific Ocean and the effect of two-dimensional maps on our thinking:

If I go out into my backyard in Tokyo and dig straight down through the center of the earth, where do I emerge?

If I get in an airplane in New York and fly to San Francisco and, maintaining the same direction, keep going, what is my next major landfall? (Hawaii and minor Pacific islands don't count.)

If I get in an airplane in Tokyo and fly to Honolulu, Hawaii, and, maintaining the same direction keep going, what is my next major landfall?

If I connect San Francisco, Tokyo, and Manila (Philippines), what geometrical figure results?

I want to fly from New York to Singapore by the shortest possible route. I have unlimited fuel, and there are no political restrictions. Which direction do I leave New York?

Notes: First cover up classroom maps and globes. My university library is 26 stories tall, a major depository for government documents and other materials. It possesses no globe. Apparently, non-book items in the collection have to be flat for storage.

JAPANESE IMPERIALISM: THE NINETEENTH CENTURY

Editor's Introduction: The last reading dealt with the cultural impact of the West on Japan. The West also had an enormous effect on other aspects of Japanese life. For example, Japan was forced to sign treaties that gave Western nations and their citizens special privileges in Japan. Nevertheless, Japan was not colonized by the West. In fact, Japan herself soon joined the ranks of the exploiters.

Many factors led Japan, in the years after 1868, to attempt to extend her influence in Asia. For one thing, Japan experienced a growing need for raw materials. For another, Japan's success in modernizing her society seemed to many Japanese to justify taking an active role in "modernizing" the rest of Asia. Many Japanese leaders were all too ready to judge other cultures by Japanese standards and to find these other cultures inferior.

We see some of these factors at work in the next selection, again by Fukuzawa Yukichi, whose ideas on equality, education, and international relations were presented in the last reading. Only a very few years after writing that essay, Fukuzawa sang a very different tune. If a man like Fukuzawa can support imperialist policies, we can expect to find very little opposition among Japanese to the creation of a Japanese empire. [19]

IT IS NOT LONG since the foreigners came to our country, and up till now they have not had time to harm or disgrace us very much, so that most people are not particularly worried about them. But those who truly have their country's welfare at heart must judge the foreigners by what they have done and are doing in the rest of the world.

To whom did the present America once belong? The Red Indians, who were originally masters of the country, were driven out by the white men, so that the position of host and guest has entirely changed. The civilization of America is thus not really America's at all, but the white man's.

And besides, what about the various Eastern countries and the Pacific Islands? Have the European countries really respected the rights and interests and integrity of the countries with which they have come into contact?... The Sandwich Islands [Hawaii] since their discovery by Captain Cook in 1778 are said to have progressed in civilization much more quickly than the neighboring islands. But their population, which was 3,400,000 when they were discovered, had dropped to 140,000 by 1823—so that in the space of fifty years the population had decreased each year by 8 percent.

... What exactly is this thing known as "civilization"? For the people of these islands it meant that they gave up the bad custom of cannibalism, but also that they became slaves of the white man. In the case of an enormous country like China, the white men have not yet been able to penetrate into the interior and have left their mark only on the coast—but it looks very much as though in the future the Chinese Empire will become European territory.

Wherever the Europeans come, the land ceases to be productive, and trees and plants cease to grow. Worse still, the human race sometimes dies out. If people understand these things clearly, and at the same time realize that Japan is an Eastern country, they must inevitably fear for the future, even though up till now Japan has suffered no great harm from foreign intercourse. [1876]

Western nations call themselves "Christian nations" and make a clear distinction between themselves and everyone else. The word "nations" in their so-called Law of Nations does not refer to all the nations in the world, but only to those that happen to be Christian.

The Law of Nations has never been seen to operate in non-Christian countries. It is thus something based entirely on custom and sentiment....

There are some Western scholars, certainly, who deplore this and advocate a truly fair and impartial Law of Nations, but in practice it usually works out in the very opposite way. Take, for example, the cruel way in which the British have ruled the Indians for some years past.... But if one says that the Indians are treated in this way simply because they are weak, it should follow that the many weak countries in the West would also be treated in the same cruel way.

The fact that they are not treated in this way proves that it is not differences in strength but differences in race and kind which are the cause of differences in treatment. Indeed, if it should happen that one of the small countries of their own kind should suffer calamity, someone will always go to their aid.

This is what they call the Balance of Power. Some people try to maintain that the Balance of Power is governed by considerations of political advantage, but this is not to be believed. What really underlies it in practice is the sentiment men bear towards people of their own kind. For whatever excesses Westerners may commit in Eastern countries, no one would dream of lifting a finger against them. [1881]

Since ancient times it has been the custom for countries to make treaties with each other. These documents always profess in the most solemn terms principles of friendship between the two countries. But what is the point, may I ask, of such solemn and high-sounding principles?... Nations are just like merchants, who care only for profit and give no thought to duty, and who exchange contracts with each other only to watch for the first opportunity of breaking them. Merchants, however, will hesitate to break their bonds for fear of proceedings in a law court. But there is no law court in the world to deal with broken bonds between nations. Thus the factor deciding whether promises shall be kept or not, and whether treaties possess authority or not, is the relative wealth and strength of the two countries....

But the point I am trying to make now is that our country is in the greatest danger. Moralists may tell us to sit back and wait for the day when war will cease, but as I see it the Western countries have already greatly developed their military techniques and are likely to develop them even further in future. Lately they have been inventing new and curious weapons every day, and their armies have been daily increasing in size.

All this may be useless and stupid, but when others treat one stupidly one can only do the same back to them. When others use violence we must be violent too. When others use deceitful trickery we must do likewise. And when one is taken up with stupidity, violence, and trickery one has no time to think of right and proper moral behavior. I said before somewhere that nationalism was a temporary expedient but I confess myself to be a supporter of this expedient. [1881]

✑

We cannot wait for our neighbor countries to become so civilized that all may combine together to make Asia progress. We must rather break out of formation and behave in the same way as the civilized countries of the West are doing.... We would do better to treat China and Korea in the same way as do the Western nations. [1885]

Japan's Hollywood, 1991

Like America's Hollywood, Japan's Hollywood is suffering from the competition of videos. Unlike America's Hollywood, Japan's Hollywood usually loses out to a foreign Hollywood. Every year since 1985, American films have earned more in Japan than have Japanese films.

Films in 1991 Earning over ¥1 Billion ($8 Million) in Japan

Domestic Films	Revenue (US $)	Foreign Films	Revenue (US $)
Doraemon Festival	14.4	Terminator 2	40.0
Dripping with Memories	14.4	Home Alone	27.2
It's Tough Being a Man	11.3	Pretty Woman	24.8
Toei Animation (Spring '91)	11.2	Total Recall	19.2
Toei Animation (Summer '91)	10.4	Dances with Wolves	12.2
Chibi Maruko-chan	9.6	Godfather Part III	10.2
Dohten	8.4	Rocky 5	8.4
Fukuzawa Yukichi	8.4	Neverending Story	8.4
Hug Me as Many Times as the Waves Come In	8.4	Robin Hood	8.0

Like America's Hollywood, Japan's Hollywood is targeting younger and younger audiences. Five of 1991's top nine films were cartoons, and "Doraemon Festival" aims at the elementary school crowds.

Yet the Japanese industry has produced some of the greatest films of all time ....

Source: Adapted from *Focus Japan* 19:7 (July 1992).

THE FACTORY SHIP

Editor's Introduction: The economic development of Japan—either before the Pacific War or after—has not come without its costs, including the degradation of the environment, the destruction of a sense of community, and the imposition of hardships on large segments of the population. As in Europe and the United States, working people suffered—in sweat shops, in child labor, in low standards of living. This suffering produced activists who worked to change the conditions and writers who wrote to draw attention to the conditions. In the United States in the early twentieth century, writers like Upton Sinclair (*The Jungle*) exposed conditions in industry; in Japan, Kobayashi Takiji was the most famous of the so-called "proletarian" (i.e., worker) writers.

Kobayashi, author of *The Factory Ship* (1929), lived most of his short life in Hokkaido, the northern island of Japan. From Hokkaido, factory ships—ships with fishermen to catch crabs and canners to can them, all on the same ship—went out into the northern seas. Kobayashi based his book on actual events, although he himself did not witness them. Much of the book contains language and incidents that are too stark and brutal to include here. [20]

.... "WHAT A HELL OF A PLACE I chose to come to!" The fisherman who spoke had once worked at a factory in the Shibaura district of Tokyo. In the wake of this outburst, talk shifted to life in the factories. To the laborers from Hokkaido, who could scarcely imagine what a factory was like, it sounded like a fine place. The man said, "If even one of the hundred things we put up with here had happened where I used to work, there would have been a strike."

As if this were a cue, the men began one after another to tell about what they had done before. Construction work on national highways. Irrigation work. Railway construction work. Harbor construction and land reclamation. Opening up of new mines. Clearing wasteland. Loading and unloading ships. Sardine fishing. The men had all done a hitch at one of these jobs, before signing up on the ship.

In the eyes of the capitalists, the laborers on the Honshu had become arrogant and recalcitrant. Besides, the market was pretty thoroughly exploited and the entrepreneurs had reached an impasse. So they had begun to extend their rapacious claws into Hokkaido and Sakhalin. There, as in the colonies of Korea and Taiwan, they could exploit brutally with an absolutely free hand, knowing full well that they were above censure. In the barracks of workers recruited for the construction of national highways and railways, men were beaten to death, their lives valued no more than those of lice....

Many men in the construction gangs died of a combination of beriberi and overwork, but, since there was no way to dispose of their corpses, they were left lying about for several days. In the dusky areas behind their shacks they could see, sticking out from under straw mat covering flung over the bodies, pairs of dull-looking, yellowish-gray legs that had shrunk in some strange way so that they looked like those of children.

"Their faces were covered with flies. When I passed by, they all flew up in a cloud!" A worker coming into the barracks spoke in disbelief.

The workers started in on their jobs while it was still dark and continued until they could see nothing but the silvery flashes of their picks. So miserable were they that they envied the prisoners working in a nearby jail. But the Koreans suffered most. They were maltreated by everybody—the foremen, the section, and even their own fellow workers, the Japanese.

A policeman stationed in a village about four or five miles from the construction site would occasionally trudge the full distance, notebook in hand, just to check up on the men. He sometimes stayed until evenings, sometimes overnight. But he never once showed up at the men's quarters. As he finally turned homeward his face would be flushed, and, muttering incoherently, he would urinate in the middle of the road, spraying here and there like a fireman fighting a brushfire.

In Hokkaido, each railway tie literally represented the clay-colored corpse of one worker. And in harbor reclamation work, each piling was the body of a worker claimed by beriberi. They might have been the human pillars buried alive in ancient times. In Hokkaido, workers were referred to as "octopuses" since, to keep itself alive, the octopus will eat its own tentacles, if it must. What real difference was there basically between the workers and this sea creature? They could be exploited in the most primitive way without a moment's concern for public opinion. Enormous profits accrued in this way. The maltreatment of workers was justified under such catch phrases as "Development of National Resources." Oh, they were shrewd all right! Workers starved and were beaten to death for the sake of the nation.

"It's a miracle I got away from that place alive! I'm thankful for that. But if they work me to death on this ship, it'll be the same thing, won't it? What a joke!" The man laughed, his voice unnaturally loud, then he stopped and turned to one side with a look of anguish.

It was the same at the mines. To open a new mine, the capitalists used wave after wave of laborers (who were, after all, as expendable as guinea pigs) to determine the existence of gas accumulations or other risks. (This was the same method the military hero General Nogi had used in capturing Port Arthur from the Russians.) There was no more concern for the men than for used paper tissue. The walls of the mines were literally strengthened, layer upon layer, by flesh torn from the workers' bodies like filets of fish. Here, too, the isolation from the cities permitted conditions that made the skin crawl. Sometimes a crushed thumb or little finger would be seen among the lumps of coal being trundled out in a handcar, but the women and children who saw it were trained not to make a fuss over that sort of thing. Their faces expressionless, they would merely push the car on to the next station. This was the coal that moved gigantic machines for the profit of the capitalists.

All the miners had puffy, lusterless yellow skin and the vacant stare characteristic of men long shut up in prison. It was obvious that their health was being ruined by the lack of sunshine, the poisonous air with its coal dust and toxic gases, and the unnatural temperature and pressure levels.

"If you've worked in the mines for seven or eight years, that means you've spent the equivalent of at least four or five full years underground without seeing the sun. Think of it—four or five years!"

But this was of little concern to the capitalists, who could mobilize any number of replacements despite the appalling conditions. When winter came, there was no dearth of workers who flocked to the mines.

Then there were the "frontier farmers"—peasants who had migrated to Hokkaido. The poor farmers on the main island who were about to lose their land were stirred up by skillful propaganda films with titles like "The Opening Up of Hokkaido," "A Solution to the Population and Food Problems: The Encouragement of Immigration," and (here was something spun out of the phantasies of boyhood) "The Immigrant Millionaire." But in contrast to the rosy picture painted for them, the farmers found, when they finally got to their destination, they were herded onto land that, under its four- or five-inch cover of loam, was clay. Around the plots of richer arable land were posted notices of ownership. Isolated in their cabins without even potatoes to eat, families starved to death, and their bodies lay undiscovered until after the spring thaw. There were many such cases—a neighbor living two miles away might come by when

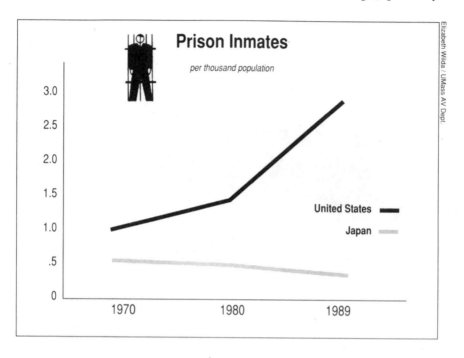

Elizabeth Wilda / UMass AV Dept.

Japan's prison population in 2004 was 76,413 individuals. The U.S. prison population at the end of 2003 was about 2,100,000. (Neither figure includes those in juvenile facilities.) How do these figures change the two lines in this chart?

the snow was melting and discover the entire family dead, half-chewed bits of straw sticking out of their mouths.

In the rare case where a farmer managed to fight off starvation and cultivate the wilderness for ten years, the land would be taken away from him just when he had transformed it into a productive farm, and it was hard for him not to believe that this had not all been prearranged. The capitalists, that is to say, the moneylenders, the banks, the aristocracy, and the rich, knew that when they made their paltry loans to the farmers—so small that the money was hardly missed—they were certain of its returning to them in the form of fertile land, as black as the fur on a plump cat. Recognizing a good thing when they saw it, sharp-eyed operators, out for quick profits, flocked to Hokkaido. So the farmers found their land being carved up by both groups. In the end, they were reduced to what they had been in Japan proper—tenant farmer. It was only then that the truth finally sank in—they had been taken in. All of them had crossed the Tsugaru Strait into snowbound Hokkaido intending to make some money and then return to their birthplaces. Among the workers on the factory ship there were many such disillusioned farmers who had been driven off their land by others.

The dockhands on board the ship had experiences much like those of the fishermen. While idling away their time in Otaru at boarding houses that were under surveillance by entrepreneurs, they had suddenly been shanghaied and taken into the interiors of Sakhalin and Hokkaido, where they were worked cruelly. If one of the deckhand lost his footing while working, he would be crushed flat in an instant under a roaring avalanche of lumber. Many a man was flicked into the ocean, as lightly as though he were a flea, his skull cracked when a log being lifted by rattling winches, its bark loosed by water, veered and swung against his head.

On the main island, the laborers who refused to die banded together and resisted the capitalists. But the laborers in the "colonies" were completely isolated from such movements. Their suffering was already unbearable, yet each time they stumbled they picked themselves up only to find that, like a snowball, they had added another layer onto their crushing load.

"What's going to happen to us?"

"They're going to kill us. That's clear enough."

A silence fell over the group, as words died in their throats.

Then the stutterer blurted out impulsively, "I'll g-get him before he gets me!"

Gentle swells slapped against the sides of the ship. Steam seemed to be escaping from a pipe somewhere on the upper deck; there was a soft, ceaseless whistling sound as of an iron kettle boiling over.

Before going to bed, the fishermen removed their jersey or flannel undershirts, now stiff as a dried cuttlefish with sweat and oil, and spread them over the stove. After the shirts had warmed, men standing near the stove would lift one, holding it by the edges, and shake it, showering lice and bedbugs onto the hot stove, where they sizzled, sending up a smell like burning human flesh....

At first the men were allowed to bathe every other day, to remove the choking stench of sweat and fish. But after a week or so on the high seas, the baths were spaced at every three days and, after a month, once a week. Finally, it was down to twice a month. This was ordered as a means of conserving water. The captain and the superintendents, however, bathed every day, which was, apparently, not considered a waste of water. The men's bodies were stained with the juice of the crabs, and for days on end there was no way to get rid of it. No wonder the men were infested by lice and bedbugs. When the men undid their loincloths, black specks fell out of them, and the loincloths left a red band on the skin around the belly, maddeningly itchy. Lying in their bunks, the men heard everywhere the sounds of violent scratching. A small coiled spring would seem to move under their bodies, followed instantly by a sharp bite. Tossing and turning brought no relief from the agony, which lasted until it was time to get up. Their skin turned scaly as though with scabies.

"You look like a dead louse."

"That's just about what I am." The man couldn't help laughing.

Editor's Postscript: How do we assess *The Factory Ship*? What questions should we ask of it? Important questions have to do with the author's life and thought. Who was he? Why did he write?

Kobayashi was born in 1903 to a poor farm family. He spent most of his life in Hokkaido. He graduated from commercial school in 1924 and later failed the university entrance exam; so he remained a bank clerk. His interest in labor issues was in part a function of hard times in the 1920s; it led him into political activity and brought him to the attention of the secret police.

The Factory Ship was banned as soon as it appeared. One passage in the work earned him six months in jail for insulting the emperor; his political activities led the bank to fire him. Police pressure soon forced him underground, but in February 1933 the police captured him, and within six hours he was dead. The police reported that he died of a heart attack, but the heart attack—if there was one—came after torture and beating.

Kobayashi himself discussed his aims in writing *The Factory Ship:*

There are no heroes in this work—no leading characters or persons such as you would find in works dealing with the lives of individuals. The collective hero is a group of laborers.... There have been other short stories that depicted groups, but I believe this is the first time it has been attempted in a long work. It was a risk and a difficult task from every standpoint. Anyway, I believe that the treatment of the group is the line along which proletarian literature must develop in the future. If my work serves this purpose, I shall be satisfied.

It follows, then, that I have rejected all attempts at depicting character or delving into psychology.... Detailed descriptions of character and psychology are gradually being eliminated from proletarian [working class] literature. But I think I have done my best not to bore my readers, which is often the danger in such an endeavor.

All sorts of stylistic devices are being used at present in an attempt to popularize proletarian literature. These are significant attempts, but there is something in them that smacks of an "intellectual style" and makes them seem no more than clever pieces. There is no force in them capable of shaking up a public toiling in the real work-a-day world. The public will subconsciously resent any kind of "intellectual" approach. I believe I have found the answer to this problem by (a) making my works overwhelmingly proletarian in approach and content, and (b) attempting to imbue my works as much as possible with these qualities. I also wonder if the light touch and the fast tempo found in the new proletarian works do not, despite all good intentions, have too "modern" a feeling. *The Factory Ship* has none of the lightness of touch or quickness of tempo currently in favor. Neither does it have any of the clever "intellectual" touches I mentioned earlier. I have tried to make this work feel as "proletarian" as possible....

In this work I have dealt with the unique form of labor found on the crab-processing ships, but this does not mean I have prepared an exhaustive description of what such a ship is like. Rather, I have tried to show (a) that this is a classical example of the exploitation being carried out in the colonies and new Japanese territories; (b) that when we step outside of the industrialized areas of Tokyo and Osaka, we see that the present condition of eighty percent of the laborers throughout Japan is exactly like conditions that exist in the factory ships; and (c) that it was a fitting method by which I could clearly (also transparently) exemplify the interlocking network of the international web formed by the military and business....

The proletariat cries out that it is utterly opposed to imperialist wars, but I wonder how many workers in Japan really understand why they must protest. Nevertheless, they must be made to understand. This is a matter of the utmost urgency. If I were to describe only the brutalities within the army, I could elicit merely righteous indignation; they are acts against humanity. But I would not have touched on the mechanisms of imperialism that move the army itself, nor upon the economic basis of imperialist wars. The imperial armed forces, the *zaibatsu*, international relations, and the workers; these four elements must all be seen together in their true relationships. For this purpose, I felt that the factory ship provided the most appropriate stage.

JOLLY GREEN GIANT GOES TO JAPAN

Pillsbury & Co. of Minneapolis (75%) and Nippon Suisan Kaisha Ltd. (25%) have formed a new company, Green Giant Frozen Foods, to sell frozen foods in Japan. Sales for the first year are expected to reach $15 million.

Source: *JETRO Monitor*, May 1992.

IMPERIAL JAPAN, 1940

Editor's Introduction: The Japanese empire remained relatively stable from 1910 to 1930. There were crises and threats, and World War I had its effects; but Japan's overseas possessions remained the same: Korea, Taiwan, and an economic edge in Manchuria.

But in the 1930s things changed. In part because of the Great Depression, in part because of events in Asia and elsewhere, in part for other reasons entirely, Japan moved to expand its military control. It set up a puppet government in Manchuria (1932), expanded its area of control into North China, and stumbled into a major war against China (1937 to 1945). Isolated diplomatically by Great Britain and the United States, Japan turned to Nazi Germany.

In 1941, after the United States and its allies cut off Japan's oil, Japan added them to the list of its opponents by attacking Pearl Harbor and other sites in the Pacific.

In June 1940, Foreign Minister Arita Hachiro delivered the following radio address. [21]

.... IT SEEMS TO BE A MOST NATURAL STEP that peoples who are closely related to each other geographically, racially, culturally, and economically should first form a sphere of their own for coexistence and coprosperity and establish peace and order within that sphere, and at the same time secure a relationship of common existence and prosperity with other spheres. The cause of strife which mankind has hitherto experienced lies generally in the failure to give due consideration to the necessity of some such natural and constructive world order and to remedy old irrationalities and injustices....

It is in this spirit that Japan is now engaged in the task of establishing a new order in East Asia. It is extremely regrettable, therefore, that there should be those who not only fail to understand Japan's great undertaking based upon this fundamental principle but, on the contrary, obstruct establishment of peace in East Asia by supporting the regime of Chiang Kai-shek. We have urged them to reconsider such an attitude in the past, and now we intend further to urge

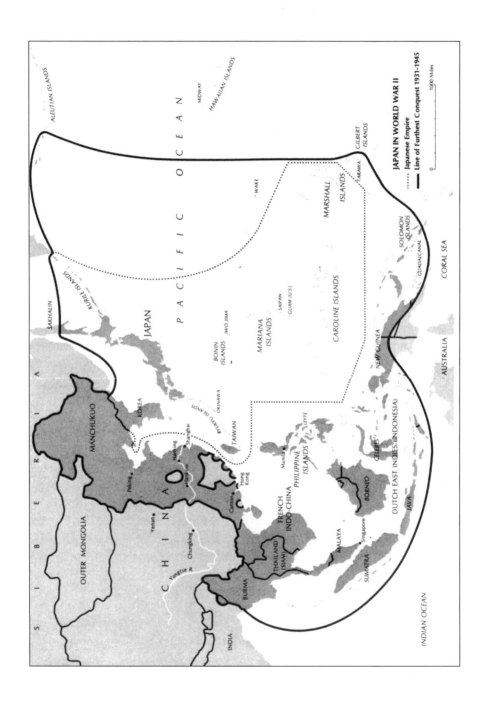

JAPAN IN WORLD WAR II
Japanese Empire
Line of Furthest Conquest 1931-1945

0   1000 Miles

their serious reflection. We are determined to leave no stone unturned in order to eradicate all activities for assisting Chiang Kai-shek.

Sometimes there are those who would disapprove a change in the *status quo* by force of arms regardless of the reasons therefor. It is for the purpose of bringing about a just and permanent peace that Japan has been fighting in China for the past three years. Her employment of armed force is an act looking beyond the immediate present. The sword she has drawn is intended to be nothing other than a life-giving sword that destroys evil and makes justice manifest.

Countries of East Asia and regions of the South Seas are geographically, historically, racially, and economically very closely related to each other. They are destined to help each other and minister to one another's needs for their common well-being and prosperity, and to promote peace and progress in their regions. Uniting of all these regions under a single sphere on the basis of common existence and insuring thereby the stability of that sphere is, I think, a natural conclusion. The idea to establish first a righteous peace in each of the various regions and then establish collectively a just peace for the whole world has long existed also in Europe and America. This system presupposes the existence of a stabilizing force in each region, with which as a center the peoples within that region are to secure their coexistence and co-prosperity and as well the stability of their sphere. It also presupposes that these groups will respect [one] another's individual characteristics, political, cultural, and economic, and they will cooperate and fulfill one another's needs for their common good....

Japan, while carrying on vigorously her task of constructing a new order in East Asia, is paying serious attention to developments in the European war and to its repercussions in the various quarters of East Asia, including the South Seas [Southeast Asia] region. I desire to declare that the destiny of these regions in any development therein, and any disposal thereof, is a matter of grave concern to Japan in view of her mission and responsibility as the stabilizing force in East Asia.

LOST NAMES

Editor's Introduction: The Japanese empire was not welcomed by most Asians who were drawn into its orbit. In China and Korea, in the Philippines and in the Dutch East Indies (Indonesia), Japanese actions antagonized the very people the Japanese claimed to be helping.

From 1905 until 1945, Korea was under Japanese control. Richard Kim, the author of the following selection, was born in Korea in 1932. The event he describes, a poignant example of colonial domination, actually took place in 1940. Kim now lives in the United States. [22]

.... BUT, AFTER ALL, there is no school that morning—for me and a few other children, that is. When I arrive at the school, our teacher is already in our classroom. He is a young Japanese, a recent graduate of a college in Tokyo. He is twenty-four years old, soft-spoken, and rather gentle with the children. He is lean, in fact, so lean that we give him a nickname the moment he is assigned to our class: Chopstick. Always pale-faced and looking in poor health, he likes to recite Japanese poetry in class, though we hardly understand it....

"Well," he says.

And I bid the children rise from their chairs, and, when they do, 1 command them to bow to our teacher. We all bow our heads to him; then we sit down.

"Today," he says, without looking at us, holding up the piece of paper in front of him, "I must have your new names. I have the new names of most of you in this class, but the principal tells me that some of you have not yet registered your names. I shall call your old names, and those who are called will be excused from the class immediately, so that they can go home and return with their new names, which have been properly registered with the proper authorities in town. Do you understand what I am saying?"

Without waiting for our reaction, and still without looking at us, he calls out several names. My name is called.

"You may be excused," he says, crunching the piece of paper into a ball in his fist. "Report back as soon as you can."

He gets down from the platform and says, "The rest of you will remain quiet and go over your homework." With that announcement, he abruptly turns away from us and walks out of the room.

I put my shoes on outside the classroom and, brushing aside the questions from the bewildered children, I start running away from the school as fast as I can in the blinding snow and choking, icy wind, running and skidding and stumbling in the deep snow. My new name, my old name, my true name, my not-true name? I am plunging and slogging through the snow, thinking, "I am going to lose my name; I am going to lose my name; we are all going to lose our names."

⁂

My grandmother says, "Leave the boy home. He will catch cold."

My father says, "No, Mother. I want him to come with me. I want him to see it and remember it." My father is wearing a Korean man's clothes: white pantaloon-like trousers, with the bottoms tied around his ankles, a longsleeved white jacket, a blue vest, and a gray topcoat. My father is seldom seen in our native clothes, except when he has to attend a wedding or a funeral. He is wearing a black armband on the left sleeve of his gray topcoat. He is not wearing a hat.

"Have some hot soup before you go," says my grandmother.

"No, thank you, Mother," says my father, holding my hand. "Stay with Father and keep an eye on him."

My grandmother nods. "It is the end of the world," she mutters angrily. "Damn them! damn them!"

"Come on," says my father to me.

Outside, by the west gate, four of my father's friends are waiting for us. They are dressed like my father—all wearing black armbands on the left sleeves of their gray topcoats. I bow to them, but no one says a word either to me or to anyone else. On the small stone bridge outside the gate, they pause for a moment, whispering among themselves. The stream is frozen and covered thick with snow. Passers-by bow to the group. The four men—my father's friends—are the bookstore owner, an elder of our Presbyterian church, a doctor, and a farmer who also has an apple orchard. The snow is slashing down on us, and my ears are cold, even with ear muffs on. Snowflakes get inside my collar, making me shiver. We walk down the street; my father is in the middle of the group, holding my hand. I slip on an icy patch and stumble, and the bookstore owner helps me up and holds my hand. In the snow-covered open-air market place, which is closed down during the winter, the wind howls even more strongly, shrieking through the electric wires and telephone poles. The snow is beating down so hard that I have

Tokyo Teacher Embattled Over War History

Tokyo—Masuda Miyako is a 23-year veteran of public schools here. Like many Japanese history teachers of her generation, she dislikes new textbooks that frame Japan as the victim in World War II.

Yet until last year, Masuda, who calls herself "pretty ordinary," rarely went out of her way to disagree. Few teachers do.

But when a Tokyo city councilman in an official meeting said, "Japan never invaded Korea," her history class sent an apology to Korean President Roh Moo-hyun—an action that sparked her removal from her classroom.

"I feel it is my job to tell the truth; it is what I spend my life doing. When something looks crooked, I don't like it. I feel I want to straighten it out. If you are straight, it's better for everyone. I explain and teach the past. But I am now suspended as a history teacher for doing that...."

Source: Robert Marquand, *The Christian Science Monitor*, November 22, 2005.

to bow my head and face sideways, but the men are walking straight up, occasionally returning, in silence, the bows from the other men on the street. We go past the town hall, past the Japanese department store and shops, and through the main street, where most of the shops are—the bakery, the barber shop, the watch shop, the restaurant, the clothing store, the bicycle shop, the grain store, the pharmacy, the doctor's office, the dentist's office, the hardware store, the bank, the grocery store—and the townspeople are looking out from their shops and offices—some bowing to us, some waving at us—and, as we continue down the main street, we are followed by other people, and more and more people join us as we come near the end of the main street. My father and the bookstore owner are still holding my hands, and I have to try hard to keep up with the men, though they are walking very slowly. At the end of the main street, we come to an intersection and turn to the right. It is an uphill road, and the snow-laden wind whips down from the top of the hill, almost blowing me off my feet, and I feel the men's hands tighten their grips on mine. At the top of the hill, there is a small Methodist church and, across from it, the police station. We struggle up the snow-packed hill, by the long stone wall of the police station, and enter its main gate. Inside, on the station grounds, in the deep snow, a long line of people barely moves along. We walk over the crackling snow and stand at the end of the line. We exchange bows with the people standing in line. No one says anything—I, my father, the bookstore owner, the doctor, the farmer, the elder of our church, and all those people who have preceded or followed us....

I am freezing with cold, I stamp my feet, crushing the icy snow on the ground. Without a word, the bookstore owner opens the front of his topcoat and pulls me inside and covers me up, except for my face, which is snuggled against the back of my father. He turns, looks at me, and fixes my ear muffs. He neither says a word to me nor smiles at me. I know when to keep quiet.

The line, hardly advancing, gets longer and longer. New people are lined up even outside the station grounds.

Someone comes to us. Someone from the front of the line. He is a young Korean man. He bows to my father. "Please, sir," he says, "come and take my place."

My father shakes his head. "I will wait for my turn here. Thank you anyway."

He stands silent for a moment.

"It is all right," my father says. "Go back to your place."

He bows to my father once more and says, before he returns to the front of the line, "I am dying of shame, sir"; then, his words nearly lost in the howling snow, "I don't know what I can do."

A little while later, a Japanese policeman comes toward us. When he comes near to us, I can tell that he is an inspector. He is wearing a black cape. I see his long saber peering out of the bottom of his cape. I can hear the clank the saber makes against his black leather riding boots. He salutes my father. He has a long turned-up mustache. "It is an honor," he says to my father, "to see you in person here. You could have sent one of your servants."

My father is silent.

"Please come with me," says the Inspector. "I can't have you lined up out here like a common person. Please."

"I will wait for my turn, just like everyone else," says my father. "They have been here longer than I have."

"Come with me," insists the Inspector. "Please."

Afraid and, to my shame, trembling, I look up at my father.

My father looks at the Inspector and then at his friends.

Other people are watching us.

I feel the hands of the bookstore owner tighten on my shoulders.

"If you insist," says my father.

The Inspector looks down at me. "You must be freezing," he says. His white-gloved hand reaches out for my snow-covered hair.

I duck my head inside the topcoat of the bookstore owner.

"Bring the boy with you, by all means," says the Inspector. I hear my father's boots crunching on the snow. I free myself out of the bookstore owner's hands and nearly bump into the back of my father.

He takes my hand. "Come with me."

The Inspector walks beside my father. His black cape is billowing in the wind and snow, flapping and flapping—and his saber jingling and clanking. We walk toward the front door of the granite station building. As we pass by the people in the line, they bow to my father silently. My father's head is bowed, and, without looking at the people, he goes slowly, holding my hand.

The Inspector opens the front door and holds it for us. A Korean detective inside the building quickly bows to my father. "You really didn't have to come in person, sir," he says in Korean. "I would have been glad to have registered your new name for you if I had known you were coming in person. In this cold."

We are inside the station. Other people in the line are admitted inside one at a time. The air is steamy and warm. The hallway is swarming with black-uniformed policemen, all wearing sabers. The wooden floor is slushy with melting snow.

The Inspector ushers us into a large room immediately to the right of the hallway by the door. There are two big tables, each with a policeman sitting behind. At each table, by the side of the Japanese policeman, a Korean detective sits on a chair, apparently interpreting for those Koreans who cannot understand Japanese.

The Korean detective who met us at the door brings a chair from the back of the room. He offers it to my father.

My father does not sit down.

The Inspector tells the detective to bring some tea.

One of the men sitting at one of the tables facing the Japanese policeman cannot speak Japanese and has to have the words interpreted. The man is old; he helps out in the open-air market place on market days, doing odd jobs.

The Japanese policeman, dipping a pen in an inkwell, does not lift his face from a large ledger on the table when he says to the Korean detective by his side, "Tell the old man we will pick out a name for him if he can't make up his mind."

The Korean detective picks up a sheet of paper and shows it to the old man, translating the policeman's words.

The old man shakes his head, looking at the paper, which contains a long list of names. "Anything," he mumbles. "It doesn't matter."

The Korean detective does not translate those words. Instead, he puts his finger on one of the names and says, "How about this one, old man?"

The old man says, "It doesn't matter which. No one's going to call me by that name anyway—or by any other name."

"Then, this will be recorded as your new name." The Korean detective tells the policeman the old man's "new" name—a Japanese name.

"All right," says the policeman. He writes the name in the ledger. "What about his family members?"

The Inspector comes back into the room, accompanied by another Japanese policeman. I know him. He is the Chief of Police.

My father exchanges bows with the Chief of Police.

The Chief of Police says, "Such inclement weather, and you honor us by being here in person. Is this your son?"

I edge nearer to my father.

The Chief of Police, a short man with bushy eyebrows and large eyes behind dark brown tortoise-shell glasses, looks at the Inspector and says, "Well, I trust the Inspector here will take care of your matter as speedily as he can. Anything, anytime I can be of help or service, please call on me. I am, indeed, honored by your presence here in person."

My father and he exchange bows again. The Chief of Police goes out of the room, his black leather riding boots jangling and dragging his spurs on the wet floor.

My father takes out a piece of paper from his vest pocket. He hands it to the Inspector. "I assume," he says, "this is what you want, Inspector. I hope you will be pleased."

The Inspector looks at the paper. "Yes, yes," he says. "Iwamoto.... Ah—it is a very fine name, sir. It does justice to your person. It reminds me of your house by the mountain and, also, of your orchard, with all those rocky mountains around it. I will have it registered. You needn't wait for the certificate, needless to say. I will have someone bring it to your house later."

"Iwamoto" ... "Iwamoto." I mouth the name. Our new name. My new name. "Iwa"—rock. "Moto"—root ... base ... foundation. "Rock-foundation." So this is our "new" surname, our Japanese "family" name.

"Come," my father says to me.

The Korean detective leads us out, with the Inspector by my side. At the front door, which the detective holds open, the Inspector gives my father a salute. "I thank you, sir, for taking the trouble to come in person."

We step out into the cold. The snow is turning into a blizzard. The long line of people is still standing outside, hunched and huddled, rubbing their ears and faces, stamping their feet in the snow. My father pauses for a moment on the steps, one arm around my shoulders, and says:

"Look."

Afraid, bewildered, and cold, I look up at his face and see tears in his eyes.

"Take a good look at all of this," he whispers. "Remember it. Don't ever forget this day."

I look at all those people lined up, from the steps all the way to the gate and outside. I feel a tug at my hand, and I follow him down the steps. We walk by the people slowly, my father not speaking. They bow to him, some removing their hats. My father, bowing back, approaches the group of his friends still in line. In silence, they shake hands.

Then, we move on along the line of people standing in the snow. Some shake hands with my father; most of them merely bow, without words. We are outside the gate. There, too, a long line has formed and is still forming, all the way down the hill, past the gray stucco Methodist church ... and I am thinking. "We lost our names; I lost my name; and these people are all going to lose their names, too, when they walk into the police station, into that half-empty large hall, when a 'new' name, a Japanese name, is entered in the big ledger with a pen dipped into a dark blue inkwell...."

৵

About four miles out of town, between our house and the orchard, the cemetery lies at the foot of a hill that gradually rises up to become a craggy, rock-strewn, barren mountain. It is what the townspeople call a common burying ground, one that is used by poor people who cannot provide their dead with a private cemetery—with the hope that, someday, when they can afford a family burial plot, they will exhume the dead and move them to their own, private graves. My family is not poor—now; it was poor in the days of my great-grandfather, when he was young, and, of course, before their time. All our known ancestors are buried in the common burying ground, where I am now plowing through the deep snow in the wailing wind—my grandfather's parents and my grandmother's parents are buried next to each other.

Twenty or thirty people are moving about the burying ground. Some are in white; some, in gray, like my father and my grandfather. All are shrouded with white snow; now, some are kneeling before graves; some, brushing the snow off gravestones; some, wandering about like lost souls....

When we are in front of the graves of our ancestors, my father wipes the snow off the gravestone. The names chiseled on the gravestones are filled with ice, so that I can barely distinguish the outlines of the letters.

The three of us are on our knees, and, after a long moment of silence, my grandfather, his voice weak and choking with a sob, says, "We are a disgrace to our family. We bring disgrace and humiliation to your name. How can you forgive us!"

He and my father bow, lowering their faces, their tears flowing now unchecked, their foreheads and snowcovered hair touching the snow on the ground. I, too, let my face fall and touch the snow, and I shiver for a moment with the needling iciness of the snow on my forehead. And I, too, am weeping, though I am vaguely aware that I am crying because the grown-ups are crying....

The snow keeps falling from a darkening sky, millions and millions of wild, savage pellets swirling and whishing about insolently before they assault us with malicious force. I watch the people everywhere, all those indistinct figures engulfed in the slashing snow, frozen still, like lifeless statuettes—and I am cold, hungry, and angry, suddenly seized with indescribable fury and frustration. I am dizzy with a sweet, tantalizing temptation to stamp my feet, scratch and tear at everything I can lay my hands on, and scream out to everyone in sight to stop— *Stop! Please stop!*—*stop* crying and weeping and sobbing and wailing and chanting.... Their pitifulness, their weakness, their self-lacerating lamentation for their ruin and their misfortune repulse me and infuriate me. What are we doing anyway—kneeling down and bowing our heads in front of all those graves? I am gripped by the same outrage and revolt I felt at the Japanese shrine, where, whipped by the biting snow and mocked by the howling wind, I stood, like an idiot, bowing my head to the gods and the spirit of the Japanese Emperor ... and I remember my father's words: "I am ashamed to look in your eyes. Someday, your generation will have to forgive us." ...

And—with the kind of cruelty only a child can inflict on adults—I scream out toward those frozen figures:

"I don't care about losing my name! I am just cold and *hungry!*"

And only then do I give in to a delicious sensation of self-abandonment— and I begin to cry.

My father is at my side. "We'll go home now."

With tear-filled eyes, I look up at him. "I am sorry, but ..."

"Yes?"

"But—what good can all of this do? What good will all of this do for us?" I say defiantly, flinging my arms wide open to encompass the burying ground, with all its graves and the people; "What good will all this do to change what happened!"

To my surprise, he says quickly, "Nothing."

"Then, why do you? ..."

"That is enough now," he says. "Someday, you will understand." ...

It is dark, and, with the coming of darkness and the night, the wind is dying down, and the snow is falling straight and calmly. The blurry figures of the people move about the burying ground like ghosts haunting the graves in the snow.

At the bottom of the hill, my father asks, "Would you like me to carry you on my back?"

I nod unabashedly and climb onto his back, nuzzling my frozen face against him, clinging to his broad shoulders.

And so, in such a way then, the three of us, the three generations of my family, bid farewell to our ancestors in their graves, which we can no longer see in the heavy snow, and join the others from the town to find our way back to our home.

Today, I lost my name. Today, we all lost our names—February 11, 1940.

Editor's Postscript: Kim's moving account is very effective literature. How trustworthy is it as history? Consider these points. First, Kim was the son of a Christian minister in largely Buddhist Korea; his father was a noted patriot (that is, from the Japanese point of view, an agitator). His family was wealthy and educated when most Koreans were too poor to afford an education. So in many ways, Kim was atypical.

Second, Kim wrote this account in English and published it in 1970, 30 years after the fact. Kim was then 38, a professor of English at the University of Massachusetts. In between 1940 and 1970, Kim had served in the Korean Army (1950-1954) during the Korean War, gone to Middlebury College (1955-1959), earned three M.A. degrees (at Johns Hopkins, Iowa, and Harvard), become a U.S. citizen (1964), and written two best-selling novels in English. Is this excerpt from this third major work, *Lost Names*, truth or fiction? Are these the thoughts of an eight-year-old boy, or 40-year-old thoughts put into the mouth of an eight-year-old boy?

Regardless, February 11, 1940, happened. It was one of the clumsiest and most ethnocentric acts of a Japanese colonial administration that created enemies of Japan throughout East and Southeast Asia.

IV
THE WAR YEARS

WORLD WAR II

Editor's Introduction: Only 18 months after Foreign Minister Arita's address in June 1940, the Japanese empire collided head-on with the United States. Japan's attack on Pearl Harbor precipitated the Pacific War; it also brought the United States into active involvement in World War II in Europe.

What lay behind the war? The issues were not simple, and even today we have no definitive answers. In the following essay, an American historian explores some aspects of the road to Pearl Harbor. [23]

ON DECEMBER 7, 1941, a strike force of the Japanese Navy launched a surprise attack on the American naval base at Pearl Harbor in Hawaii. The effect was devastating: four battleships sunk and four damaged; 230 planes destroyed or heavily damaged; 2,400 dead and 1,300 wounded. The attack brought the United States into World War II. It unified Americans in opposition to the Japanese war aims. It reinforced the widespread belief that the Japanese were not to be trusted.

The Japanese leaders had not expected the attack on Pearl Harbor to have these effects. They had hoped, instead, that a sudden crippling blow would break the American will to resist. What were the issues at stake between the United States and Japan in 1941?

During the 1920s, the Japanese had pursued a policy of cooperating with the other great powers in Asia. But in the 1930s, the Japanese became disillusioned with the policy of cooperation, convinced that it did not afford sufficient protection for their national interest. For this reason they decided to go it alone, to secure by whatever means necessary the sphere of influence to which they felt entitled.

That sphere of influence was not restricted to the main islands of Japan. The home islands were woefully deficient in raw materials. Hence, from the very early stages of Japan's defense planning, it was apparent that Korea and Manchuria must be incorporated economically into the Japanese empire. Similarly, the countries of Southeast Asia, with their rubber and oil, attracted Japanese attention.

Along "battleship row" in Pearl Harbor lie the *USS West Virginia*, the *USS Tennessee*, and the *USS Arizona* (sunk in the attack on December 7, 1941). Photo from Wide World Photos.

Thus Japan's planning for national security presupposed an area of control far beyond the territorial confines of the Japan we know today—in effect, a Japanese version of the Monroe Doctrine.

There were other factors in Japanese planning. Most Japanese leaders were strongly anti-Communist, and they feared the spread of Russian influence into Asia. China was absorbed in a civil war. The specter of a Communist victory in China caused nightmares for Japanese planners; and even without so dire a prospect, continued instability in China seemed to threaten Japan's interests.

The growth of American power in the Pacific was another major factor. What, wondered the Japanese, were the real intentions of the Americans? Why was the United States intent on expanding her naval power? Why was she adamant in her support of China against Japan?

For their part, the Americans really had no well-thought-out Asian policy. A long tradition of contacts with China (including a large missionary effort) and an instinctive sympathy for the underdog, combined with American fears of Japanese power in the Pacific, led the United States to support China. Japan's alliance with Nazi Germany in fact never amounted to much, but it greatly alarmed the United States. The final straw was Japan's military action in China and, in 1940-41, Indochina.

For all its economic and military power in the 1930s, Japan had an Achilles heel: oil. Japan in 1941 produced just over 10 percent of her peacetime oil needs. The other 90 percent had to be imported. The bulk of Japan's imports (80 percent) came from the United States, whose oil production was 700 times greater than Japan's.

The United States responded to Japan's move into southern Indochina by cutting off all oil shipments to Japan (July 1941). This action brought issues to a head: Either the Japanese would back down, or they would take military action to secure their own supplies of oil.

The Japanese chose not to back down. On December 7, 1941, Japan invaded Southeast Asia and simultaneously struck at Pearl Harbor. The decision to go to war was taken with great reluctance. Here are the words of the Japanese Prime Minister, Tojo, at the end of a crucial government conference (November 5, 1941):

> If we enter into a protracted war, there will be difficulties.... The first stage of the war will not be difficult. We have some uneasiness about a protracted war. But how can we let the United States continue to do as she pleases, even though there is some uneasiness? Two years from now we will have no petroleum for military use. Ships will stop moving. When I think about the strengthening of American defenses in the Southwest Pacific, the expansion of the American fleet, the unfinished China Incident [Japan's war with China], and so on, I see no end to difficulties. [24]

The war did become "protracted." Japan soon lost the initiative. America brought her vastly superior power to bear, and Japan's fate was sealed.

Six decades after Pearl Harbor, some historians have begun to question the wisdom of American policy in the prewar period. Why was the United States hostile to Japanese expansion in the 1930s? This question has a special sting, for in the postwar years the United States has supported actively Japanese economic penetration of Southeast Asia. What was the American national interest in 1941? Would a softer line with the Japanese have avoided war in 1941 and yet protected America's basic interests?

Were the Allies wise in taking the decision to cut off Japan's supplies of oil? Were no less drastic remedies available? In 1990 the United States and its allies went to war in the Persian Gulf. Most observers agree that the importance of oil from the Gulf was a primary factor in the decision to go to war against Iraq's Saddam Hussein. The parallel with Japan's energy crisis of 1941 is far from exact, but perhaps it will lead to a re-evaluation of America's policy and Japan's response.

These issues will not be settled for many years. What does seem clear about the road to Pearl Harbor is this: For reasons of national security the Japanese attempted to gain a dominant position in Asia. In the 1930s, when China was turned inward and Russia was only beginning to develop her Asian strength, this goal was not an un-realistic one. However, the United States placed herself squarely in the path of Japanese ambitions. The result was the Japanese attack on Pearl Harbor and the war that followed it.

TWO IMPERIAL
RESCRIPTS

Editor's Introduction: The Japanese emperor, Hirohito, had little influence on the decision to go to war in 1941. If anything, he leaned toward peace. At one point, he expressed his views by quoting a poem written by his grandfather, the Emperor Meiji: "Since all are brothers in this world/ Why is there such constant turmoil?" But once his ministers had made up their minds, Hirohito gave his seal of approval to their decision. His countrymen learned of that decision in the Imperial Rescript, or proclamation, reprinted below.

Four years later, the Japanese government surrendered. In this second decision the emperor played a very active role, in effect ordering his ministers to accept the Allies' demand for surrender. Again, his countrymen learned of the decision in an Imperial Rescript. Needless to say, these rescripts present only one side of a very complex picture. [25]

Declaring War on the U.S.A. and Britain
December 7, 1941

WE, BY GRACE OF HEAVEN, Emperor of Japan, seated on the throne of a line unbroken for ages eternal, enjoin upon ye, Our loyal and brave subjects:

We hereby declare war on the United States of America and the British Empire. The men and officers of Our army and navy shall do their utmost in prosecuting the war. Our public servants of various departments shall perform faithfully and diligently their appointed tasks, and all other subjects of Ours shall pursue their respective duties; the entire nation with a united will shall mobilize their total strength so that nothing will miscarry in the attainment of our war aims.

To insure the stability of East Asia and to contribute to world peace is the farsighted policy which was formulated by Our Great Illustrious Imperial

Dr. Seuss and Japan at the Time of Pearl Harbor

Dr. Seuss (Theodor Seuss Geisel, 1904-1991) grew up in Springfield, Massachusetts, went to Dartmouth College in New Hampshire, and spent time in Europe before working in New York City (1927-1942). All four of his grandparents had been born in Germany, and as a child in Springfield, Dr. Seuss himself attended German-language church services. He knew much about Europe, but he had virtually no contact with Asia.

During the year before the Japanese attack on Pearl Harbor (December 7, 1941) and the year after, Dr. Seuss drew editorial cartoons for the New York newspaper *PM*. *PM* had a small circulation, and its politics were distinctly left.

On December 9 and 10, 1941—that is, only days after Pearl Harbor—Dr. Seuss drew these editorial cartoons. Judging solely from these cartoons, what can we say about Dr. Seuss's attitude toward Japan? Consider, for example, the relative size of the figures and their activities. How serious a threat to the United States is Japan? Is the depiction of the Japanese racist? What happens when cartoonists draw

Source: "Richard H. Minear, *Dr. Seuss Goes To War* (New Press, 1999).

people (or Uncle Sam) as animals or birds? Not long after the war, Dr. Seuss published *Horton Hears a Who*. That story about an elephant who saves a civilization on a speck of dust does not mention Japan, yet beneath the surface it surely relates to Japan and the U. S. Occupation of Japan then in progress.

Grandsire [the Meiji Emperor] and Our Great Imperial Sire succeeding Him, and which We lay constantly to heart.

To cultivate friendship among nations and to enjoy prosperity in common with all nations has always been the guiding principle of Our Empire's foreign policy. It has been truly unavoidable and far from Our wishes that Our Empire has now been brought to cross swords with America and Britain.

More than four years have passed since China, failing to comprehend the true intentions of Our Empire, and recklessly courting trouble, disturbed the peace of East Asia and compelled Our Empire to take up arms. Although there has been re-established the National Government of China, with which Japan had effected neighborly intercourse and cooperation, the regime which has survived at Chungking, relying upon American and British protection, still continues its fratricidal opposition.

Eager for the realization of their inordinate ambition to dominate the Orient, both America and Britain, giving support to the Chungking regime, have aggravated the disturbances in East Asia.

Moreover, these two Powers, inducing other countries to follow suit, increased military preparations on all sides of Our Empire to challenge us. They have obstructed by every means Our peaceful commerce, and finally resorted to a direct severance of economic relations, menacing gravely the existence of Our Empire.

Patiently have We waited and long have We endured in the hope that Our Government might retrieve the situation in peace, but Our adversaries, showing not the least spirit of conciliation, have unduly delayed a settlement, and in the meantime they have intensified the economic and political pressure to compel thereby Our Empire to submission.

This trend of affairs would, if left unchecked, not only nullify Our Empire's efforts of many years to stabilize East Asia, but also endanger the very existence of Our nation. The situation being as it is, Our Empire for its existence and self-defense has no other recourse but to appeal to arms and to crush every obstacle in its path.

DESIGNING BOEING'S B777

Five Japanese manufacturers have sent nearly 300 engineers to help Boeing develop its new B777 passenger airplane that seats 350. Mitsubishi Heavy Industries, Kawasaki Heavy Industries, and Fuji Heavy Industries had agreed previously to share 21% of the total development and production work.

Source: *JETRO Monitor*, February 1991.

The hallowed spirits of Our Imperial Ancestors guarding Us from above, We rely upon the loyalty and courage of Our subjects in Our confident expectation that the task bequeathed by Our Forefathers will be carried forward, and that the source of evil will be speedily eradicated and an enduring peace immutably established in East Asia, preserving thereby the glory of Our Empire.

Announcing Japan's Surrender*
August 14, 1945

To Our good and loyal subjects:

After pondering deeply the general trends of the world and the actual conditions obtaining in Our Empire today, We have decided to effect a settlement of the present situation by resorting to an extraordinary measure.

We have ordered Our Government to communicate to the governments of the United States, Great Britain, China, and the Soviet Union that Our Empire accepts the provisions of their joint Declaration [Potsdam Declaration].

To strive for the common prosperity and happiness of all nations as well as the security and well-being of Our subjects is the solemn obligation which has been handed down by Our Imperial Ancestors, and which We lay close to heart. Indeed, We declared war on America and Britain out of Our sincere desire to ensure Japan's self-preservation and the stabilization of East Asia, it being far from Our thought either to infringe upon the sovereignty of other nations or to embark upon territorial aggrandizement. But now the war has lasted for nearly four years. Despite the best that has been done by everyone, the gallant fighting of military and naval forces, the diligence and assiduity of Our servants of the State, and the devoted service of Our 100,000,000 people, the war situation has developed not necessarily to Japan's advantage, while the general trends of the world have all turned against her interest. Moreover, the enemy has begun to employ a new and most cruel bomb, the power of which to do damage is indeed incalculable, taking the toll of many innocent lives. Should We continue to fight, it would result not only in the ultimate collapse and obliteration of the Japanese nation but also in the total extinction of human civilization. Such being the case, how are We to save the millions of Our subjects or to atone Ourselves before the hallowed spirits of Our Imperial Ancestors? This is the reason We have ordered the acceptance of the provisions of the joint Declaration of the Powers.

We cannot but express the deepest sense of regret to our Allied nations of East Asia, who have consistently cooperated with the Empire toward the eman-

---

* *Nippon Times,* August 15, 1945.

cipation of East Asia. The thought of those officers and men as well as others who have fallen in the fields of battle, those who died at their posts of duty, or those who met with untimely death and all their bereaved families pains Our heart night and day. The welfare of the wounded and the war-sufferers, and of those who have lost their homes and livelihood, are the objects of Our profound solicitude. The hardships and sufferings to which Our nation is to be subjected hereafter will be certainly great. We are keenly aware of the inmost feelings of all ye, Our subjects. However, it is according to the dictate of time and fate that We have resolved to pave the way for a grand peace for all the generations to come by enduring the unendurable and suffering what is insufferable.

Having been able to safeguard and maintain the structure of the Imperial State, We are always with ye, Our good and loyal subjects, relying upon your sincerity and integrity. Beware most strictly of any outbursts of emotion which may engender needless complications, or any fraternal contention and strife which may create confusion, lead ye astray, and cause ye to lose the confidence of the world. Let the entire nation continue as one family from generation to generation, ever firm in its faith in the imperishability of its divine land, and

On September 2, 1945, representatives of the Japanese government stand stiffly at attention at the surrender ceremonies on the battleship *USS Missouri*, anchored in Tokyo Bay. Photo from Wide World Photos.

mindful of its heavy burden of responsibilities and the long road before it. Unite your total strength to be devoted to the construction for the future. Cultivate the way of rectitude, foster nobility of spirit, and work with resolution so that ye may enhance the innate glory of the Imperial State and keep pace with the progress of the world.

GIRL, 14, CONQUERS TANGLEWOOD WITH 3 VIOLINS

That was the title of the front-page report in the *New York Times*, July 28, 1986. It began: "Prodigious talent for a performing musician has three components: technical skill, artistic mastery and, rarest of all, that strange combination of pluck and luck that allows the artist to triumph in sudden crises."

The "girl" was Midori (the *Times* was so excited it didn't even get her name straight). The event was a concert at Tanglewood. The crises: in the final movement of the Bernstein Serenade, a broken E string (Midori borrowed the violin of the concertmaster and kept going); then a second broken E string (Midori borrowed a second violin and kept going, virtually without flaw).

Midori has gone on since then to become one of the world's most famous performing artists.

ICHIKŌ IN 1944

Editor's Introduction: Ichikō was prewar Japan's most prestigious and selective higher school. It accepted only seventeen-year-old boys; it trained them in foreign languages and other subjects for three years before sending them on to the nation's best universities. Students lived in dormitories and sang school songs and participated in all sorts of school activities.

In 1944, Japan was at war. In fact, Japan had been at war with China since 1937 and since December 7, 1941 with the United States and its allies. As the fortunes of the war turned against Japan, higher-school students and university students were increasingly called on for labor service (in factories or arsenals) or for military duty.

The author, Takeyama Michio, was a member of the faculty and a dormitory manager; he accompanied students to at least two work sites. What does this entry tell us about relations between Ichikō students and ordinary Japanese? Between the students and the military? What does it tell us about Japan in 1944? [26]

1944 WAS A MOST DIFFICULT year for our school.

Since the spring of 1944, second-year students had been working at a factory in Hitachi, 75 miles northeast of Tokyo. Young people being young people, even in hard times they fashioned their own lives. But doing so in those times was completely unacceptable. In particular, in that militarized factory town, Ichikō student life itself was defiant and provocative. Sometimes it was taken as insulting.

The school borrowed a vocational-school dorm; the teachers there had often said to their pupils, "The Ichikō students will arrive soon. Model yourselves on them." But soon after we arrived, the teachers stopped staying that. Instead, they warned: "Don't ever imitate them!"

At night, under complete blackout, the entire city turned dark. Only our dorm on the hill above the ocean had lights on, unshaded. Seeing this, the townspeople worried. At the time American submarines were already a constant presence fifty miles offshore.

At the factory the students worked hard and earned trust, and they studied hard for the few hours in the day after they returned to the dorm. But to outsiders, the ways of Ichikō students were beyond understanding. They walked in big groups, singing as they went. That was what drunks or crazy people did. Walking in the rain, they covered themselves from head to toe with their capes. Encountering these weird figures, girls grew frightened and ran away. What the people of the town had expected, of course, was that Ichikō students above all others would show the way in their "absolute faith in victory." To reassure people that this was not false, an illusion, the students would have learned to follow to the letter the behavior the times called for: clothes, rules, salutes, and the like. But our students maintained neither this illusion nor this behavior.

Leaving their own world behind, these young people had come here to work in a weapons arsenal. And here is what they saw. For example, when, at the ringing of a hand bell, they enter the cafeteria, they find several hundred vocational-school pupils sitting there. Up front is one aluminum bowl, and each waits with his own lunch box for lunch to be given him. The pupils range widely in age, some of them already adult in appearance, some still childish. Their expressions are uniformly empty and horribly docile. If asked the sum of three plus four, some of them would count on the fingers of both hands, so every stage of the meal, too, takes place on command.

There is a large Shinto altar high in front and here, on a step below it, the supervisors are lined up, epaulettes on their shoulders. All through the meal, some of the supervisors walk about keeping watch.

On command, the entire hall stands, bows to the altar, and observes a moment of silence. On command, they sit back down, and the several hundred recite in unison. Our students term these words an incantation; ancient words of ritual blessing, they express gratitude for the meal and for the good fortune of prosperity under the emperor's reign.

When this is over, again on command, one squad leader per table stands up. In sequence, the pupils raise their lunch boxes high and incline their heads. The squad leader then takes these boxes and dishes up the food. Thus begins the meager meal.

Our tables were in a long line under the windows. If our students didn't arrive on time, they neither bowed nor recited the incantation. For the vocational school, control via regimentation was a practical necessity, so the cafeteria observances became a fractious issue. But days passed without any solution being arrived at, and finally a cold, tough atmosphere of callousness between them and us became the solution.

As I ate on the high step, I often thought I had seen it before, as a prison scene in a movie.

This cavalier attitude on the part of our students was a cause of worry for the teachers who had accompanied them. We made excuses and apologized to the townspeople; we scolded and pleaded with the students. During the war, we lived a strange contradiction.

Our shaky position was as follows. That the country lose the war and fall to ruins was of course not something we desired. Yet we couldn't bring ourselves to hope that those now ruling us should win. But as of now they were the country. There was no way to change that. To separate leaders from country and topple them ourselves was inconceivable.

Military training in the schools was under the supervision of the military. It had to be a daily affair. The chief of the Military Affairs Bureau of the Utsunomiya Division, I believe it was, appeared one day unannounced at the dorm on Hatogaoka in Hitachi and, without asking to be shown, inspected the dorm and listened to the appraisals of the locals.

He reported the results to the regiment: "The lack of order defies description."

Had it not been Ichikō, the school would have been done for. But we were given a temporary reprieve—a last chance, and a second officer was assigned to the school. Moreover, the division chief, a prince, would redo the inspection. This time he would inspect the extent to which military training had become a daily affair. The deadline was announced—the end of August.

Ichikō faced its darkest hour.

Mornings at 5:20, as manager of Middle Dorm, I made the rounds ringing the wake-up bell. Then we gathered on the roof, took the roll, reported the count, observed morning ceremony, and did physical training. Then after an hour of class, the juniors went to their new place of work, a factory in Kawasaki, ten miles south of Tokyo to return after dark. Taking their deportment on the way there and back as an index of their training, the military officer assigned to the school exercised strict control, mornings in particular. As winter approached, morning meeting took place in total darkness. In the dark on the roof of North Dorm, the physical training instructor materialized, shoulders hunched against the cold, ringing the bell. Dawn broke while we were doing physical training, and the snow-capped mountains appeared beyond the reddish plain to the west, beautiful.

In early autumn the days continued bright and clear, and as far as concerned me, life in the cleaned-up dorm was surprisingly pleasant. But in October came the long rains and then the cold, befitting the problems at the front, and a sense of grim oppression was added to daily life.

Our students wore their capes against snow and cold. But out on the streets and in the factory, the capes raised eyebrows. Angry letters of protest arrived, calling it "ivory-tower romanticism." But we couldn't now take these useful capes away from our students who didn't have money for clothing. After much thought, we finally solved the difficulty provisionally: wearing the capes was okay, but whenever the students set foot outside the school gate, they wrapped on gaiters, donned air-raid gear, and an announcement was made, "Be ready for an air raid!"

The shortages were severe.

One afternoon a student returned from the Kawasaki factory ahead of time. Our students had a poor attendance record, and this was a cause of real worry for the school, so on that score the teacher assigned to the factory had a tough job. Leaving the factory early was also controlled strictly. I asked this student why he had left early, and his answer caught me off-guard: "Because I don't have shoes." He had walked home in his bare feet. "When it gets late, the streetcars are crowded, and people are always stepping on my toes. So I left early." Having said this, he entered the dorm, nonchalantly singing the dorm song in a loud voice.

Many students had minor injuries that became infected and didn't respond to treatment. It was because of malnutrition. A student named Ueno on the third floor of Middle Dorm had his instep swell up to twice normal size, and the skin became soft and transparent; underneath the dirty bandage you could see the wound. Still, whenever you inquired, he simply smiled gently and didn't take it seriously. It astonished me that about such issues young people are all in fact calm, indifferent, nonchalant, stoic.

When ordinary people got together, they always talked about food; but despite their meager diet, these young people didn't talk about food.

Thinking to add some elegance to dorm life, the school planned to put together a magazine and asked for submissions. I too wrote a piece about the dorm day. Manuscripts piled up, and after much effort things got to the proofreading stage. But among the finished pieces there wasn't a single militarist line, and that fact surprised and angered the people at the printer's. What is more, when we got finally to the printing stage, military police in plain clothes were coming and going, searching our wastebaskets, so we gave up the idea of publishing it.

Against the winter we tilled the playing field assiduously. But nothing much grew.

Alerts sounded constantly. Every last thing became a rush. Dread winter approached. Along with it, the liveliness of the dorm died, and one no longer heard voices singing dorm songs. Some students grew reckless and didn't even go out for labor duty; they stayed in bed during the day and went out at night. Their nutrition was bad, their spirits sank, and they looked miserable. Many anguished over tough questions: What point is there in this labor-force life? No matter how you look at it, can you see any raison d'etre in living this way? To resolve them, some people read recondite philosophy of history, and some agonized, unable to reach any resolution. For young people, conceptual problems turn into virtual bodily pain. Agonizing for different reasons, several of the adults deteriorated visibly.

Call-up notices came daily. Faces we had grown used to seeing were suddenly gone. At this late date there were no more send-off parties; some people stood and chatted for a bit at the shoe rack in the entryway before departing with an "I'm off now." Everyone realized his own day would come. Voices singing the sad school song, "Skies over the Capital," sung when students left for military service, rang endlessly atop the tower, in front of the buildings, and in our ears even after we returned to our own homes.

One student joined a kamikaze unit and, wearing a new military uniform, came to school to say goodbye; he died soon thereafter, as I learned a bit later. I confess: speaking with him on that occasion was tough and unendurable. Perhaps sensing my coolness, he hesitated briefly on the stairs, then went resolutely on down and left the building alone.

I was awestruck at the organization, execution, and rhetoric of the students who became leaders, regardless of their stance. Even if they only slept in class, lacked spirit, or were passive, when they got back to the dorm they were spectacularly active.

Even at such a time, some students really studied hard. They came back from the factory, hauled chairs to the only corridor with a light on all night, and set books on the chairs; squatting on the floor, wrapping their capes about them, they read with a will. This was against regulations, and it caused concern for their health, but I couldn't bring myself to put a stop to it. Walking past them late at night, I worried about them....

Scheduled for the end of August, the inspection by the prince who was divisional commander was called off because he happened to be reassigned just before then; instead, Major General Y, Director of the Military Affairs Bureau, came to inspect us—it was at the beginning of December, if I'm not mistaken.

Few of the students understood just how critical for school and dorms this inspection was.

In preparation for the fateful day, we had to put the whole school in such order that even the military couldn't find fault.

To this end we needed first to persuade the students, get them in the mood.

There were many purists: "Why dissemble by prettying up the surfaces of things for just the one day? Why not let them see us the way we are?"

In the dorm, meetings were held, and debate took place. The discussion took one of two familiar paths: people either used subjective words difficult to grasp, sometimes tracing the issue back to human fundamentals, or piled abstraction on abstraction until finally they themselves didn't understand what they were saying to each other. In South Dorm, after strenuous efforts by the dorm manager, they finally reached this conclusion: "Okay. We'll do it. But it's not to show the brass. It's to prove to ourselves that if we decide to do so, even Ichikō students can clean all this up."

On the day before inspection, I went into the toilets on each floor, braving the stench, and erased the graffiti on the walls. They were a real danger. In one room I erased a profusion of ink graffiti. For a long time this room had had graffiti all the way up to the ceiling, but at the time of the dorm reform, at considerable cost, all the dorm walls had been whitewashed. These graffiti were on top of the whitewash, so where they had scraped off the new graffiti, the old showed through. The only solution was to paste paper over the old graffiti and then write on it. The words appealed to me, but I've forgotten them.

In another room the whole wall was covered with calls for violent revolution in huge letters. That was ominous.

The rooms I had absolutely no hope of cleaning up I locked up and decided to say they belonged to second-year students still off on work service.

One cold day we cleaned up outside the dorms. We didn't have tools of any kind, so we picked everything up by hand. Dorm rain* froze, green and bubbly, and embedded in it were pieces of broken glass. These we grabbed with our fingers and pulled out. I wondered how to kill the penetrating ammonia smell from the triangular depressions beneath the windows of the dorm rooms, but there was no way.

Most students disappeared midway, but a dozen worked with a will and cleaned up the area around the dorms completely.

Inspection day arrived at last. Leather boots raising a clatter, the Director of the Military Affairs Bureau and a group of ten officers went through the dorms.

Major General Y was an older man, slight and thin and grizzled. Fidgety and short-tempered, he engaged in loud, one-way communication. He was a haughty and proud man accustomed to control and command. Entering without ceremony, he looked around, gimlet-eyed. But on this day there wasn't a single

---

*Euphemism for urine. Pissing out dorm windows was a cherished practice, part of the grunge style—"higher school barbarism"—that characterized higher-school life in Japan.

chink in Ichikō's armor. The general seemed displeased, almost as if he didn't like it.

There was an air raid that day. It was the third or fourth time that B-29s had appeared in the skies over Tokyo. In the clear early winter air, they floated calmly, violet and sparkling. Shining like a firework, a Japanese plane approached like a shooting star and rammed a B-29. Then, spinning and giving off black smoke, it fell to earth. Drawing long white frosty lines, the B-29s faded slowly into the crystalline distance.

We had dug an air raid shelter in the schoolyard. Our flawless enterprise, command, communication, and report surprised the officers.

On the second floor of Middle Dorm, General Y questioned one of the students lined up in the corridor outside their rooms and saluting: "How did you feel when you saw that plane ram the B-29?" The student answered, "I was sorry 'Japanese science isn't up to the task.'" This was a popular phrase at the time. The general nodded. Then he asked, again in a loud voice, "So what do you think we should do now?" The student froze and, face red, couldn't come up with an answer. Pointing at the chest of the student, the general said, "You students—that's your responsibility. Right?" and walked on.

The inspection ended without incident. The general said nothing to the school, but on departing, he supposedly commented to the officer assigned to the school, "Satisfactory."

Watching him leave, I said: "If the Director of the Military Affairs Bureau has the time now to come inspect a place like this, the war must be going fine." The man standing next to me responded, "No. He's got time because things aren't going well."

Thus, the danger passed for the present, and the school regained the standing it had enjoyed before.

The winter that followed was a truly bitter one. Air raids continued one after the other. Any number of times the fuel and food necessary for the large household of a thousand people seemed on the point of running out. During this time military police in civilian clothes came and went at the school.... There was also the dilemma of how to evacuate the school itself out of Tokyo. The pupils scattered to several places—from Yamagata in the north to Shizuoka in the south, lived in dispersed lodgings, and did labor service. Some became firemen and, when air raids came, raced to their assigned posts in the dead of night. In May a third of the school went up in flames. But in July, when Tokyo was already largely destroyed, the school celebrated an all-dorm dinner assembly and a culture day, listened to the orchestra, and presented research reports....

What Do These People Have in Common?

Igawa Kei, Iguchi Tadahito, Iwamura Akinori, Jōjima Kenji, Kashiwada Takashi, Kuwata Masumi, Matsui Hideki, Matsui Kazuo, Matsuzaka Daisuke, Okajima Hideki, Ōka Tomokazu, Ōtsuka Akinori, Saitō Takashi, Suzuki Ichiro, Taguchi Sō.

Here's a hint: one of them was 2001 American League Rookie of the Year/Most Valuable Player and Gold Glove outfielder (2001-2006) and 2007 MVP of the All-Star Game. The first Japanese to play in the U.S. major leagues was Murakami Masanori in 1964-65; there have been thirty-two in all.

HIROSHIMA AND NAGASAKI

Editor's Introduction: The costs of the war for Japan were incalculable. Over two million Japanese were killed, and many more injured. Japan lost her empire abroad and her economic machine at home.

Consider the following passage from the official U.S. Strategic Bombing Survey (December 1946):

> By July 1945, Japan's economic system had been shattered. Production of civilian goods was below the level of subsistence. Munitions output had been curtailed to less than half the wartime peak, a level that could not support sustained military operations against our opposing forces. The economic basis of Japanese resistance had been destroyed. This economic decay resulted from the sea-air blockade of the Japanese home islands and direct bombing attacks on industrial and urban-area targets.

The "urban-area targets" mentioned were cities, not factories or military positions within the cities, but the cities themselves. The report continues:

> The urban-area incendiary raids had profound repercussions on civilian morale and Japan's will to stay in the war. Sixty-six cities, virtually all those of economic significance, were subjected to bombing raids and suffered destruction ranging from 25 to 90 per cent. Almost 50 per cent of the area of these cities was leveled.

Fire-bombing was employed "in the belief that the industrial results of urban-area attacks would be far more significant than they had been in Germany, because of the greater fire vulnerability of

Japanese cities and the importance of small industry to Japanese war production." The results described in the report were "achieved" before President Truman decided to use against Japan the atomic bomb our scientists had developed for use against Hitler. American planes dropped atomic bombs on Hiroshima (August 6) and Nagasaki (August 9).

The poet Tōge Sankichi (1917-1953) was 28 years old when the U.S. dropped the first atomic bomb on Hiroshima. Far enough away from the center of the city to survive, he died eight years later of other causes.

Tōge had mixed feelings about the war even before Hiroshima. Here is an entry from his diary for May 29, 1945; he was in the Tokyo area, and the POW is an American airman shot down over Tokyo. [27]

I saw an enemy POW, who had parachuted to the edge of Kikuna Pond and had been captured, under arrest. From less than a meter away, I observed him for some time. He was on a bicycle-drawn trailer, hands tied behind him, blindfolded, and legs stretched out, accompanied by two soldiers; one wore a sword,

This official Air Force photo suggests the extent of the damage inflicted by the atomic blast in the heart of Hiroshima. Photo from the Wide World Photos.

and one was an interpreter. He appeared to be a youngster of about 20, with gray hair, a big nose, childish lips tightly clenched; he wore a shirt and pants and leather shoes. His neck rose stiffly from his breast; what thoughts did his breast contain?

The crowd (in reality, there were ten or twelve people, still not unruly) surrounded him and watched silently; there were whispers, someone saying softly, "Wire would be better to tie him with," another saying, "Isn't there something we can do for him?"

Just before the trailer began to move again, someone caught the guards napping and suddenly landed a good kick on the POW's legs, limp and pale, stretched out over the metal bumper in front of us. The POW held back his pain with an "Oh!" and pulled in his legs, and the soldier angrily pulled his pistol. The person quickly fled, melting into the crowd, and the trailer began to move and pulled away.

I returned, deep in thought.

Without falling into animal hatred (nay, I may suffer *because* I can't easily do so), taking the path of intellectual affirmation, I suffer greatly trying to hate him. Indeed, my sense of intellectual struggle is deep.

He too is a young man and probably to some degree feels a sense of righteousness. I can't have a sense of righteousness strong enough to destroy his and to engulf me. For me the slogans—co-prosperity sphere, liberation of oppressed peoples, and the like—are only intellectual concepts and are not sublimated to beliefs; so I have a weakness: I cannot hate him firmly and deeply with my mind.

> ❧Not until 1950 did Tōge begin to write of the atomic bomb in poetry; by that time he was 33 and a member of the Japanese Communist Party. But in a very brief period of time Tōge then composed the most famous poems of Hiroshima. Here are two: [28]

August 6

That brilliant flash—who can forget it?
In a split second, 30,000 in the streets vanished;
the screams of 50,000 pinned under in pitch black
died away.

The churning yellow smoke thinned to reveal Hiroshima:
buildings split, bridges fallen,
packed streetcars burned,
an endless heap of rubble and embers.

Soon a procession of the naked, crying, walking in bunches,
trampling on brain matter:
charred clothes about waists,
skin hanging like rags
from arms raised to breasts.

Corpses at the Parade Ground, scattered about
    like stone statues;
at the river's edge, too, fallen in a heap, a group
    that had crawled toward a tethered raft,
turning gradually, under the burning rays of the sun,
    into corpses;
in the glare of the flames piercing the night sky,
the area where Mother and Brother were pinned under alive—
it too went up in flames.

In the feces and urine on the floor of the arsenal
a group of schoolgirls who had fled lay fallen;
bellies swollen like drums, blinded in one eye,
    skin half-gone, hairless, impossible to tell
    one from the other—
by the time the rays of the morning sun picked them out,
they had all stopped moving;
amid the stagnant stench, the only sound:
flies buzzing about metal washbasins.

The stillness that reigned over the city of 300,000:
who can forget it?
In that hush
the white eyes of dead women and children
sent us
a soul-rending appeal:
who can forget it?

At the Makeshift Aid Station

You girls—
weeping even though there is no place for tears to come from;
crying out even though you have no lips to shape the words;
reaching out even though there is no skin on your fingers
    to grasp with—
you girls.

Oozing blood and greasy sweat and lymph, your limbs twitch;
puffed to slits, your eyes glitter whitely;
only the elastic bands of your panties hold in your swollen
    bellies;
though your private parts are exposed, you are
    wholly beyond shame:
to think
that a little while ago
you all were pretty schoolgirls!

Emerging from the flames that flickered gloomily
in burned-out Hiroshima
no longer yourselves,
you rushed out, crawled out one after the other,
struggled along to this grassy spot,
in agony laid your heads, bald but for a few wisps of hair,
    on the ground.

Why must you suffer like this?
Why must you suffer like this?
For what reason?
For what reason?
You girls
don't know
how desperate your condition,
how far transformed from the human.

You are simply thinking,
thinking

of those who until this morning
  were your fathers, mothers, brothers, sisters
(would any of them know you now?)
and of the homes in which you slept, woke, ate
(in that instant the hedge roses were torn off; who knows
  what has become of their ashes?)
thinking, thinking—
as you lie there among friends who one after the other
  stop moving—
thinking
of when you were girls,
human beings.

Let Us Be Midwives
Untold story of the atomic bombing

  Kurihara Sadako (1913–2005), an activist on the left most
of her life, was in Hiroshima on August 6. Like Tōge, she was
far enough away from the city center to escape uninjured. She
wrote on Hiroshima for 45 years, in the process expanding her
vision to include Japan as victimizer as well as victim. In August 1945, the very month in which the bomb fell, she wrote
"Let Us Be Midwives!" [29]

Night in the basement of a concrete structure now in ruins.
Victims of the atomic bomb
jammed the room;
it was dark—not even a single candle.
The smell of fresh blood, the stench of death,
  the closeness of sweaty people, the moans.
From out of all that, lo and behold, a voice:
"The baby's coming!"
In that hellish basement, at that very moment,
a young woman had gone into labor.
In the dark, without a single match, what to do?
People forgot their own pains, worried about her.
And then: "I'm a midwife. I'll help with the birth."
The speaker, seriously injured herself,

had been moaning only moments before.
And so new life was born in the dark of that pit of hell.
And so the midwife died before dawn, still bathed in blood.
Let us be midwives!
Let us be midwives!
Even if we lay down our own lives to do so.

When We Say "Hiroshima"

In 1972, Kurihara wrote "When We Say 'Hiroshima." The
foreign military bases to which she refers are American bases.
Since 1945, American troops have been stationed in Japan, first
as an army of occupation and then, after 1960, as a military ally.
[30]

When we say "Hiroshima,"
do people answer, gently,
"Ah, Hiroshima"?
Say "Hiroshima," and hear "Pearl Harbor."
Say "Hiroshima," and hear "Rape of Nanking."
Say "Hiroshima," and hear of women and children in Manila
thrown into trenches, doused with gasoline,
and burned alive.

Say "Hiroshima,"
and hear echoes of blood and fire.

Say "Hiroshima,"
and we don't hear, gently,
"Ah, Hiroshima."
In chorus, Asia's dead and her voiceless masses
spit out the anger
of all those we made victims.
That we may say "Hiroshima,"
and hear in reply, gently,
"Ah, Hiroshima,"
we must actually lay down
the arms we were supposed to lay down.

We must get rid of all foreign bases.
Until that day Hiroshima
will be a city of cruelty and bitter bad faith.
And we will be pariahs
burning with remnant radioactivity.

That we may say "Hiroshima"
and hear in reply, gently,
"Ah, Hiroshima,"
we first must
wash the blood
off our own hands.

Hiroshima and the Emperor's New Clothes

෨ It is in this sense that Kurihara wrote the following poem in
1981. The occasion was the visit to Hiroshima of the Japanese
prime minister. In the Japanese version of the European fairy
tale, "emperor" becomes "king" or "monarch;" the standard
Japanese term for the Japanese emperor is a different word entirely. So Kurihara's "emperor" is really the prime minister. This
translation uses idiomatic English— "black is white, and white
is black"—for a Japanese expression— "what is isn't; what isn't
is." Kurihara's point is that the Japanese government has always
refused to acknowledge that American forces in Japan have
been equipped with nuclear weapons. [31]

Chubby,
glossy face shiny with sweat,
the emperor of the new clothes,
his (nuclear) belly button plain to see,
says he's coming to Hiroshima.
He says he'll pay his respects at the atomic cenotaph.
Can he really stand
belly-button-bare before the monument
that says "the mistake shall not be repeated"?
The emperor of the new clothes,
who says black is white

and white is black
and makes lies and fraud state policy,
says he's coming,
bare belly button and all.
In Hiroshima
not only the children
but also the old people, the men, the women
laugh, get angry
at the chubby emperor's
belly-button antics.

In April he pays his respects at the shrine to war,
in August he pays his respects at the atomic cenotaph.
Repeating flat contradictions every day—
in the country across the sea
he says what they want him to say;
here at home, for domestic consumption,
he says black is white
and white is black.
But Hiroshima will not be fooled.
O, you 200,000 dead!
Come forth, all together,
from the grave, from underground.
Faces swollen with burns,
black and festering,
lips torn,
say faintly, "We stand here in reproach."
Shuffle slowly forward,
both arms, shoulder high,
trailing peeled-off skin.
Tell them—
the emperor of the new clothes
and his entire party—
what day August 6 is.

                              —August 1981

V
THE OCCUPATION,
IDENTITY, AND
PATRIOTISM

TWO CONSTITUTIONS

Editor's Introduction: Defeat in World War II brought many changes to Japan. First and foremost, it led to military occupation by the Americans. For seven years, from 1945 to 1952, Americans exercised ultimate authority in Japan.

The status of the emperor was an immediate focus of American concern. Before and during the war, the Japanese government had made much of the emperor's "godhood." The emperor, it said, was the direct lineal descendant of the Shinto Sun Goddess; he was "the Sun Goddess living in the present." Loyalty to the emperor therefore had powerful religious overtones.

Brought up to believe in the separation of church and state, Americans looked askance at this. How could democracy flourish under a "divine" emperor? In response to American pressure, the emperor inserted an extraordinary passage into his New Year's Day, 1946, address to the nation. "The ties that bound the Japanese people to their emperor," he said, "did not depend on the false doctrine that the emperor was divine."

This announcement was confusing to most Japanese. They had never considered the emperor a "god" in the Western sense of that word. But there was little to do but go along.

A second change in the status of the emperor was much more important. It affected his constitutional position and powers. Here is the Preamble and Article I of Japan's prewar constitution.

The Constitution of the Empire of Japan

Preamble

Having, by virtue of the glories of our Ancestors, ascended the Throne of a lineal succession unbroken for ages eternal; desiring to promote the welfare of, and to give development to the moral and intellectual faculties of Our beloved subjects, the very same that have been favored with the benevolent care and affectionate vigilance of Our Ancestors; and hoping to maintain the prosperity of the State, in concert with Our people and with their support, We hereby promulgate, in pursuance of Our Imperial Rescript of the 12th day of the 10th month of the 14th year of Meiji [1881], a fundamental law of State, to exhibit the principles, by which We are to be guided in Our conduct, and to point out to what Our descendants and Our subjects and their descendants are forever to conform.

The rights of sovereignty of the State We have inherited from Our Ancestors, and We shall bequeath them to Our descendants. Neither We nor they shall in future fail to wield them, in accordance with the provisions of the Constitution hereby granted.

We now declare to respect and protect the security of the rights and of the property of Our people, and to secure to them the complete enjoyment of the same, within the extent of the provisions of the present Constitution and of the law.

The Imperial Diet shall first be convoked for the 23rd year of Meiji [1890] and the time of its opening shall be the date when the present Constitution comes into force.

When in the future it may become necessary to amend any of the provisions of the present Constitution, We or Our successors shall assume the initiative right, and submit a project for the same to the Imperial Diet. The Imperial Diet shall pass its vote upon it, according to the conditions imposed by the present Constitution, and in no otherwise shall Our descendants or Our subjects be permitted to attempt any alteration thereof.

Our Ministers of State, on Our behalf, shall be held responsible for the carrying out of the present Constitution, and Our present and future subjects shall forever assume the duty of allegiance to the present Constitution.

Chapter 1. *The Emperor*

Article 1. The Empire of Japan shall be reigned over and governed by a line of Emperors unbroken for ages eternal.

> A new constitution was issued in 1947, and this document remains in force today, without amendment. Written under heavy American pressure, it may, indeed, have been written by Americans. There were some Japanese who contended in 1947 that they could not understand the text of the new constitution (the Japanese text) because they did not know English.
>
> Few people agree about the ultimate meaning of the changes embodied in the new Japanese Constitution. What real difference, after all, does an amendment to the American Constitution make in

your life? Does your attitude toward the President of the United States depend on what is written in the Constitution? How much do you really know about the American Constitution?

In any case, however, it seems likely that the role of the emperor in Japanese politics and thought has changed significantly. Here are the preamble and first article of Japan's current constitution.

The Constitution of Japan

Preamble

We, the Japanese people, acting through our duly elected representatives in the National Diet, determined that we shall secure for ourselves and our posterity the fruits of peaceful cooperation with all nations and the blessings of liberty throughout this land, and resolved that never again shall we be visited with the horrors of war through the action of government, do proclaim that sovereign power resides with the people and do firmly establish this Constitution. Government is a sacred trust of the people, the authority for which is derived from the people, the powers of which are exercised by the representatives of the people, and the benefits of which are enjoyed by the people. This is a universal principle of mankind upon which this Constitution is founded. We reject and revoke all constitutions, laws, ordinances, and rescripts in conflict herewith.

We, the Japanese people, desire peace for all time and are deeply conscious of the high ideals controlling human relationship, and we have determined to preserve our security and existence, trusting in the justice and faith of the peace-loving peoples of the world. We desire to occupy an honored place in an international society striving for the preservation of peace, and the banishment of tyranny and slavery, oppression and intolerance for all time from the earth. We recognize that all peoples of the world have the right to live in peace, free from fear and want.

We believe that no nation is responsible to itself alone, but that laws of political morality are universal; and that obedience to such laws is incumbent upon all nations who would sustain their own sovereignty and justify their sovereign relationship with other nations.

We, the Japanese people, pledge our national honor to accomplish these high ideals and purposes with all our resources.

Chapter 1. *The Emperor*

Article 1. The Emperor shall be the symbol of the State and of the unity of the people, deriving his position from the will of the people with whom resides sovereign power.

> *Editor's Postscript:* One fundamental goal of the American Occupation was to "demilitarize" Japan, to prevent Japan "from being a menace to the United States and the other countries of the Pacific area." Japan had threatened the Allies through her military might. Therefore, the reasoning went, remove Japan's military capability.
>
> The result of this logic is Article 9 in the present Constitution, which reads as follows:
>
> > Aspiring sincerely to an international peace based on justice and order, the Japanese people forever renounce war as a sovereign right of the nation and the threat or use of force as means of settling international disputes.
> >
> > In order to accomplish the aim of the preceding paragraph, land, sea, and air forces, as well as other war potential, will never be maintained. The right of belligerency of the state will not be recognized.
>
> Voices were raised very soon in opposition to Article 9. What is a nation if it has no armed forces? Can it survive? Will it not always be dependent on powerful neighbors? Can you imagine the United States without a Pentagon? In fact, Japan today does maintain armed forces, called "Self-Defense Forces" to circumvent Article 9.

THE 1946 CONSTITUTION: ONE HISTORIAN'S VIEWS

Editor's Introduction: Ienaga Saburō is the single most famous Japanese historian of the twentieth century. Born in 1913, Ienaga spent all but a few years of his professional life in schools, first as student (1919-1937), then as teacher in a higher school (1941-1943; higher school students were elite males between the ages of seventeen and twenty), then at a university in Tokyo (1944-1977). Though of service age in the 1930s, he was physically frail and exempted from duty. He wrote many scholarly books. But he is most famous for three suits he lodged and fought against the government for its censorship of his textbooks (1965-1997). Despite a few lower-court judgments in his favor, Ienaga ultimately lost all the suits in the Supreme Court. But as one colleague put it, he "will win in the court of history." Ienaga was nominated for the Nobel Peace Prize in 2001* by a large group of scholars from around the world (the prize that year went to the UN and UN Secretary General Kofi Annan); he died in 2002.

Here are two passages from his autobiography (1977). The first describes his initial reaction to the 1946 Constitution; the second shows his later reaction and the connection between Constitution and Ienaga's lawsuits. [32]

.... AT THE TIME OF ITS PROMULGATION, I did not grasp the epoch-making significance of the Constitution of Japan. Minobe's theories [Minobe was the leading liberal interpreter of the Meiji Constitution] construed the Meiji Constitution as constitutionally as possible and tried to realize within its framework the highest possible degree of democracy; paradoxically, his ideas may have been one factor preventing me from understanding the epoch-making significance of the postwar revision of the constitution.

---

*The nomination and other materials are available: vcn.bc.ca/alpha/Ienaga/letter.htm.

At the time I did not know that the original draft of the Constitution of Japan—the so-called MacArthur draft—had been drawn up by the Occupation's General Headquarters; my first contact with the Constitution of Japan was when I read what was published in the newspapers as "the government draft." Popular sovereignty, the renunciation of war, and unconditional guarantees of fundamental human rights were this constitution's fundamental ideals, and as far as they were concerned, far from being opposed, I was in full agreement in principle. Still, I was not deeply moved.... My slowness to catch on is a source of embarrassment to me today....

I was one of those spineless characters who during the war had taken no action in opposition to the war, had watched powerless from the sidelines as my country met destruction, and could only stand by as many of my generation went to their deaths. The fact that any opposition I might have attempted would have had no effect at the time was irrelevant; the experience left me with spiritual scars. I did not want to let the deaths of several million countrymen be in vain.

The rejection of war and the protection of the fundamental human rights that the Constitution of Japan established—weren't they an inestimable heritage bought with the noble blood of my countrymen? The Constitution of Japan was not merely the pride of the Japanese people; it held epoch-making significance in human history. The people should protect those basic ideals of the constitution at all costs and, each according to his own strength, give their all to oppose attempts to destroy these ideals or render them hollow. And isn't it the responsibility in particular of my generation, which survived that tragic war, to see that the people do so?

The Constitution of Japan was in force, yet textbooks true to its spirit were blocked from publication, and to swallow one's bile [at censorship] was to allow the destruction of the constitution or its hollowing out. Leave victory or defeat out of account—by fighting all the way in the courts and appealing broadly to the public outside the courts, I would sound the alarm.... If I could only get the people to understand how frightening it is when the state controls the content of education, how horrendous the result when the people give the state a blank check, victory or defeat in the courts would not matter. That was the fundamental motive that led me to embark on the [first] suit.

> *Editor's Postscript:* In the first Gulf War, Japan paid for a significant portion of the total American costs of the war. In 1992, it sent Self Defense Forces on a non-combat mission as part of UN forces in Cambodia. In September 1992, the *New York Times* reported, "Eight

Japanese cease-fire observers arrived in Cambodia today without fanfare, becoming the first ground troops to be deployed abroad by Japan since World War II." September 11, 2001, emboldened the Japanese government to urge revision of the Constitution of Japan, in particular, Article 9. And after the initial American victory in the second Gulf War, Japan sent "non-combat" Self-Defense troops to a quiet area of Southern Iraq in 2004; they were withdrawn in 2006.

Here is Ienaga in an interview in 1990: "Under the constitution's 'land, sea, and air forces...will never be maintained,' it's strange that there are Self Defense Forces at all—and dispatching them overseas? That's out of the question. Despite the fact that this hollowing out of the constitution proceeds rapidly, not that many people react sharply against it."

PATRIOTISM
RE-EXAMINED

Editor's Introduction: Japan today is a highly cosmopolitan society. The major works of all traditions—Western, Chinese, Indian—are all available in Japanese translation. Indeed, Japanese students spend more time studying other countries than studying Japan.

Late in 1968, when most Japanese universities were shut down by student strikes, a group of more than 1,200 Japanese students responded to a public-opinion survey that asked which books had influenced them most deeply and which politicians they most admired. The students ranked Dostoevski's *Crime and Punishment* first and his *The Brothers Karamazov* third. Second was a Japanese novel written in the early twentieth century. Also among the top 10 were *The Stranger*, by Albert Camus, Pearl Buck's *The Good Earth*, Tolstoy's *War and Peace*, and a German novel of protest. Twelve of the top 20 books were not Japanese but Russian, French, German, or American.

A similar pattern emerged from the answers about politicians the students respected. To be sure, a very large number of the students (more than 60 percent in the case of the most prestigious school, Tokyo University) asserted firmly that they respected no politician. Among those who did respond, the top four were John F. Kennedy, Lincoln, Lenin, and Churchill. The two most respected Japanese politicians tied with Charles de Gaulle for *fifth* place. Also among the top 20 were Mao Tse-tung, Ho Chi Minh, Nehru, Gandhi, Che Guevara, Fidel Castro, Napoleon, Franklin Delano Roosevelt, and Robert F. Kennedy. Only four of the top 20 were Japanese.

One of the most successful novelists of contemporary Japan is Ōe Kenzaburō, Ōe's typical hero is a modern man who happens to have been born in Japan. The dilemmas these heroes face are not exclusively Japanese.

Ōe's concerns range widely. Not merely a novelist, he is a leading conservationist, and one of his books, *The Day the Whale Became Extinct*, is a plea for the preservation of the whale. Ōe holds no romantic illusions about Japanese nationalism but he is not an outright cynic either. [33]

AT HIROSHIMA AIRPORT, they sell oysters packed in barrels. You can leave Tokyo in the morning, meet a friend for lunch in Hiroshima, and have fresh oysters for dinner in Tokyo that night. Tokyo and Hiroshima television show the same Westerns, too. The Tokyo man and the Hiroshima man who discussed business during the day separate in the evening and then watch the same television program in Hiroshima and in Tokyo. There is nothing extraordinary about this, it has occurred to everyone. Japan today is linked from one corner to the other, unified, simplified. Time has whittled away at Japan until, in 1965, the entire country is no larger than any of the tiny villages you might have found ... one hundred years ago.

But even you, who learn from watching television about everything that happens in this country, from the most important to the most trivial incident, even you must be ignorant of two deaths that occurred in Hiroshima during the past few weeks, the deaths of two young people. Yet the Japanese State was directly responsible for the first of these two related deaths and, as any Japanese with heart must feel, responsible for the second death too. The first death was attended by nausea and terrific pain in the joints, the second was the tranquil suicide of a young girl in utter despair.

There lived in Hiroshima a young man of 23 who was four years old when the Bomb fell. In his late teens, the boy's white cell count began running high, and he entered the Atomic Bomb Hospital. The specialists there saw immediately that he had leukemia. Ours is the age of space flight, yet leukemia, the so-called cancer of the blood, remains an untreatable, fatal disease. All that can be done is to halt temporarily the increase of white cells, to compel the disease to take a "summer vacation." In this case, the Hiroshima doctors managed to extend the vacation for a period of two years. But when the summer vacation is over, leukemia comes back to work and absolutely, unfalteringly, abducts its victim's life.

This particular young man expressed the desire to go to work while his temporary recovery lasted. The doctors, concealing the fact that he was in the grips of such a disease (no one would have hired him otherwise), found the youth a position at a printing company. And he did very well at his job. So well, in fact, that *Life* magazine carried an article about him, a cheerful young man dedicated to his work, which conveyed the impression of a healthy, new Hiroshima. Before long,

A young intellectual makes a point
in a coffee-bar conversation.
Photo by Doug Hurst.

he fell in love with a girl who worked in a music store, and they were soon engaged to be married.

Then the two-year period of grace expired, the agonizing nausea returned,
and the young man went into the hospital again, where he died.

One week after his death, the boy's fiance appeared at the nurses' office at
the Atomic Bomb Hospital; she had come to express her gratitude, and she
brought with her a set of porcelain deer, one horned and powerful looking, the
other small and feminine. She was calm, apparently in perfect control of herself.
The next morning, the girl was found dead from an overdose of sleeping pills, a
suicide.

That same week, in Tokyo, the Japanese Government conferred the First
Order of the Cordon Bleu on the man directly responsible for the bombing of
Hiroshima. The Secretary-General of the Cabinet, grinning, had this to say:

"My house was gutted in the air raids too, but that's 20 years forgotten. Why
shouldn't we present a medal to a soldier who bombed our cities during the war?
In fact, the gesture represents the kind of open generosity that befits the people
of a great nation."

To the *Life* readers in America who remember having seen a few years ago
some pictures of a cheerful youth who had experienced the horrors of the Bomb,
to those readers I would like to report what happened to that boy and his lover

two years afterward. To the Secretary General of the Cabinet I say that tragic, outrageous suffering is still resulting, right now, this very minute, from an incident *20 years forgotten.*

The youth who died of leukemia had a right to demand reparations from the Bomb which, if you will, sowed the seeds of disease in him when he was just a baby, to demand compensation from the war itself and from the State that brought about the war. None of the responsibility was his, yet 20 years later, as an individual, he became a victim of the war at the cost of his own life. If the State felt compelled to confer honors, it was to just such a young man that the medal of honor should have gone, though of course he would have refused it.

In fact, the young man did receive a medal, a real one, the suicide of the young girl who loved him and followed him in death. She was 20, born and raised after the war, and so she had nothing whatsoever to do with it. Yet she substituted for the State and, sacrificing her own life as an individual, as he had done, made of herself a medal for the young man. She, too, had the right to demand from the war and from the State reparations for the tragic loss of her fiance, yet even at the moment of death, she did not criticize her country. Ten days apart, without a word to one another, the two lovers moved on to the land of death.

But this is not to say that these young lovers sacrificed themselves to their country because they loved it; quite the opposite must have been the truth. The boy was silent precisely because he knew that the State could do nothing for his leukemia, that bitter silence. The girl determined, how resolutely! that the entire world, including the nation called Japan, was not worth one dead young man, so she committed suicide. Foreknowing that the State and this great wide world could never afford her anything that could come even close to taking his place, she chose death. Turning her back on the State and on the world, she demonstrated with her own life that nothing so valuable as the dead boy would ever be discovered anywhere again. And what if a representative of the State and of the world at large had visited that Hiroshima music store and asked her not to die, *please, Miss, recognize that the State and the world, that all the people still living are worth more than that dead boy, and go on living;* most certainly she would have refused. *I'm finished with you* she would have said, *Japan has nothing to do with me now, not any more, and neither does the rest of the world, either.* When the young man died, the country called Japan, the entire second half of the twentieth century world, ceased to have any value for her whatsoever, she proved it beyond doubting with her suicide. And what a bitter taste it leaves in the mouth, this abject girl's heroic suicide.

And yet, with the radioactive material that sowed the seeds of death in that boy's body still playing the leading role in world government, what man on the

Three teenagers chat on a
Tokyo street. All were born
long after 1945, when the
atomic bombs fell and Japan
surrendered.
Photo by Doug Hurst.

face of this earth today can say YOU ARE MISTAKEN to a girl resolved to die?
What can we do ourselves, save remain silent with bitter hearts?

Japan's postwar generation knows that it has the right to deny its own country, to say to Japan, not with the magnificent eloquence of the Hiroshima girl
who committed suicide, nor in the voice of urgent defiance, but in tones appropriate to everyday life, to say *I'm through with you. I have nothing to do with
you now.* The awareness of this right is the most beneficial wisdom the postwar
democratic age possesses, but it is probably the most burdensome wisdom, too.

Before the war, when the Emperor's absolute authority cast a shadow in
which all men stood, there must have been times when a patriotic man could not
be sure whether his patriotism was merely the instinct of a slave in bondage to
the State, or whether it was truly human will, a thing he had selected freely and
for himself. The wills left behind on Edajima Island by the *kamikaze* pilots hor-
rify because they are so clearly a mixture of this slavish instinct and individual,
human volition.

While discovering patriotism may be extremely difficult for the postwar
Japanese (difficult because, in times of peace more than in times of emergency,
patriotism is in an inconspicuous state, commonplace as body temperature,
which is not to say that it has been lost because it is not feverish. On the contrary,
it continues to function in a normal, everyday way), we may assess our patriot-

ism without reservations once we have managed to discover it for ourselves. This is because such patriotism has real value, has nothing to do with the predictable habits of a slave, because free men not bound to the State have willed it for themselves. And patriotism such as this must be a source of pride and pleasure, both for the State at which it is directed, and for the citizens who feel it. Our freedom reaches to the most fundamental levels; we are not bound to the State; the right to deny is ours—in this sense, the most beneficial wisdom of the postwar age.

Conversely, however, this awareness must be considered the most burdensome wisdom, a serious handicap, because the state of freedom is ever accompanied by uneasiness.

A good friend of mine once said to me:

"I got out of college six years ago and now I'm an assistant section chief at a pretty decent company; in other words, the most ordinary kind of citizen, the rank and file, and yet somehow I feel suspended, you know, apprehensive. And recently, I find myself saying 'I don't belong' all the time."

I don't belong? What did he mean by that, I asked.

Just that, *I don't belong.* Like at breakfast, when I read the newspaper, and it says that some politicians who were expelled from the Communist Party have formed a new party—I say to myself *I don't belong* to the Communist Party and *I don't belong* to the splinter group either. I think if there were ever a revolution I'd just wait around to see who had won. Needless to say, I'm not a rightist and *I don't belong* to the Conservative Party either. When the elections come up I vote for some Independent who seems like a nice guy.

"In the train on the way to work I look at a weekly magazine, and there are pictures of a Soka Gakkai rally and athletic meet. [The Soka Gakkai is a postwar Buddhist group with an extraordinary zeal for spreading its gospel. It claims millions of members.] And I think to myself, *I don't belong* to the Soka Gakkai. I have a feeling that the Independent I like in the next elections will be forced out of the running by the Komeito [the political organ of the Soka Gakkai], and yet I have no inclination to try and influence anyone else to vote for him.

"The magazine carries pictures of the Emperor too. But *I don't belong* to the sentimental pyramid that installs the Imperial House at its apex.

"Even when I'm at work, I sense that *I don't belong* to my company, not really, and when somebody drags me to a meeting where they show North Korean movies, I have the feeling that *I don't belong to Japan* the way these new Koreans belong to their country. I'm a Giants fan, too, but *I don't belong* to a rooting club. What do you think? I mean, is this not belonging complex something special to me? Anyway, there's no need to worry, I'm not the kind of guy who gets more and more neurotic until he has to hang himself—I *don't belong* to that club either."

Two young cyclists flash the peace sign at an American photographer.
Photo by Doug Hurst.

To hear my friend talk, you might think that he wanted desperately to participate in some political party or religious group, to belong to something, anything. Actually, such is not the case. This particular form of freedom suits his temperament well, and his disposition is probably shared by the average Japanese citizenry in general, or at least by the "unbelonging" rank and file, who far outnumber those Japanese who do belong. Though my friend feels vaguely apprehensive about his state of freedom, at the same time he is perfectly aware that he has no desire for any state other than freedom. Force him to participate in something like the old fashioned military system and he would immediately develop a "restrictions" complex.

Consequently, my friend, along with the millions of rank-and-file citizens just like him, has no choice but to select consciously this state of "unbelonging" as his own attitude. Now if, having redefined ourselves as "unbelongers," we rank-and-file citizens can maintain the stance that we represent, then there is no reason on earth why we should feel inferior to those who do belong. After all, the so-called "age of postwar democracy" was launched when we were liberated from a myriad restrictions belonging to the old Japanese order, and merged into a vast body of *petit bourgeois* who do not belong.

The year 1965, which commemorates the one hundredth anniversary of the Meiji Restoration, has been a year for discussing the rebirth of nationalism. And for the past several years now, there has been a tendency to intensify nationalism, sometimes innocently, sometimes in suspicious ways for dubious reasons. At any rate, a classical and orthodox version of prewar nationalism, the kind engendered in people who feel themselves essentially and inseparably bound to the State, has been revived, and is now asserting its authority. Those embracing this brand of nationalism conceive of themselves as a kind of organ which, were it cut away from the nation called Japan, would surely wither and die. But we members of the *unbelonging* rank and file, we millions, are not likely to grow ardent in support of any nationalism which requires us to sacrifice ourselves unreasonably, for we have experienced the sensation of being free of the State. Even if we should become infected, the fever would not last long....

We rank-and-file citizens know that the right to deny Japan is ours and yet, except for a trifling number of international exceptions, we remain here. In other words, we elect to be Japanese as an act of individual and free will. And it is in the soil of this attitude that a new nationalism, different both from prewar nationalism and from its opposite, internationalism, will sink its roots and send up a mighty trunk.

I would like my attitude toward my country to reflect precisely this kind of nationalism. I want to remember the 20-year-old Japanese girl who not only denied Japan but bid farewell to the entire world. If there exists a state whose image could have inspired that devoted girl to go on living as a Japanese even after she had lost her fiance, then that state, or one just like it, will be the flower that blossoms at the summit of the new nationalism.

THE JAPAN THAT
CAN SAY NO

Editor's Introduction: Japan and the United States have been allies
since the end of the American Occupation of Japan in 1952. During
these six decades, Japanese governments have cooperated with U.S.
policy in Asia and the rest of the world. That cooperation has included American military bases in Japan (there are still bases in Japan
today), nuclear weapons on those bases (successive Japanese governments have chosen to ignore their presence), logistical support for
the American war in Vietnam, and refusal to recognize China until
1972 or to go against U.S. policy in the United Nations.

The relation between the two allies was unequal in its early
stages—the United States enjoyed clear dominance, and that in-
equality grated. Some Japanese thought Japan should not follow U.S.
policy so slavishly; some Americans thought Japan was "getting a free
ride" because the American military played so large a role in Japan's
defense.

More recently, however, Japanese economic success and American economic problems have added to the earlier strains. We saw
some of those strains in the previous selection. Many American
politicians want Japan to pay American military bills (Japan did pay
$9 billion of the $51 billion that constituted the American military
cost of the Gulf War), to open its markets wider to American goods,
and to spend more money improving the life of the average Japanese. In particular, Americans react against Japanese purchases of
highly visible property in the U.S.: Rockefeller Center, Columbia
Pictures, the Seattle Mariners. And Japanese react, often angrily, to
the American reaction.

Ishihara Shintarō, the author of the following selection, is a
major figure in contemporary Japanese politics. Born in 1933, he
started as a filmmaker, has written many books and won a number of
literary awards, and since 1968 has been a member of the Diet. In

Japan, his book *The Japan That Can Say No* (1989) has sold over one
million copies. In the United States, the Pentagon thought the book
significant enough to print an unauthorized translation. The following excerpts are from the authorized translation. [34]

About 1987, the United States began using a new tactic against Japan. Given
Gorbachev's popularity in the West and the reduced threat from the "evil empire," Japan bashing became even more frequent. It was open season on Tokyo as
one politician after another made wild, emotional attacks. Instead of carefully
weighing all the facts, Congress went off half-cocked. Several members, for example, smashed a Toshiba radio-cassette player to bits with sledgehammers on
the steps of the Capitol. That was a disgraceful act.

The Technology Card

During my April 1987 visit to Washington, politicians hinted at a detente with
the Soviet Union, implying that the two Caucasian races would soon be on much
friendlier terms, leaving Japan out in the cold. Our foreign policy makers must
not be intimidated by this absurd threat. We control the high technology on
which the military power of both countries rests. Unfortunately, Japan has not
used the technology card skillfully. We have the power to say no to the United
States, but we have not exercised that option. We are like a stud poker player with
an ace in the hole who habitually folds his hand.

The American lawmakers I met with bristled when I said they had no cred-
ibility because Congress, ignoring administration goals, so often acted erratically
and selfindulgently. "The best example is Prohibition," I said. "No legislative assembly worthy of the name would pass such a law." They laughed with embarrassment....

[When I was in Washington] ... the mood was venomously hostile. In con-
versations with several members of the Senate and House of Representatives
who I knew well, I said matter-of-factly that I thought racial prejudice was behind the trade friction between our two countries, and I cited several specific
examples. American politicians get upset about such terms as racism, but those
I spoke to finally conceded, with a wry smile, that I had a point. Interestingly, at
first they had insisted prejudice was not a factor, and then said it might stem
from the Pacific War. In my opinion, lingering distrust from World War II could
not be the only reason.

Westerners, subconsciously at least, take great pride in having created the
modern age. During my meetings with politicians in Washington, I said, "I
admit that Caucasians created modern civilization, but what bothers me is you

seem to think that heritage makes you superior. In the thirteenth century, however, the Mongols under Genghis Khan and his successors overran Russia and
eastern Europe, reaching almost to Vienna and Venice. Mongol armies destroyed
every army and fortress in their path, plundering and raping. Caucasians adopted
Mongol-style haircuts and shaved eyebrows, and even the Mongols' bandy-
legged gait. Just as Orientals of today are crazy about the clothing and hairstyles
of the Beatles, Michael Jackson, and Sting, Occidentals of Genghis Kahn's time
copied Mongolian ways. Even women liked the new styles.

Eventually, the Mongol empire disintegrated, but some people trace Western fear of Asians—the concept of the yellow peril—to the slaughter and pil-
lage committed by the Mongol forces. Whatever the reason, Japanese should
not forget that Caucasians are prejudiced against Orientals.

The U.S. Choice: Racism or World Leadership

American prejudice was clearly evident in a discussion I had with a senior U.S.
navy officer. The U.S. Navy places a powerful sonar unit that can detect unusual
objects on the bows of civilian tankers and container ships. Called the Amber
System, its purpose is to locate nuclear submarines. The sonar cannot distinguish
between U.S. and Soviet subs; it just flashes a sighting report to the Pentagon.
The U.S. Navy knows the location of its own subs and can determine if the object is friend or foe.

I suggested to the officer that the Amber System be installed on Japanese
merchant vessels, which sail all the tanker and cargo routes and have well-trained,
reliable crews. Japan could collect raw intelligence data for the U.S. Navy to analyze. The officer said that Japan's help would not be necessary. I pressed the
idea, noting that Soviet subs outnumbered the U.S. underwater fleet. He replied
that he could not ask Japan's merchant marine to participate. If West Germany
or Britain made such an offer, I asked, would you install the Amber System on
their vessels? The officer candidly answered that the Pentagon would.

Americans feel that they cannot trust Japan. We cannot decode the sonar
signals, but still they choose not to ask us to collect the data. U.S. admirals would
probably even ask the Russians before they asked the Japanese! The Japanese
people should be aware of how deeply biased Americans are....

Today, the modern era is in its terminal phase. An awareness of its imminent
demise had made Americans, the most powerful Caucasians since World War
II, increasingly emotional, almost hysterical, about Japan. Both societies are in a
similar transitional phase, which makes the rivalry more intense. The kind of
trade friction that exists between Japan and the United States would not occur
if a West Germany, Britain, or Australia had achieved our economic power and

standing. When pressed about racism, many Americans honestly admit their feelings. But that is not enough. They must purge themselves of bigotry. Given the power and importance of the United States, Americans especially should understand that the world is at one of those moments of epochal change. Technology, manufacturing, and economic power are gradually shifting from the West to the East. Whether that means the Age of the Pacific has dawned, I do not know. But I am certain that despite the ethnic and racial diversity of the U.S. population, persistent discrimination by the white power elite against Japan and other Asian countries will undermine U.S. leadership of the free world.

As the modern civilization created by Caucasians comes to an end in the last decade of the twentieth century, we are on the verge of a new genesis. Japanese, and Americans, too, are shaping this age. American politicians must explain to the American people that times have changed. In fact, however, other U.S. opinion leaders—businessmen, for example—are more aware of the profound transition under way than the political leadership. Americans, with their scant few centuries of history, have never experienced the shift from one major historical period to another. They emerged as the premier world power only decades ago, toward the end of the modern era. That Japan, an Oriental country, is about to supplant them in some major fields is what annoys the Americans so much.

Japanese, of course, must also prepare for the new era. They must become more cosmopolitan and less insular. Sony chairman Morita Akio, proud and confident of his company's excellent products, personifies this urbanity. Other Japanese as well, buoyed by our technological prowess and flourishing culture, should be more self-assured. We do not have to be arrogant, but if we continue to feel inferior, Japan cannot be the mainspring of the new genesis. To bear the great responsibilities that lie ahead, Japanese must change their attitudes and self-image....

Americans: Look in the Mirror!

I realize that these are very trying times for Americans. Until very recently, the United States was the unrivaled military and economic leader of the free world. Now, suddenly, Japan seems to have usurped that economic power. Americans from all walks of life are upset, frustrated, and worried about their country.

Most of America's woes are self-made, but some prefer to blame Japan, saying that our market is closed to U.S.-made products and we are an unfair trader. Those who cannot take stock of themselves—whether an individual, company, or nation—face an uncertain future. I want to believe that the United States,

Cartoon copyright © 1992, *Boston Globe*. Distributed by Los Angeles Times Syndicate. Reprinted with permission.

with its enormous underlying strength, will pull itself together and come roaring back. Yet there are many worrisome signs.

In October 1989, *Newsweek* reported that most Americans viewed Japan as a greater threat than the Soviet Union. The word "threat" might be appropriate if Americans had attempted to put their house in order. Instead, Congress looks to Japan for a scapegoat, uses high-handed tactics, and tries to push us around. To confuse a hypothetical military foe with an economic competitor and stick a ridiculous label like "threat" on us shows how dangerously confused the United States is. It would be fairer and more productive if Americans stopped the arm-twisting and sanctions and got their country back into shape.

Japan can help by compromise and cooperation, but the outcome depends primarily on American efforts. Let's be candid. America's problem is not Japan's economic strength but its own industrial weakness. As many senior Japanese executives have pointed out, the fundamental cause is the endemic shortsightedness in U.S. boardrooms. Some uninformed Americans make long lists of the evils of Japanese-style management and demand corrective action. Of course, there are impediments to free trade in Japan, but our businessmen are always ready to make reasonable adjustments. Before pointing the finger at Tokyo and Osaka, Americans should deal first with the host of problems in their own backyard....

The Rockefeller Group Inc.'s sale of Rockefeller Center to Mitsubishi Estate Co. for $846 million is an example. RGI executives decided they could make quicker profits by investing their money in stocks, bonds, and money-market accounts than from real estate holdings. RGI approached a total of seventeen Japanese firms, including Mitsubishi, Mitsui Real Estate Development Co., and Sumitomo Realty & Development Co. Finally, Mitsubishi agreed to purchase the complex.

Playing the financial market does not help an industry manufacture products or render services; in the long run, it only weakens the company. The phenomenon recently reared its ugly head in Japan, too, and the government is considering a capital gains tax and other measures to cool the speculative fever. The authorities are acting because a preoccupation with quick paper profits saps managerial energy.

In a great many of the U.S. corporations with a "ten-minute" mentality, ownership and management are completely divorced. Stockholder demands for high dividends not only encourage management to play the money game but also hamper efforts to enhance profitability through research and development (R&D), new products, boosting sales, and gradually acquiring a larger market share. Admittedly, Matsushita Electric is an unusual case of the "ten-year" approach. When an entrepreneur like Konosuke Matsushita not only owns the company but personally runs it and is responsible for operations, including the livelihood of thousands of employees, he must have a long-term vision. The employment contract of the average American CEO is for only a few years. If profits dip, he is quickly sent packing. The system forces the president to concentrate exclusively on short-term gains. This is the basic difference between the frenetic style of U.S. corporations and the relatively long-term approach of Japanese firms that stress steady market expansion.

I am not suggesting that Japanese companies are in all respects superior to U.S. firms. However, I do feel that the United States would be better off if the strident critics of Japan, who seem resentful of our economic growth, would shut up for a while and do their homework. They should analyze objectively what makes Japanese companies tick, study the solid suggestions to improve productivity made by American experts, and use this data to turn U.S. firms around....

I hope the United States is not too proud to roll up its sleeves and do whatever is necessary to revive its manufacturing industry and economy. Then, America's enormous potential in high-technology fields will bloom and contribute to the next era. U.S. attacks on Japan's trade practices and demands for reforms are not a black-and-white issue; some points are valid and others are not. One thing, however, is certain: Americans should take a cold shower and calm down.

Newsweek said of Sony's $3.4 billion purchase of Columbia Pictures that "this time the Japanese hadn't just snapped up another building; they had bought a piece of America's soul." But who put it up for sale? The attacks on Mitsubishi Estate Co. were equally unfair. Tsuboi Hajime, chairman of Mitsui Real Estate, told me at the time, "The Rockefeller Group offered the site to us, too. They initiated and pushed the deal. To me, as a Japanese, the negative American reaction is very regrettable." A few days later, Sumitomo Realty chairman Ando Taro gave me a similar account.

There is a widespread feeling in the United States that Japan is buying up America. The sentimental attachment to a Hollywood institution like Columbia Pictures and a New York landmark like Radio City Music Hall is understandable. But the American public, and Japanese who attacked these purchases as provocative, should realize that it takes two to make a deal: Americans put these properties on the market.

Some Americans will still object to rich Japanese companies picking up trophy real estate in Hawaii, Los Angeles, Dallas, and elsewhere. But look at the genesis of this situation. Aside from the general excellence of Japanese-style management, there was a more immediate factor. The U.S. currency-rate policy, broached in 1985 at a meeting of the finance ministers and central bankers of the major industrialized nations (the so-called Group of Five, or G-5), made Japan a financial superpower and Washington's creditor. Japan got those billions of dollars to buy real estate as a direct result of the Reagan administration's weak-dollar, strong-yen policy.

The strategy resembled the U.S. Occupation's grand design for postwar Japan in that initial success was followed by monumental failure. As a result of our U.S.-designed pacifist Constitution, which for practical political reasons cannot be revised, Japan made itself into the kind of country Washington wanted: an industrial nation that follows the U.S. lead in foreign policy and poses no military threat to anyone. But our manufacturing sector now outshines U.S. companies.

Similarly, Reagan's devaluation of the greenback made U.S. exports more competitive and reduced the current account deficit. At the same time, however, the United States became the world's largest debtor nation. Under present circumstances, no matter what steps the United States takes to revitalize its economy, by 1995, its net debt to Japan will be at least $1.3 trillion and our total net investment in the United States will be $700 billion....

Strange as it may seem, U.S. demands on Japan boomerang; our concessions adversely affect the United States. That is precisely why, when circumstances

Blame the Japanese

By George Dawson

When the 'phone is out of order, and the roof has sprung a leak,
When the money in your paycheck barely gets you through the week,
When the baby has the colic, and your dog is full of fleas,
Don't complain to Washington — just blame the Japanese.

When the crooks are running rampant, and the judges are too lax,
When letters from the I.R.S. demand some extra tax,
When your son is quitting college, and your daughter's getting D's,
Just do what Iacocca does — and curse the Japanese.

When your taxes keep on rising, while your bank-book starts to shrink,
When pollution clouds your city, so the air begins to stink,
When the temperature is falling, and your pipes are sure to freeze,
Call upon your Congressman to bash the Japanese.

When everyone around you is complaining of the news,
And some condemn the Arabs while others blast the Jews,
Stiffen up your lip, my son, and never bend your knees —
Just be a true American, and blame the Japanese.

George Dawson is emeritus professor of economics at Empire State College of the State University of New York.

—*New York Times*
January 30, 1992

Source: George Dawson is emeritus professor of economics at Empire State College of the State University of New York. *New York Times*, January 30, 1992.

warrant, we must resolutely say no to Washington. Firmness in Tokyo should speed America's economic recovery. The fall of dictators in Eastern Europe shows the fate of those who surround themselves with yes-men....

We cannot cavalierly reject all U.S. trade demands, of course. But if both sides took tough positions ... the result would be a more positive relationship. Economic issues with large amounts of money at stake bring out the worst in Tokyo and Washington. It seems to the Japanese that U.S. emotionalism over Columbia Pictures and Rockefeller Center is a result of the Americans shooting themselves in the foot. In 1985, U.S. leaders were laughing up their sleeves at the dollar depreciation scheme they had foisted on Tokyo. It somehow misfired and instead made Japan affluent. Americans should follow the Chinese proverb, "When things go wrong, first look in the mirror." ...

The United States has not sufficiently appreciated Japan or even taken us all that seriously, because since 1945, we have been under Uncle Sam's thumb. Today, Americans may feel that Japan is getting out of hand. My own view is that Japan should not immediately disassociate itself from the U.S. security system. For our sake and that of the whole Pacific region, the special Tokyo-Washington relationship must be preserved. A breakup could destroy the budding new developments in that region. Japan should play an expanded role in the post-cold war world order. Effective use of our economic power—technology, management skills, and financial resources—at our own initiative can be the key to stable progress.

The economic dimension of the next era is already unfolding. That communism, a political doctrine no longer meaningful or functional, has remained powerful until recently is an irony of history. Prolonged obsession with ideology was a cultural lag between technology and the human beings who created it. To Japanese, as a pragmatic people inclined toward craftsmanship rather than metaphysics, the end of ideology is good news.

History shows that technology creates civilization and determines the scale and level of its economic and industrial development. Eastern Europe and the Soviet Union want state-of-the-art technology and financial aid to make them productive. What country can provide them? Only Japan. But we cannot meet this challenge alone. It must be a joint undertaking with our partner, the United States.

Japan's World Role

In its opinions about Japan, Washington is divided into the so-called Cherry Blossom Club and the Japan-bashers, with the former in the departments of State and Defense and the latter headquartered on Capitol Hill. The U.S. military and foreign service are well aware that Japan's high technology and mass-production system are indispensable to America's global strategy and consider the torrent of congressional attacks unwise. Still, the Cherry Blossoms and the Japan-bashers agree on one thing: They do not want Japan to become more powerful than it is now.

Ronald Morse, a Japan specialist at the Library of Congress, and Alan Tonelson, former editor of *Foreign Policy,* coauthored an unusually freewheeling article in *The New York Times* entitled "Let Japan Be Japan" (October 4, 1987). They wrote: "Clearly, Japan should stand on its own two feet, strategically and politically as well as economically. By continuing to treat Japan as a subordinate, America only makes the inevitable breakup speedier and nastier." Morse and Tonelson concluded that "If Japan assumes a constructive role in regional and world affairs, both countries will benefit."

The message is clear: We must think and act for ourselves and stop being a dutiful underling who leaves all the hard decisions up to the boss.

At the risk of repeating myself, the first step in that direction is to get rid of our servile attitude toward the United States. We should no longer be at Washington's beck and call. The ending of *The King and I* suggests a great beginning for Japan. As his father is dying, the young son who will become king proclaims a new era for Siam: No longer will the subjects bow like toads. They will stand erect, "shoulders back and chin high," and look the king in the eye as a proud people were meant to do.

Once Japan stands up to Uncle Sam, what will we do with our independence? What ideals do we bring to the global arena?

When Emperor Hirohito died in January 1989 and his son Akihito acceded to the throne, a new era—Heisei, or "achievement of peace"—was proclaimed that symbolizes Japan's role in the future course of civilization. The two characters that make up the word Heisei appear in such classical passages as "Tranquility achieved inside makes the outside peaceful." Japan's stability and progress will be increasingly intertwined with those of the outside world. This will be the first time Japanese play a leading role on the world stage, a task to which I think we are equal and must accept. The cooperation of many other nations, foremost among them the United States, is essential....

The conflicts among nations will be increasingly economic in nature. With the cold war over, friction on trade and investment will inevitably intensify. Over the next few years, Japan-bashing in the United States will become even more virulent. Although I see the bilateral relationship as the dominant force in the next century, before we reach that level of cooperation, U.S. policy toward Japan will approximate the stance against the Soviet Union at the height of the cold war.

First, Americans will argue that Japan is different and therefore a threat. Next, a "collective security system" will be created to block Japan's economic expansion. Then protectionist measures and sanctions against Japanese products will follow one after the other. An alliance is already being formed against Japan. Finally, there will be a witch hunt directed at everything Japanese. We must be prepared for stormy days ahead.

If we try to bend with the wind, making concessions and patchwork compromises as usual, the tempest will abate for a while, only to recur with even greater force. We must not flinch in the face of pressure. The only way to withstand foreign demands is to hold our ground courageously. No more temporizing. When justified, we must keep saying no and be undaunted by the reaction, however furious. A prolonged standoff forces both sides to find areas of agreement. That is the best way to resolve disputes, not unilateral concessions by Japan, which leave the other party unaware of how we really feel. Our lack of assertiveness in the past has led to disparaging epithets like "the faceless people." ...

But politicians and bureaucrats must realize that the time is past when Japan can be preoccupied with its own affairs. For the past forty-five years we have not had a major say in world developments. Geopolitical factors always dictated a reactive stance. Playing the leading man is out of character. Nevertheless, stage fright will keep us in the wings forever. If we know our lines and say them confidently, I am sure our performance will get rave reviews. After all, we are not an unknown understudy. Our long history and rich culture have prepared us for the limelight.

Japan-bashing is a reaction both to our moving to center stage and the impending Pacific Century. Only the uninformed or insolent would say we are unqualified for leadership. That the United States, our indispensable partner, is furiously attacking us is extremely regrettable.

It is true that postwar Japan has not taken major political initiatives. To say, however, that the country is incapable of lofty goals or thinks only of self-interest shows utter contempt for Japan. A well-funded creative aid program that combined high technology with management expertise could be the core of a Japanese vision....

SAY NO—
BUT TO WHAT?

Editor's Introduction: Ishihara Shintarō argued that Japan should say no to the U.S. as one step in its move from junior partner to full partner. He embraces the central goal of Japan's postwar state: economic development. Other Japanese, not so famous as Ishihara, would like Japan to say no, too, but their agendas are different from Ishihara's.

One such person is Kurihara Sadako, the poet and survivor of Hiroshima. Until her death in 2005 at the age of 92, she criticized postwar Japan: for its amnesia about the Pacific War, for its pursuit of economic development, for its alliance with the U.S. She wrote "The Flag, 1" in 1952: [35]

The Flag, 1

As if nothing at all had gone wrong,
the flag fluttered once more
high over the roofs
and began to dream again of carnage in broad daylight.
But no one looked up to it,
and people resented its insatiable greed
and gnashed their teeth at its monstrous amnesia.

Beneath that flag
each morning,
dizzy from malnutrition,
we were made to swear the oath of slaves
and send off
fathers and brothers
wearing red sashes and waving that flag.
Ever since it flew over ramparts on the continent,
that flag has believed fanatically
        in the dream of empire.
From far Guadalcanal

to the cliffs of Corregidor.
It drove our fathers and husbands
into the caves of Iwojima and Saipan,
starved them like wild beasts,
and scattered their white bones.

Ah! Red-on-white flag of Japan!
The many nightmarish atrocities carried out
        at your feet.
Manila and Nanjing, where they splashed gasoline
        over women and children
and burned them alive—
consummate crimes of the 20th century.
Yet today the flag flutters again, shameless,
all those bloody memories
gone;
fluttering, fluttering in the breeze,
it dreams once more of redrawing the map.

Indictment of Japan

◌ "Indictment of Japan" is a poem of 1973. The "criminal gang" landing once more on an island south of Japan refers to the fact that in 1972 the U.S. restored Okinawa to Japan. [36] ◌

In Japan
there is a city where black rain falls, still invisible
(in that city nothing ever happens except that
abstract monuments and buildings
are forever going up),
but they say no one has seen the crooks.
The mayor likes ceremonies:
in summer, before the cenotaph,
he proclaims to the world
"a new order with no killing,"
and in the fall he stands on the reviewing stand
reviewing the troops
and encouraging killing.

In Japan
there are countless beaches and valleys
where resentment swirls black as tar.
Criminal factories go into operation

(though the crooks are in plain sight,
they cannot be arrested),
spew poison,
and fish and shellfish putrefy and dissolve.
People shuffle along in pain,
dance like cats,
and die frenzied deaths.
And at points all along the shoreline
are places that turn the sky blood-red night and day,
and people inhale the cloudy gas
cough horribly,
turn yellow, and die.

In the sea to the south of Japan
there is an island
where poison gas and nukes lie concealed
        under the briers
and even the sun is American-made.
The criminal gang that twenty-eight years ago
starved the islanders,
gave them handgrenades,
and forced them into mass suicides
lands once more,
wearing green camouflage suits,
and says they're there to defend the islanders.

The Japanese archipelago has grown overheated
and the landscape is stained the color of blood;
still night and day
a stuck record
sings over and over,
"Everything's just fine!"
"Everything's just fine!"
In 1973 the summer of the defeat has grown distant,
and things have come full circle—
Japan now the seventh largest military power,
defense budget in the billions.
In the distance I hear the wolf-like howls
of democrats who have grown fangs,
and I cannot rest.

Who are they,
who were they—the order-givers

who deserted brave underlings in the jungle
and have lived twenty-eight years snug and warm?
What was my own purpose in life during those years?
And what am I doing now?
We can't let the dead
be killed once again.

Gold and Nukes

In "Gold and Nukes" (1982), Kurihara uses the myth of Midas to attack nuclear weapons and nuclear power. [37]

Once upon a time
there was a king who loved gold.
He was given the power
to turn absolutely everything
he touched
to gold.
One day the king's young daughter
came to his room, cried, "Daddy,"
and threw her arms around him.
In his embrace
she turned to solid gold.

Nowadays
there are kings
who love nukes more than gold,
and they have been given the power
to destroy humankind
the instant
their hands touch the button.
As if competing at soccer,
these kings
competed at testing
atomic bombs.

All over their countries
they wove fine nets of nuclear-bomb factories
and nuclear power plants.
The death ash
crossed boundaries and oceans
and spread throughout the world.
Gradually and surely, the bodies of those who absorb
        radiation are eaten away,
develop leukemia and cancer,

their hair falls out, red spots appear,
they vomit blood and die.
Even so, the kings keep repeating that all is well:
"We can't be sure the one causes the other."

Just as the daughter of the king who loved gold
turned into a statue of gold,
the kings' daughters develop leukemia.
Even so, I doubt that the kings
will stop their game of nukes.
Babies in their cradles
all over the world
and children running about with bright smiles
will be burned black as charcoal,
and the globe will turn into an uninhabited star
that can never again support life.
In the dark wind
uranium and helium
go on singing
their song without words.

Editor's Postscript: Ishihara and Kurihara agree on very little. Ishihara's book sold over one million copies; Kurihara's poems go largely unnoticed. But their disagreement gives some sense of the range of debate within Japan today.

VI
TEXTBOOKS AND
THE TEACHING
OF HISTORY

A JAPANESE
TEXTBOOK

Editor's Introduction: The Japanese Ministry of Education must approve textbooks before they can be used in Japan's classrooms. As we have seen ("The Japanese Constitution: One Historian's Views"), that certification process led to thirty years of lawsuits. In all the lawsuits the Supreme Court upheld the right of the Ministry to screen textbooks before publication.

In 1995, there were four approved textbooks for Japanese History A. ('A' denotes a focus on modern and contemporary history; 'B' denotes surveys of all of Japanese history.) *History of Contemporary Japan* (Tokyo: Yamakawa) was one of the most widely used 'A' textbooks. It listed four authors, all male. It consisted of 176 pages of text; it had twelve chapters and a conclusion. Five chapters (65 pages) covered prehistory to 1868; five chapters (80 pages) covered 1868-1945; one chapter (11 pages) covered the American Occupation; one chapter (12 pages) covered Japan since 1952.

These pages are three of the eight dealing with World War II. [38]

太平洋戦争要図

8. 日本の敗北

**戦局の悪化と
国民生活の荒廃** 日本の真珠湾奇襲攻撃によって，アメリカの国論は沸騰し，挙国一致で戦争に突入した❶。はじめ日本に有利であった戦局は，1942（昭和17）年6月，**ミッドウェー海戦**で日本海軍が敗北したのをきっかけに逆転した。翌年，アメリカ軍を中心とする連合国軍が本格的な反攻を開始すると，ガダルカナル島の敗退をはじめ，日本軍はつぎつぎと後退をかさねた。そして，1944（昭和19）年7月，南洋諸島中の重要な軍事拠点であったサイパン島がアメリカ軍に占領され，東条内閣は退陣に追いこまれたが，あとをついだ小磯国昭内閣も戦争を続けた。
1880～1950

政府・軍部は国のあらゆる生産能力を軍需目的に集中したが，アメリカの巨大な生産力には追いつけなかった。働きざかりの青年が兵士として戦地におもむいたため，労働力不足は深刻となった。**学徒勤労動員**や **徴用** によって，中等学校以上の男女学生・生徒や中高年の人人まで，軍需工場などで労働に従事させられた。また，そのころ日本の植民地だった朝鮮の人々や，支配下におかれていた中国の人々が日本本土に **強制連行** されて，工場や鉱山などでの労働にかりだされた❷。

1943（昭和18）年10月には，**学徒出陣**がはじまり，1944（昭和19）年夏以降，大都市の学童たちが 空襲 の危険をさけて，あいついで地方に疎開した（**学童疎開**）。

❶ アメリカの西部諸州に住んでいた10万人以上の日系人は，戦争がはじまると家や土地をすてさせられ，強制収容所に収容された。アメリカ市民権をもつ日系2世のなかには，アメリカ合衆国への忠誠のあかしとして志願し，アメリカ軍に入隊したものも多かった。

❷ 1943（昭和18）年に朝鮮に，1945（昭和20）年には台湾に徴兵制が適用されて，朝鮮・台湾の人々も戦場にかりだされた。女性のなかには，戦地の軍の慰安施設ではたらかされたものもあった。また，植民地に対しては同化政策がいっそう進められ，朝鮮の人々は1939（昭和14）年以来，姓名を日本式にかえさせられた（創氏改名）。

The Pacific War

8.   Japan's Defeat

Deterioration in the War Situation and Collapse of Life at Home

American public opinion, aroused by the sudden Japanese attack on Pearl Harbor, launched into the war in a spirit of national unanimity.[1] The fortunes of war, at first favorable to Japan, began to turn from the time of the Japanese navy's defeat in the **Battle of Midway** in June 1942 (Showa 17). The following year, Allied — mainly American — forces began their counteroffensive in earnest; from the fall of Guadalcanal onward, the Japanese army made a succession of withdrawals. Finally in July 1944 (Showa 19), Saipan, one of the most important military bases of the South Pacific islands, was occupied by American forces, and the Tojo government was driven to resign, although the succeeding Koiso Kuniaki (1880–1950) government still continued the pursuit of the war.

The government and military concentrated the nation's entire productive potential on supplying military essentials, but it was no match for the huge productivity of the United States. Since young men in their prime had all gone as troops to the front, the shortage of labor became acute. Under systems of **mobilizing students** and older people, school children and students, both male and female, at junior high school and above, together with the middle-aged and elderly, were set to work in military arms factories and the like. Besides this, inhabitants of Korea, then a Japanese colony, and of the parts of China under Japanese control were **forcibly sent** to Japan proper and set to work in factories, mines, and elsewhere.[2]

In October 1943 (Showa 18), university and trade college students began to be taken into the forces (the **Student Forces**), and from summer 1944 (Showa 19) on schoolchildren in the major cities were steadily evacuated to the country to escape the danger of air raids (the **mass evacuation of schoolchildren**).

[1] With the beginning of the war, more than 100,000 Americans of Japanese descent living in the western states of the U.S. were forced to leave their homes and land and were placed in concentration camps. There were many second-generation Japanese-Americans, holding U.S. citizenship, who volunteered and served in the U.S. forces as a sign of their loyalty to the United States.

[2] In 1943 (Showa 18) and in 1945 (Showa 20), respectively, conscription systems were put into effect in Korea and Taiwan under which Koreans and Taiwanese were sent off to the battlefield. Some of their women too were obliged to work in "relief facilities" for troops in the battle zones. Policies of assimilation were stepped up still further in Japan's colonies, and from 1939 (Showa 14) onward Koreans were obliged to change their names to Japanese-style names.

防空訓練 もんぺに防空頭巾という服装で，バケツリレーなどによる消火訓練をさせられた。実際のB29の焼夷弾による空襲に対しては，ほとんど無力であった。

学童の集団疎開 集団疎開は1944(昭和19)年7月ごろからはじまり，親もとをはなれた児童41万人あまりが，地方の旅館や寺などに収容された。疎開児童たちは深刻な空腹になやまされた。写真は群馬県妙義山麓に疎開した東京の国民学校の児童たち。

　政府・軍部は戦局の悪化についての真相を国民に知らせなかったが，生活必需品の欠乏や食糧不足は深刻化し，国民の戦意はしだいにおとろえていった。

　敗　戦　連合国側では，1943(昭和18)年11月，アメリカ・イギリス・中国の3国首脳が**カイロ宣言**を発表して，日本の敗北まで協力して戦いぬくこと，日本の植民地を独立または返還させることなどをあきらかにした。

　1944(昭和19)年末以降，アメリカ空軍による**日本本土空襲**が激しくなった。とくに，1945(昭和20)年3月の東京大空襲では東京の下町がほとんど焼きつくされた❶のをはじめ，全国のおもな都市は，空襲でつぎつぎに焼野原となった。同年4月アメリカ軍は**沖縄本島に上陸**を開始し，日本軍は激しい戦闘の末，同年6月ほとんど全滅した❷。

　ヨーロッパ戦線では，1943年9月イタリアが連合国に降伏し，1945年5月にドイツも降伏したので，日本はまったく孤立無援となってしまった。鈴木貫太郎内閣は，同年6月，日本と中立関係にあったソ連を仲介とする和平工作に着手した。しかし，すでに同年2月，アメリカ・イギリス・ソ連3国首脳が，第二次世界大戦後のドイツ問題を協議したヤルタ会談で，ドイツ降伏の2～3カ月のちにソ連が対日参戦することなどをとりきめた，**ヤルタ協定**がむすばれていた❸。

　1945(昭和20)年7月，ふたたび3国首脳はベルリン郊外のポツダムで会談し，アメリカ・イギリス・中国3国(のちソ連も参加)の共同宣言として，**ポツダム宣言**を発し，日本に降伏をよびかけた。鈴木内閣

❶ 1945(昭和20)年3月9～10日のB29大型爆撃機百数十機による東京大空襲で，約10万人の住民が死亡した。その大部分は婦女子をふくむ非戦闘員であった。

❷ 沖縄の戦闘で，日本側は軍人約10万人，民間人約10万人，合計約20万人が死亡した。アメリカ軍の戦死者は約1万2000人といわれる。

❸ ソ連の対日参戦はヤルタ協定の秘密条項でとり決められたが，ソ連はその代償として，南樺太の回復や千島の獲得を認められていた。

Air raid training Women wearing the baggy cotton trousers called *mompe* and padded air raid hoods were put through firefighting drills using bucket relays and the like. Such training was almost useless in the face of the actual incendiary raids by B29 bombers.

Mass evacuation of schoolchildren Mass evacuation began around July 1944 (Showa 19), more than 410,000 children being taken from their parental homes and accommodates at inns, temples and so on in the provinces. The evacuated children suffered from severe hunger. The photograph shows children from a people's school in Tokyo evacuated to a district near the foot of Mt. Myogi in Gumma prefecture.

The government and military kept the public in the dark concerning the deterioration of the war situation, but the increasingly serious lack of daily necessities and shortages of food progressively sapped the nation's will to fight.

On the Allied side, the leaders of the U.S., England, and **The Defeat** China issued the **Cairo Declaration** in November 1943 (Showa 18), affirming that they would continue to fight alongside each other until the defeat of Japan, and that Japan's colonies would be given their independence or returned (to their former owners).

From the end of 1944 (Showa 19) onward, **raids on the Japanese main islands** by the U.S. air force were stepped up. In the great raid on Tokyo in March 1945 (Showa 20) in particular, almost all the low-lying business and commercial areas of Tokyo were razed by fire,[1] while principal cities and towns throughout the country were one by one reduced to ashes in the raids. In April of the same year, U.S. forces began **landings on the main island of Okinawa**, where Japanese forces, after intense fighting, were almost entirely wiped out by June.[2]

On the European front, Italy surrendered to the Allies in September 1943, followed by Germany in May 1945, leaving Japan entirely isolated and unsupported. In June of that year, the Suzuki Kantaro (1867–1948) government sent out peace feelers, using the Soviet Union — which had a treaty of neutrality with Japan — as intermediary. However, at the Yalta Conference in February of that year, in which leaders of the U.S., Britain, and the Soviet Union discussed the question of Germany following the end of World War II, leaders of the three nations concluded the **Yalta Agreements** under which it was agreed, among other things, that the Soviet Union should join the war against Japan two to three months following the German surrender.[3]

In July 1945 (Showa 20), the three leaders held further talks at Potsdam on the outskirts of Berlin, and issued the **Potsdam Declaration** as a joint declaration by the U.S., Britain, and China — later to be joined by the Soviet Union — calling for Japan's surrender. The Suzuki government, which had been sounding out ways of ending the war, had hopes of peace

[1] In the great Tokyo air raid of March 9–10, 1945 (Showa 20), carried out by around 150 B29 large bombers, some 100,000 inhabitants were killed, most of them noncombatants, including women and children.

[2] In the fighting on Okinawa, some 200,000 Japanese died: approximately 100,000 military personnel and approximately 100,000 civilians. The number of American troops killed is said to have been approximately 12,000.

[3] Soviet participation in the war against Japan was provided for a secret clause appended to the Yalta Agreement, under which it was agreed that the Soviet Union, in return, should recover southern Sakhalin and be given the Kuril Islands.

原爆投下で廃きょとなった広島（上）と長崎（下）

❶ 原子爆弾による死者は，広島で約20万人，長崎で約7万人と推定されている。今日でも放射線障害などによる被爆者の死亡が続いている。

❷ 戦争終結によって，約60万人の軍人，民間人がソ連軍の捕虜となり，シベリアやモンゴルに送られ，強制労働に従事させられた。そのうち約6万人が死亡したといわれる。

❸ 第二次世界大戦における日本の人的被害については正確な数字はわからないが，軍人・民間人をあわせて死者・行方不明者約300万人，国内の被害家屋は240万戸におよんだと推定される。

は終戦の道を模索していたが，ソ連をつうじての和平工作に期待をかけ，はじめポツダム宣言を黙殺すると発表したので，アメリカは，同年8月6日広島に，ついで8月9日長崎に原子爆弾を投下し，一瞬のうちに両市を壊滅させ，多数の一般市民を殺傷した❶。その間，8月8日にはソ連が日ソ中立条約を一方的に破棄して日本に宣戦を布告し，満州・樺太・千島などに侵入を開始した❷。

鈴木内閣は天皇の裁断という異例の形をとって，軍部の一部にあった戦争継続論をおさえ，1945（昭和20）年8月14日，ポツダム宣言の受諾を決定して，これを連合国側に通告した。翌8月15日，天皇自身のラジオ放送をつうじて，国民にこれをあきらかにした。

こうして，6年にもわたって，全世界に空前の惨害をもたらした第二次世界大戦は，枢軸陣営の敗北によって終わりを告げた❹。

Hiroshima (above) and Nagasaki (below) laid waste by atomic bombs

[1] The numbers killed by the atomic bombs are estimated at approximately 200,000 in Hiroshima and 70,000 in Nagasaki. Even today, victims of atomic bombing are still dying from the after-effects of radiation.

[2] With the conclusion of the war, some 600,000 military personnel and civilians were taken prisoner by Soviet forces and sent to Siberia and Mongolia, where they were set to forced labor. Approximately 60,000 of them are said to have died.

[3] No accurate figures are available for human losses incurred by Japan in World War II, but it is estimated that the dead and missing, military personnel and civilians included, totaled some 3 million and that the number of houses destroyed within Japan totaled 2.4 million.

maneuvers via the Soviet Union, and at first announced that it would ignore the Potsdam Declaration, so America **dropped atomic bombs** on Hiroshima and Nagasaki on, respectively, August 6 and 9 of the same year, destroying the cities instantly and killing or wounding large numbers of ordinary citizens.[1] In the meantime, on August 8, the Soviet Union arbitrarily abrogated the Soviet-Japanese Neutrality Pact, declared war on Japan, and began to invade Manchuria, Sakhalin, and the Kurils.[2]

On August 14, 1945 (Showa 20), the Suzuki government decided to accept the Potsdam Declaration, sidestepping calls for continuation of the war from among the military by resorting to the unusual expedient of a personal decision by the emperor, and informed the Allies accordingly. On the following day, August 15, the nation was informed of this decision via a personal broadcast by the emperor himself.

Thus World War II, which had wrought unprecedented havoc throughout the world over a period of six years, came to an end with the final defeat of the Axis.[3]

Editor's Postscript: In Japan, the Ministry of Education guards the textbook gate. In the United States, textbook publishers perform that role, and school systems and/or Boards of Education are normally free to choose any text they please, although in a few states the state Board of Education selects a short list of textbooks that it deems qualified. But the main concern of the publishers, normally, is profit. What effects might that have on the textbooks?

In 1989 the Ministry of Education set this goal for Japanese History 'A' textbooks:

> To give an understanding from a historical viewpoint of the course of Japanese history, taking care to make students think about the process of the establishment and development of modern society in relation to the international environment as it affected Japan, so as to foster in them the ability to think historically and develop their awareness as citizens of Japan and as Japanese living in international society.

What purpose do textbooks serve? What are the qualities of a good textbook? Of a poor textbook? Who writes textbooks?

How different is this textbook in format (layout, illustrations, style) from an American history textbook? (The original size of this textbook is 7" x 10", larger than the reproductions here.)

Do history textbooks cover the most recent history? Why is that difficult to do? How important are textbooks? More important than exams? More important than classroom information? More important than teachers? How do we tend to read textbooks? "Will it be on the exam?"

Japan's Nobel Prize Winners

Japanese scientists have won 12 Nobel Prizes, including three in Chemistry, three in Physics, and two in Literature. The most recent winners are Koshiba Masatoshi (2002) in Physics, and Tanaka Kōichi (2002), Noyori Ryūji (2001), and Shirakawa Hideki (2000), all in Chemistry.

Source: *Japan Now*, November 2002.

Tokyo Teacher Punished for Pacifist Stance

Refusal to Sing Wartime Anthem Comes As Japanese Schools Push National Pride

TOKYO—When the national anthem started playing during a ceremony this year at Tachikawa Daini Junior High, Nezu Kimiko, a soft-spoken but resolute home ec teacher, refused to stand and kept her mouth shut while others sang around her. A self-described pacifist, Nezu said she has done the same thing ever since the Diet designated the "Kimigayo" as the national anthem in 1999. She opposes the song because it was the same one sung as the Imperial Army set forth from Japan calling for an "eternal reign" of the emperor. Previously, her protest brought nothing more than harsh stares from some students and parents. But in October 2003 the Tokyo school board ordered that the anthem must be respected. In May, shortly after the incident at Tachikawa, she was suspended for a month. Officials warned that another offense could lead to her dismissal after 34 years of teaching. The school board reaction was part of an effort by Tokyo and other school districts to enforce a new sense of pride in being Japanese. The measures were strongly backed by Ishihara Shintarō, governor of Tokyo and outspoken nationalist.

Source: Anthony Faiola, *Washington Post*, August 30, 2005.

LIES MY TEXTBOOKS
TAUGHT ME

Editor's Introduction: What do textbooks teach? What should they teach? These are questions that need answering, whether the textbooks are Japanese or American. In the following essay, I lay out aspects of the recent debate about Japanese textbooks. I take my title from the book by James Loewen, *Lies My Teacher Taught Me*, which offers useful criticisms of American textbooks.

IN 2000 THE CONTENT of Japanese textbooks became an international issue. Why? In that year a right-wing group in Japan decided to compile a text with the explicit aim of giving Japanese children an increased sense of pride in their nation. The new text received the approval of the Ministry of Education.

In Japan, the Japanese government (through its Ministry of Education) screens potential textbooks for content; textbooks that fail to gain Ministry approval cannot be used in the public schools. That process was the cause of the famous lawsuits of Professor Ienaga Saburō, who claimed that government certification infringed on his rights. The Japanese courts, notoriously reluctant to hold the government guilty, ruled that textbook certification was not unconstitutional even if specific actions the Ministry of Education took against Professor Ienaga were wrong. (In the U.S., publishing companies play the screening role, but the result is similar—subject matter that offends a significant group will not survive.)

So the Japanese government becomes a natural target of protest, both for Japanese and for foreign countries. Many Japanese, including teachers and historians, objected to the new textbook. Other nations—most notably, those nations that had suffered at the hands of the Japanese in the Pacific War—raised concerns about that new textbook. China and South Korea were vociferous in their attacks.

Here is a statement by one of the authors of the new textbook:

Studying history is not the same as passing judgment on the injustices and inequities of the past with present-day yardsticks. Each
period in history had its own notions about right and wrong and its
distinctive ideas about what constitutes happiness. In the introduc-
tory section of the history textbook for middle school that our Japanese Society for History Textbook Reform has prepared, we urged that
history stop being treated like a court in which the figures and actions of the past are called to judgment....

The annexation of Korea must also be viewed in the proper context. In the early 20th century, maintaining equilibrium among the
great powers was an important part of international policy. Following the Russo-Japanese War [1904-05], Russia hoped to thwart
America's advances into Manchuria and thus sought a reconciliation
with Japan. Brought together by common interests, Japan and Russia signed an agreement delineating the boundaries of their respective
spheres of influence in Northeast Asia. In return for accepting
France's colonial rule over Indochina and U.S. control of the Philippines, moreover, Japan won recognition of its colonization of the Korean Peninsula. And as the price for winning Britain's
acknowledgment during talks to renew the Anglo-Japanese alliance,
Japan accepted an obligation to defend India as Britain's ally.

Japan's colonization of Korea was not simply a bilateral issue,
therefore, but part of a complex international balancing act among
the great powers. The attempt to frame this historical development
in a broader context has been criticized as an attempt to legitimize
Japanese aggression, but such charges ignore historical reality....

Many have noted that our textbook represents an attempt to
overcome a 'masochistic' tendency in the teaching of history. I rather
think the aim is to rectify the absence of common sense.... We are
not bound to a single ideology; rather, we are opposed to the history
that has been taught thus far from ideologically biased viewpoints.*

As you can see, this author assumes that it is possible to teach history without an "ideologically biased viewpoint." But the group of which he was a member stressed the need to oppose "masochistic" history—the tendency to blame
Japan too much. Is that stance itself ideological?

One of the critics of the new textbook offered this rejoinder:

---

*Nishio Kanji, "Rekishi kyōkasho: Mezashita no wa jōshiki no kakuritsu," in *Asahi,* April
4, 2001; translated in "Four Views of the Textbook Issue," *Japan Echo* 38.4 (August
2001), pp. 33-34.

The present is always defined by the past, regardless of whether one is discussing national traits, socioeconomic trends, living conditions, or human rights. Without an accurate grasp of history, it is not possible to live in the present and future with a proper self-awareness. Knowledge of history is indispensable for both the state and the individual.

People's deep interest and desire to learn the truth about the past are quite natural, and history education must satisfy this desire. From the Meiji era (1868-1912) to the end of World War II, however, the teaching of history focused on filling children's minds with a sense of national superiority and instilling a uniform sense of allegiance to the state. This effort required that children be taught not so much important historical facts as "historical tales" that appealed to their impressionable minds. Needless to say, the consequences of such a policy included a war fought by "one hundred million hearts beating as one" [a wartime propaganda slogan that overstated the population of Japan—then about 70,000,000—and stressed national unity].

The starting point of postwar education was an admission of these mistakes. An effort was made to present historical facts as they were and to have pupils think about them to enable them to draw their own conclusions on how they should live as contributing members of the state and the international community.

The middle school text submitted for authorization by the Japanese Society for History Textbook Reform...is an unabashed attempt once again to plant nationalistic seeds in youngsters' minds. It makes no mention of how the Imperial Rescript on Education was utilized to enforce loyalty to the emperor and the state.... Instead, the proposed textbook simply describes the rescript as identifying a code of behavior befitting citizens of a modern state. At every turn there are attempts to distort facts and justify Japan's conduct, such as by assigning part of the blame for the annexation of Korea and the invasion of China on the other parties involved....*

How should nations confront their imperialistic pasts or presents? That is a serious question. Is it ideological to confront those pasts? Is it ideological to sugar-coat those pasts?

Here are excerpts from the Preface ("On Studying History") of the controversial new history textbook:

*Nagahara Keiji, "Rekishi kyōkasho: shijitsu yugameru jiyū wa nai," *Asahi*, April 26, 2001, translated in "Four Views of the Textbook," *Japan Echo*, 38.4 (August 2001), pp.34-35.

There are likely many people who think that to study history is to learn facts about the past. But that is not necessarily so. To study history is to study how people in the past thought about the past....

To study history is not the same as to make judgments on and indict the injustices and unfairnesses of the past in terms of today's standards. In the various ages of the past, each age had its own particular virtues and vices, its own happiness....

Let's stop thinking of history as something fixed and unchanging. Let's stop assigning right and wrong to history, stop applying today's morality to make of history a court of judgment. Let's look at history with free, unprejudiced eyes; let's pile up many viewpoints and ascertain the facts with care.*

Can we separate history and morality? Can we study history and not apply "today's morality to make of history a court of judgment"? Consider the implications of this approach in the United States: how should we study the treatment of Native Americans? Of slaves? Of women? Of other minorities? Should American textbooks include views from abroad? Should American museums present exhibits about the darker sides of U.S. history?

In 1937, when the Japanese army seized the Chinese nationalist capital of Nanjing (or Nanking), many Chinese—soldiers and civilians—died at the hands of the Japanese. Although there will never be an exact figure, estimates of the numbers killed range up to 300,000. Japanese accounts often cite a figure of 200,000; Chinese accounts often emphasize the higher figure. Many American texts refer to the event as the Rape of Nanjing or the Nanjing Massacre, and it is one of the most notorious Japanese atrocities of the war. Japanese textbooks of the mid-1990s mentioned it routinely. Here is one mainstream Japanese textbook: "In Nanjing the army massacred large numbers of Chinese people, including not only prisoners of war, but women and children. [A footnote adds: "It has been said that 200,000 people were slaughtered by the Japanese army in this incident, which was condemned internationally as the 'Nanjing Massacre.'"] From about 1940 the Japanese army destroyed the lives of the Chinese people in a three-pronged strategy of burning, killing, and pillaging villages in North China, where the anti-Japanese movements were centered."**

The new text does mention Nanjing: "Thinking that if it captured Nanjing, the capital of the Nationalist government, Chiang Kai-shek would surrender, the Japanese army seized Nanjing (at that time many civilians, too, were casual-

---

* Atarashii rekishi kyōkasho (Tokyo: Fusō sha, 2001),

** Chūgaku shakai, Osaka: Osaka shoseki, 1993); translation in *Japanese School Textbooks: Japan in Modern History—Junior High School*, ed. International Society for Educational Information (Tokyo: Shobundo, 1994), p. 321.

ties of the Japanese army. Nanjing Incident)." Readers are then directed to a later section dealing with prosecution of Japanese war crimes after the war, which reads as follows: "At the Tokyo trial, it was determined that in 1937 during the Sino-Japanese war when the Japanese army seized Nanjing, it killed many Chinese (Nanjing Incident). Still, as to the facts of this incident, doubts about the documents have also been raised, and there are various opinions, and even today the debate continues."*

Statements such as these aroused the opposition of many scholars both in Japan and abroad. Here is a statement of protest against the textbook signed by several hundred non-Japanese scholars:

> We the undersigned support the efforts of Japanese historians, educators, and citizens to ensure that textbooks are consistent with values of peace, justice, and truth. We join them in protesting the recent decision of the Japanese Ministry of Education and Science to approve a new textbook that tramples on these values.... Although historians and educators inside and outside Japan raised important questions about the text, it passed Japanese government textbook screening in early Spring 2001 and is now approved for use in 2002 in junior high schools.
>
> History textbooks and instruction are the primary means whereby younger generations learn about their past. Indeed, for many people, school textbooks provide the most systematic introduction to the past that they will ever receive. Textbooks should, therefore, provide students with truthful accounts that reflect the finest achievements of historical research. This is all the more important in Japan, since school textbooks bear a government imprimatur because of Japan's system of government screening.
>
> History textbooks are not merely the repository of society's understanding of the past; they also convey what we as a society choose to remember and represent as the core of civic knowledge. They convey to students ideas about local, national, and global citizenship, and thereby help to shape our future. It is precisely because of this characteristic of textbooks that their content has been so fiercely contested, particularly during the last half century and more in Japan as elsewhere.
>
> At the dawn of the twenty-first century, we recognize the mistakes committed by the human race in the last century, including the atrocities associated with colonialism and war. Reconciliation and reorientation to build a new global community in which humanity prevails are our urgent tasks. It is, therefore, imperative that school

---

*Atarashii rekishi kyōkasho, pp. 270-271, 295.

textbooks present knowledge and values that contribute to making our world more democratic, peaceful, and just.

The new Japanese history textbook is unfit as a teaching tool because it negates both the truth about Japan's record in colonialism and war and the values that will contribute to a just and peaceful Pacific and world community. Its chauvinistic history, in overemphasizing what its authors call the "bright side" of the nation and disregarding the "dark side," fundamentally distorts the history of Japan and Asia....

It details war atrocities committed by the Allied forces and Nazi Germany, while virtually ignoring Japan's own (e.g., the cruel experiments of the biological warfare unit 731 and the massacre of the Chinese population in Singapore). It refers to the Nanjing Massacre but minimizes its importance by referring to "points of doubt" about the event....

All nations have disgraceful chapters in their histories. Teaching history today requires comparative and international perspectives that help students examine and reflect on such problems. We should not forget painful events but learn from them, because such lessons are the first step toward reconciliation. Like our colleagues in Japan, we too face important historical issues that we have yet to deal with effectively in our textbooks and in public discourse. But we join them now in expressing concern about the ideological orientation of this textbook and the effects it will have both in (mis)educating students and poisoning the relationship between Japan and neighboring countries that experienced Japanese invasion and rule.*

The publishers of the new text hoped to capture 10 percent of the market for this textbook. In fact, for the first year only two local school boards adopted the text—in both cases to be used by children with learning disabilities. That result was in part a response to the domestic and international furor the text aroused. As a trade book, in bookstores for the general public, the text sold very well indeed, over 500,000 copies—many to readers eager to learn for themselves the cause of the furor. (When did a textbook ever get read by people who didn't have to take a test?)

To be sure, part of the concern in Japan and elsewhere about this right-wing text has to do with other recent aspects of Japanese policy: the attempt to revise the Constitution's Article 9, which outlaws the maintenance of military forces; the dispatch of Japan's Self-Defense Forces first to Cambodia and then to Iraq (in

---

*International appeal, Summer 2001.

support of the U.S. in the second Gulf War); the push to expand the UN Security Council and make Japan a permanent member. All of these raise questions about the long-term goals of Japan's recent governments.

How about textbooks in use today in our own schools? What would Japanese or Russian or Mexican historians think of them? Do these textbooks include Japanese or Russian or Mexican points of view? Do they favor a U.S. government point of view? Do they discuss "disgraceful chapters" in U. S. history? In 2007, the famous documentary film-maker Ken Burns released a PBS documentary on World War II that includes no treatment of the role of U.S. Hispanics. Is that a problem? Should it be?

What is history?

Used by permission of cartoonist Roger Dahl.

JAPAN AND ASIA:
A TEXTBOOK TREATMENT

Editor's Introduction: Japan's wartime policies and behavior cast a long and dark shadow over Japan's postwar relations with Asia. For example, a Japanese victory in men's soccer over China in summer 2004—59 years after the end of the war—caused Chinese soccer fans to burn the Japanese flag and make anti-Japanese statements that harked back to the war. Successive Japanese governments have attempted to put this issue to rest, but it resurfaces periodically, in particular when prominent figures attempt to whitewash the past or when the prime minister pays a visit to the shrine to Japan's war dead, Yasukuni.

In the following selection, one Japanese textbook of the 1990s deals with this issue. This text was one of the most widely used at the time; this passage is a "topic for study," a two-page section set off from the main narrative and including one photograph, of the Shinto shrine Japan set up in Seoul in 1925.

As you read it, ask yourself how your U. S. textbooks deal with topics of which most American citizens are less than proud: the treatment of Native Americans, of women, gays, and other minorities, and of various countries that became the objects of American military action.

Even the language is loaded. *Kankoku* is the Japanese pronunciation of the accepted Korean term for Korea today. (*Koku* means land or country, and so this term was not in use during the long years of Chinese rule before 1900.) *Chōsen* is the term the Japanese gave to Korea during the era of Japanese rule. *Kankoku* is the title in use today in South Korea. The title's "People of Korea" carries a different nuance, less formal, than "Korean people." [39]

The People of Korea [Chōsen]
Under Japanese Colonial Rule

At the outset of the 20th century, via three successive treaties between Japan and Korea [Kankoku], Japan grasped complete control of Korea's domestic politics and foreign policy; then, in 1910 (Meiji 43), Japan brought about the signing of a treaty of annexation and turned Korea into Japanese territory. Korea became a Japanese colony and was ruled by a Governor General of Korea [Chōsen].

In the 1920s, a policy of "amalgamating homeland and Korea" was proclaimed under the name of "enlightened politics." But when the 1930s arrived, as Japan's aggression against the Chinese mainland progressed and in hopes of turning Korea into its supply line, Japan proclaimed a policy of "same ancestors, same roots," which stressed that Japan and Korea had the same ancestors and the same roots; and at the end of the 1930s, Japan took a further step beyond the "amalgamation" of homeland and Korea to proclaim that "Homeland and Korea are one." Together with steps toward the wartime structure at home, a policy was developed of turning Koreans into "subjects of the empire." This "subject" policy turned Koreans into "imperial subjects," that is, subjects of the emperor; in practice, it compelled Koreans to worship at Shinto shrines, to be educated as Japanese, to use the Japanese language, and to change their names to Japanese names.... In May 1942 a Cabinet decision was taken to implement the conscription of "Korean compatriots." ...

Beginning in the late 1920s, the numbers of Koreans crossing the straits to Japan increased gradually, but in July 1939 the rounding-up of Koreans began under the guise of "the transfer of Korean laborers to the homeland," and in March 1943 the forced rounding-up of Koreans began in both fact and law. Then, in October 1944 national conscription was applied to Koreans. In order to make good the shortage of labor in Japan, some 700,000 people were rounded up by force, taken to Japan, and put to work in mines, factories, and construction sites, and many women were rounded up and sent as comfort women to the front lines in China, the Philippines, Indonesia, and Okinawa; they became sacrifices to Japan's war....

In November 1993 then-Prime Minister Hosokawa visited the Republic of Korea and at a joint press conference with Korean Prime Minister Kim (born 1927) stated: "Through Japan's colonial control the people of the Korean peninsula were robbed of the opportunity to study their own language in their schools, caused to change their family names to Japanese names, and made to experience unbearable hardship and suffering as comfort women and conscript workers; as victimizer, Japan reflects sincerely on its actions and offers its deep apologies."

Japan and the Japanese must reflect on the past and, having done so, work to establish new friendly relations with Korea [Chōsen] and China and the other Asian nations.

These university students, "examination hell" behind them, concentrate in a Tokyo classroom. Photo by H.W. Silvester. Rapho Guillumette Pictures.

TEXTBOOK CERTIFICATION: DOES IT SERVE A PURPOSE?

Editor's Introduction: The following discussion involves Kariya Take-hiko, a young professor of education, and three anonymous individuals. 'A' is a public middle-school social studies teacher who has taught for twenty years and worked as author and editor with a textbook publisher for ten years. 'B' is director of the editorial department of a textbook publisher. 'C' is editor-in-chief at a company that publishes supplementary educational materials. 'A,' 'B,' and 'C' prefer anonymity because of their positions. [40]

Kariya: Could you explain the steps of the production process?

'B': The first step is to select authors and have them do the writing. This part is the same as for ordinary books. But in the case of textbooks, once the author has written up a draft, we compare it with the textbooks that other companies have put out, and we have actual schoolteachers look at it and submit their opinions.

Kariya: I assume you start once the Ministry of Education issues its standards.

'A': In practice, the work starts before the standards. At the textbook company with which I'm involved, there's already an editorial board at work looking ahead to the new standards we anticipate will be issued in 2010.

Kariya: I understand the writing of textbooks involves teams of dozens of people, including university faculty members and middle and high school teachers, but how is the work of writing split up?

'A': It's somewhat different in the case of elementary school texts, because teachers don't specialize in particular subjects, but in the case of social studies texts for middle school and high school, we usually have university professors do the writing. Then we have middle and high school teachers look at the texts and make suggestions for items that the professors aren't familiar with—for example, student activities like mock trials or research on local history—along with requests for the addition of particular phrases that they might want to have included at, say, the middle school level.

Kariya: Textbook publishing companies presumably want to produce textbooks that will be readily adopted. Does this lead to clashes within the editorial boards between what the company wants and what the authors want in terms of content?

'A': That sort of clash hardly ever occurs. But one difference between the company and the authors is that the company tends to be more concerned about the physical makeup of the book. In the case of social studies texts, the practice now is to have the material to be covered in a one-hour class presented as a single two-page spread. Also, the texts are

Self-portrait of Japanese teens. Photo by Morisaki Minoru, from *Japan Forum*; used with permission.

printed in full color, and the company stresses the visual elements. If there are lots of photographs, that means less space for written text. Sometimes the authors complain because it's necessary to cut out some of the background information that they want to include as a supplement to the factual presentation so that pupils can understand the material more thoroughly.

Kariya: So after about a year of work writing the text and having it reviewed and discussed by an editorial board, it gets submitted for certification.

'B': That's right. The textbooks are submitted with blank covers so the examiners won't know the company involved. The application must be accompanied by documents including an 'editorial outline' listing the authors and the distinctive features and a table comparing the contents with the standards. Several months later, there is a meeting.

Kariya: Please explain.

'B': On the appointed day, a group of people go to the Ministry. Usually this consists of two or three people from the publisher and three or four of the principal authors, about six or seven people in all, though sometimes there are as many as ten. When they enter the room, they are given a "statement of certification opinions," which lists the examiners' comments about specific passages.

In the past it was a closed-door environment, and there was some gratuitous pressure, but now the opinion documents are made public, and the atmosphere of the meetings is friendly, at least on the surface.

Kariya: I assume those on the publishing side are aware of what sorts of terminology and content are likely to result in comments from the examiners. Does this cause the companies to impose self-restraint in deciding how far to go with contents?

'A': Back when the opinions were presented verbally and not in writing, publishers would try to catch the tone and nuances of what the examiners said and revise the textbooks accordingly.

'B': Nowadays, though, it seems that examiners are not attaching comments to passages that wouldn't have made it through the screening in the past. I'd say certification as a whole has become more lenient.

Kariya: Do textbook authors have the same impression?

'A': I think there has been considerable relaxation. Basically the material will be approved unless there are problems with factual content, and the number of comments has decreased sharply. This is probably due in large part to the fact that comments are now made public.

Kariya: Has the fact that textbook passages about modern history have developed into diplomatic issues caused the Ministry to decide to allow more leeway?

'C': I would say so. It looks to me as if the Ministry has drawn up a set of rules to avoid being criticized as leaning to the right.

Kariya: But with left-leaning texts coming under criticism as "masochistic," authors have probably started to restrain themselves. So isn't the result likely to be a shift toward the right?

'A': It does seem that overall there's a tilt toward the right.

> *Editor's Postscript:* Who is not represented in this discussion? Which authors are likely to be approached by textbook companies? What are the results—positive and negative—of joint authorship? Who likely has the final say? Ministry? Publisher? Authors? Teachers? What about textbook "consumers"—students? It would be nice to know who makes the decision when a given school decides among "certified" texts: the classroom teachers? The administrators? The school committee?
>
> Students encounter textbooks in the classroom. They seem to be absolutely unimpeachable historical "truth." What students often don't realize is that the material is the result of a long and complicated process of screening and selecting by a whole range of individuals, some of them interested first and foremost in "facts," some in ideological slant, some in profit, and some in avoiding controversy, whether domestic or foreign.

VII
NATURE AND
POLLUTION

THE TALISMAN

Editor's Introduction: Two hundred years ago, Japan had a population of perhaps 30 million. The vast majority of the people lived in the countryside and supported themselves by farming.

Today the picture is very different. Japan's present population is 128 million, and the farm population has dropped to below 14 percent. Cities with populations of 50,000 or more account for 70 percent, and 25 million Japanese live in cities with populations of more than one million.

Well over half of Japan's population lives in an area roughly the size of the state of Delaware. This area stretches for several hundred miles along the coast between Tokyo and Osaka, but it is nowhere very wide. Delaware's population is less than one million, but this Japanese megalopolis has a population of over 58 million, making it one of the most densely populated areas of the world. It may be a signpost into the future for similar areas elsewhere—for example, the coastal area of the eastern United States between Washington, D.C. and Boston.

A quiet and ordered life seems important to the development of individual identity and social stability. But how do you find quiet and order when you are one among 128 million? How do you establish your individuality?

A talisman is an amulet, or charm, often worn to fend off evil. The evil in the following short story seems to be the uniformity, the loss of identity, that the social environment forces upon its members. [41]

"I DON'T SUPPOSE you need any dynamite?"

This was the question my friend Sekiguchi asked me. I had not seen him in four or five years. We had run into each other on the Ginza, and were drinking in an upstairs room of a small restaurant.

I had been with Sekiguchi through high school. He was now working for a construction company. It was not strange that he should have access to dy-

The sameness of mass urban development afflicts Japan as it does most other industrialized nations. Photo from the Consulate General of Japan, N.Y.

namite; but the question, however peculiar an old friend he might be, was a little sudden.

"I don't know what I'd use it for."

"I have it right here if you want it."

It would be a joke, of course. I smiled and poured a new drink for him. "It would blow up right in my hands. And what is the point in carrying dynamite around with you?"

This was the story Sekiguchi told me.

My wife and I live alone in an apartment house. I put my name on the list two years ago, and got married last spring, before I had a decent place to live. And then last fall I got one of the apartments. I couldn't have been happier.

Everything seemed new and fresh.... Before that we had been with my family, a big family at that. We had only one room, and we wanted a place where we could lock other people out. Well, now we had a room with a lock. You can imagine what it meant to us.

We had it, a place of our own. But I had not been there six months before I began feeling uncertain and irritated. I felt somehow that I was disappearing. No one's fault—call it some sort of neurosis. I can't say it was his fault either, I suppose. But I can say that Kurose made things start going this way for me.

It was late one night. I had been to a party. There were no more buses, and I took a taxi and got off at the main gate. I hoped that by the time I got to my wing of the building the night wind might sober me up.

There was a man in front of me. I had the feeling that I was looking at myself from behind. He had on the same felt hat, and he had the same package in his left hand. You could tell by his walk that he had been drinking too. It was a foggy night, and I wondered if I might be seeing my own shadow.

But it was no shadow. He walked on, the image of me, I thought—and he went into Wing E, where I lived. He went up the stairs I always go up.

It was a big complex, I grant that; but I knew at least the people who went up and down the stairs I used. And I did not know him. He went up as if they were the stairs he knew best in the world. He came to the third floor and knocked on the door to the right.

It was my apartment. And then I was even more startled. The door opened and he was taken in, like any tired husband home from work.

I thought my wife must have a lover. That was it. I climbed the stairs quietly. I would catch them in the act. I put my ear to the door.

The way I felt—how can I describe it to you? I was wrong. He was not her lover. He was I myself.

No, wait. I'm not crazy. But I thought I was. I could hear her saying 'Jirō, Jirō,' and laughing and telling me what my sister had said when she had come calling that day. And I could hear my own tired voice in between. She was off in the kitchen getting something to eat, and "I" seemed to be reading the newspaper. I did not know what to think. There was another "I," that was clear. And who, then, was this I, standing foolishly in the hall? Which was "I" and which was I? Where should I go?

I had thought that I was sober, but I'm afraid I was still drunk. The confidence that I was I had left me. It did not occur to me that the man in the room was a false "I," a mistake. I opened the door only because I could think of nothing else to do with the I that was myself.

"Who's there?" she said.

"I," I finally answered.

It was quite a scene. My wife came screaming out. She looked at the other "I," and screamed again, and threw herself on me. Her lips were moving and she began to cry. The other "I" came out. His face was white.

His name was Kurose Jirō.

Sekiguchi fell silent, a thoughtful expression on his face. He poured himself a cup of sake.

"Another you," I laughed. "A fine *Doppelgänger* [double]."

He glanced up at me, but seemed to pay no attention to my words. Unsmiling, he went on with his story.

Kurose was all apologies.

When he handed me his name card I saw what the mistake had been. I lived in E-305, he in D-305. He had come into the wrong wing and gone up to my apartment.

My sister is named Kuniko. He was a civil engineer, and he had a cousin named Kuniko. His name was Jirō, so is mine. He lived alone with his wife. The coincidence was complete.

"I did think she seemed a little young. I've been married four years, after all," he said as he left. He said it as if he meant to flatter, but I was not up to being pleased. It weighed on my mind, the fact that until I opened the door neither of them had noticed the mistake.

"But I went off to the kitchen, and he sprawled out with the newspaper the way you always do. It didn't even occur to me that it wouldn't be you."

I reprimanded her, and she looked timidly around the room.

"Not just the room. They must be exactly like us themselves. You saw how he thought I was his wife. It scares me."

I was about to speak, but I did not. To mistake a person or a room—that made no difference. It happened all the time. What bothered me was that Kurose had mistaken our life for his own.

Trains and Airplanes Battle for Passengers

Bullet trains between Tokyo and Osaka (340 miles) now take two and a half hours, with top speed of 170 mph; the fastest trains run 137 times per day. The fare: $130. Round-trip shuttle flights from Tokyo to Osaka now cost about the same. The bullet trains have the edge in number of riders between Tokyo and Osaka, but the airlines now have the edge in trips to destinations west of Osaka.

Source: *Japan Now*, June 2003.

"No car day" in Tokyo dramatizes the concentration of people in the world's largest city. Photo from the United Nations.

Kurose had been mistaken for me by my own wife. And were they as alike as all that? These apartment-house homecomings?

I knew of course that all the apartments were the same. But I asked myself: had our very ways of life become standardized?

You know what apartment-house life is like. It does have a terrible uniformity about it. The qualifications for getting in, and the need to get in—they mean that the standard of living is all on the same general level. All of us are even about the same age. But it seemed to me that the uniformity had gone beyond externals. It had gone to the very heart of things.

Take for instance when I have a quarrel with my wife. The wind always brings the same kind of quarrel in through the window from another apartment. It all seems so foolish that we stop fighting. So far so good; but then you come to realize that the people in the other apartments have their quarrels on this and this day of the month and this and this time of the day, and you are no exception yourself; and—this may seem a strange way to put it—the sacredness of quarreling disappears. A quarrel comes to be no more than a periodic outburst of hysteria. Think about it. It's not very exciting.

You go to the toilet, and over your head you hear someone pulling the chain and the toilet upstairs flushes. The same thing day after day. I hadn't paid too much attention, but it began to weigh on me.

I began to wonder whether identical surroundings and identical routines were bringing us to identical emotions and identical outlets for them. And if so we were like all those toy soldiers lined up on a department-store counter. Like standardized puppets.

Where was there something that was mine? No one else's but mine? In this mass of people who so resembled one another, I was no more than one bean spread out to dry with the rest. I could not even identify myself among them all.

My wife said something that did not help matters. We were in bed. "It's very strange. I go off to the toilet, and I hear water running up above and down below. We all do exactly the same thing."

I pulled away from her. We men of the apartment house proceeded every night, as if upon a signal, to go through the same motions. And so I began to lose interest in them too. Each time my wife would whisper something to me, it would seem to me as if all through the building wives were whispering. I would hear a gale of whispers in the darkness and I would find myself frowning.

We may think we have something of our own. But we only have standardized days with standardized reactions.

It seemed intolerable. I was not a puppet!

Could I put much importance on my life when I could no longer be sure that I was myself and no one else? Could I love my wife? Believe I was loved by her?

I started to laugh, but did not. Sekiguchi was gazing earnestly at me.

Presently a faint smile came over his face.

He had always been a man, I remembered, who placed a high value on a smile.

"It's a very serious story," he said.

Smoking

Since 1988, there has been a growth in no-smoking areas and facilities—no-smoking taxicabs, trains, airlines, offices. But 49% of men and 14% of women still smoke. A year earlier, 27% said they'd like to quit, and 38% said they'd like to cut down. 95,000 deaths per year are due to smoking. Smokers often find themselves exiled to balconies, patios, sidewalks; the label for them is "fireflies"—after the glow from their cigarettes. (In 1966 49% of all adults and 84% of men smoked.)
Source: *Japan Now*, March 2003.

Recycling of Paper (2003)			
Production (million tons)	Consumption kilos per capita	Collection %	Recovery %
World	339	51.7	48.1	48.2
China	41.7	35.8	31.4	57.6
Germany	19.3	224.7	73.7	65.4
Japan	30.5	242.6	66.0	61.0
U.S.	41.7	300.8	49.4	41.8

Source: *Japan Statistical Yearbook.*

Kurose became for me the representative of all those numberless white-collar workers, all the apartment-house husbands, the toy soldiers, exactly like myself. The representative of all those numberless people who were "I."

You will have guessed that after that foggy night I did not want to speak to the man. We were too much alike, and it would seem that, as he clutched his briefcase to his chest, he was avoiding me too. He always seemed to be scurrying off.

He had become a scapegoat for all those standardized toy soldiers—I hated them through him. I rejected all those standardized articles that were "I."

I resented him. He was not I. I was not one of them, those office workers so much like myself. I was I, I was most definitely not he. But where was the difference? Where was there positive evidence to establish the difference?

I was not a random spot. I was I, a particular person with the name Sekiguchi Jirō, someone not to be substituted for another, whoever he might be. So I said over and over to myself.

And yet where were the grounds for distinguishing me from them? Was there more than my name? A name is only a tag. Aside from my name, where was the evidence that I was not a random apartment-house dweller?

I had to build it—my independence, my individuality. I had to find something to distinguish me from those numberless ones who were Kurose Jirō.

A couple of weeks ago I found it. A charm. I've kept it secret from my wife. The problem is my own private one.

This is my charm.

Sekiguchi opened the heavy leather briefcase behind him and took out a bundle just small enough to hold in one hand. It was elaborately tied up in oil paper.

"Dynamite. The real thing."

With great dexterity he undid the knots, and for the first time in my life I saw dynamite, the real thing. There were four iron tubes perhaps eight inches long, bound tightly in wire, heavy for their size.

"This is my charm—my talisman," said Sekiguchi. "We talk and talk, but we can't get away from the uniformity. But when I am of a mind to I can blow all of them up and myself too. This is what I came on. The secret that keeps me going. My uniqueness."

I handed the tubes back, and Sekiguchi turned a caressing gaze on their dark luster.

"I don't think I need any dynamite, thank you."

"Oh? That's too bad. I don't need it any more myself. I'm going to have to hunt up another charm."

"I don't know whether you're being funny or not, but it's dangerous...."

Sekiguchi raised a hand to silence me. "Make no mistake," he laughed. "You're a very lucky person. I don't need it any more, because it's not my uniqueness any more." He paused. "Did you hear the news on the radio this evening?"

"No."

He smiled a wry smile. "There was a dynamite explosion on a bus. Three people were killed on the spot. The others got by with cuts and burns. It was near my apartment house."

"How did it happen?" I felt the effects of the sake leave me.

Sekiguchi did not look at me. Slowly and deliberately he put the bundle away.

"He always did carry his briefcase around like the most important thing in his life. And he avoided me. He must have resented me as much as I resented him. He needed a charm too."

"Oh?"

Sekiguchi stretched out on the matting. His voice rose in a sort of lament. "They said it over the radio. The police think the dynamite was in a briefcase of one of the three people killed. An engineer named Kurose Jirō."

KARAOKE

Karaoke began in 1972 in Kobe, in a bar that couldn't afford live music. Instead, the bar offered tapes that had everything except the lead vocal. (Karaoke comes from kara—empty or open—and okesutora—Japanese English for orchestra. The correct pronunciation is kah-rah-oh-keh.) The first karaoke machine appeared in 1976; within a few years the machines added a video display. In 1985 came karaoke machines for home use.

Today in Japan, there are 1.3 million karaoke machines; 3,500 songs are available. 75% of Japanese between the ages of 19 and 29 have tried karaoke; so it is Japan's most popular cultural activity.

In the U.S. today, 10,000 locations offer karaoke.

Source: Based on "Karaoke: Teaching the World to Sing," *Focus Japan* 20:12, December 1993.

PURE LAND,
POISONED SEA

Editor's Introduction: In a highly industrialized and populated society it is easy to lose one's sense of self; but the process is a subtle one, and not everyone is affected. A second process within industrialized societies is far from subtle and affects everyone: the deterioration of the physical environment.

Pollution of the air and water is one effect of economic growth. Today such pollution threatens the mental and physical health of almost every Japanese. Naturally enough, it threatens most directly those who live in the vicinity of major industries. On a single day in 1970, for example, photochemical smog in the Tokyo area sent 43 students from a single high school to the hospital. Most of them were treated and released, but five remained in the hospital for two or three days. On that same day and for the same reason, some six thousand people of all ages sought medical assistance.

General debilitation, asthma, and lung cancer are some of the long-term effects of air pollution. These diseases are serious and sometimes fatal, but they are not spectacular enough to arouse a public outcry. However, Japan has some distinctive pollution diseases that are truly horrendous, and in the late 1960s public attention became riveted on these diseases and the issues they pose.

One of these ailments is the Minamata disease, named for the city in which it first appeared. In that area of western Japan, factories discharged methyl mercury wastes into the ocean. The chemical built up in the fish of the region, and when people ate the fish over an extended period of time they became victims of the disease. Over 1,000 people have already died of Minamata disease; the government recognizes over 4,000 other victims, and another 8,000 claim to be victims. The following selection from a documentary novel describes the suffering of one woman who contracted Minamata disease. [42]

This whole place is shaking: the bed, the ceiling, the floor, the door, the windows through which we can watch heatwaves dancing—all shaking and shuddering to Sakagami Yuki's convulsions. Ever since she recovered consciousness, these convulsions have been shaking her entire body.

After her convulsions started coming on every day and night, all those things with which she had always been familiar—fish, people, sky, windows—have been strangers to her gaze and to all her being. From time to time they come back to her, but only fitfully, in bits and pieces.

Though she keeps shaking incessantly, she tries to present a smiling face to the world, as she had always done when she was in good health. But as she is already over forty and has wasted away, her familiar and touching smile now withers on her lips as soon as it appears.

She tries hard, in the presence of visitors, to abide by her former surprisingly artless and honest nature. But we can see that sometimes she has to give way to fits of passion, because at such times her shaking becomes even more violent. This is because the behavior that usually revealed her honest heart cannot now be commanded by her will.

In Japan, as elsewhere, the price of affluence is environmental pollution. Photo from the Consulate General of Japan, N.Y.

"My tongue gets all tied up in knots. So if you want to understand what I'm talking about, you'll have to sort it out for yourself. It used to be really lovely out on the sea ..."

She speaks in a peculiar way, with long-drawn-out, fragmentary words, like a small child wheedling his mother and father, With her stumbling tongue she tells us she had never before spoken in this unsatisfactory and unpleasant manner, and that she feels sorry her speech has become so incomprehensible through the Minamata disease. Of course, it is not she who should feel ashamed. But we can understand it when she tells us she feels shame at having become a kind of deformed person in a freak show. "Ever since I've been like this, I've loved my husband more than ever. I give him everything my visitors bring to comfort me in my sickness. Because you see my mouth trembles so, I cannot touch them. So I give it all to him. He's taken good care of me, you know. I went to him as his second wife—from Amakusa, across the water. We'd hardly been together three years when I was struck by this queer disease. Now I can't even put my kimono to rights. My hands and body are always shaking, as you can see. They shake away all on their own, without my telling them. 'What a helpless woman you are, aren't you?' my husband tells me, as he helps me put my kimono to rights. And he tells me 'Put on these long drawers,' and he makes me put them on. (Real-ly....my ... dear... I ... real-ly ... have ... become a ... help-less... creature?) I want to get better again. My mother and father always told me I'd have to work to make a living. I had never been sick before. Before this started, my hands, my legs—every part of me was good and strong.

"It was so lovely—it was really good to work out on the sea. Whatever happens, I want to get well and row the boat again. What a state I'm in now! I'm a useless housewife.... I used to be always on the go, a real live wire I was. My hands and legs were that strong! People always used to admire the way I kept at my work. I'm always thinking of what I should be doing, even when I'm in bed. Just now, it's the time to sow barley. I must sow barley. I should be starting to knock muck [hoe or work in the paddy], too. I feel restless. Soon there'll be the grey mullet season coming along. Even in bed I keep worrying about these things.

"If I don't keep on working, our family can't make ends meet. Now I feel as if my body is gradually drifting away from this world. I have no grip. I can't grip anything firmly in my hands. I can't hold my husband's hands in mine; I can't even hold my own dear son in my arms. Well, I might be able to put up with that. But I can't even hold a bowl of rice which is the chief food in my life. I cannot hold my chopsticks. When I walk, I don't feel as if I am walking with both feet on the ground. I feel as if I'm all on my own, a long way from the earth. I feel so alone. You cannot imagine how lonely I feel. My husband's the only one I love.

He's the only one I can rely on now. How I wish I could work again, and use my hands and my legs!

"It was good, working out on the sea. My husband would pull on the main oar, and me on the side one. We would row out to pull up our cuttlefish baskets and octopus pots. Grey mullets—those fish, and octopuses they're lovely. From April to October it was always very calm off Lion Island." ...

She would keep on talking like that—always talking to herself. Mohei [Yuki's husband] would answer her in a voice if it can be called a voice—that was a series of snorts and grunts. The two were a well-matched pair. Their catches were not very big. But they kept on getting moderate catches every day.

"It was really lovely, working out at sea. Those damned cuttlefish though are mean devils, and when we catch them, they spurt their ink; but the octopuses are very lovable. We would pull up a pot and find an octopus that didn't want to come out, his feelers gripping the bottom of the pot and rolling his eyes at me. 'Hey, you,' I would shout, 'you've got to come out now you've been pulled into the boat. Get a move on. Come on out!' That's the way I used to talk to them, but sometimes he still wouldn't come out. I would bang on the bottom, but still he would seem reluctant. As a last resort, I would stuff the helve of a hand-net into the pot and so force him to get out. Once he was out, he would try to scamper away. I was always surprised to see how he could run without getting his eight legs all tangled up. I used to have to scramble after him in such a hurry it's a wonder the boat was never overturned. After I've caught him I put him in a basket and start rowing again. Then he comes out of the basket and sits there on the basket very well-behaved. 'Hey you, you're one of the family now you're in our boat. Keep in the basket!' I tell him. But he's sulking, avoiding my eyes, and I feel that's his way of showing his affection for me. We feel a deep love for the things of the sea—even for the fish we are going to eat. Oh, it was lovely in those days...

"We've had to sell the boat, now.

HURRICANE RELIEF FROM JAPAN

When Hurricane Andrew hit Florida and Hurricane Iriki hit Hawaii in 1992, the following Japanese firms and groups donated money and goods totaling over $1 million: Toyota, Honda Motors, Nissan Motors, Yamaha, Fuji Bank, JDC American, Komatsu America, Marubeni America, Mitsui & Co. (USA), Nippon Express (USA), Sony Group, Japan Air Lines, Kagoshima City (sister city to Miami).

Source: Based on *Joining Hands* 1.1, Fall 1992.

"When I was in the University Hospital, I kept thinking only of the boat whenever it was windy or raining. My husband hoisted a flag on her and launched the boat when we were married. It's like our own child. You know how much care I took of that boat? I would mop the whole body of the boat clean. Between the fishing seasons, I would pull up all the octopus pots. I would scrape all the oyster shells and barnacles and weeds off the outsides of the pots and pile them in a hole in the rocks so they would be out of the rain.

"The pots are their houses. I wanted to make their houses clean for them. Fishermen always take good care of their equipment. There's a guardian deity on every boat and there's a soul in every piece of equipment we use. No woman would ever step over a fishing rod, you know.

"Well, we had to sell the boat we had taken so much care of, after I got this queer disease. That's what I regret most of all.

I want to go to sea again.

"I can't take care of myself and so I feel sorry for my ancestors who taught me that I must make my own living and feed myself with my own hands and legs.

"In the old days they called a person like me who suffers from these convulsions a jumping jenny. But the convulsions they had in the old days were not as violent as ours. How awful it is! I can't hold chopsticks. I can't hold a rice bowl, my mouth never stops quivering. There's an attendant here who helps me with my meals. But what a performance it is! Three times a day, she puts rice in my mouth, but I always spill it, and I spill my soup too. I feel very sorry for her. Anyway, I can taste nothing. I can't take food as I keep spilling it. What a waste! Once a day would be enough for me, because they give me my food without my having to work for it....

"I can't do anything by myself. I want to get my own body back. The body I have now is not like my own.

"I never want to eat anything now. But I like a smoke. They didn't allow me to smoke before. My husband could not smoke his cigarettes in my room.

---

13 Dead as Japan Endures Hottest Ever Day

The temperature hit a record high in Japan on Thursday, killing at least 13 people across the nation this week, officials said. The mercury shot up to a record 40.9 degrees Celsius (106 degrees Fahrenheit) in Tajimi city in the central prefecture of Gifu on Thursday afternoon, according to the weather agency.

Source: AFP Press, August 16, 2007.

"When I recovered a little and began to be able to walk again I was walking down the corridor to go and be examined by the doctor when I found a cigarette end on the floor. I had not smoked since I lost my mental balance, so I was very pleased. 'Oh, there's a cigarette end! How lovely! Lovely! Just let me get my hands on it!' With these thoughts in mind, I began to direct my steps carefully toward it. But I could only walk in a zigzag way. I tried to stand still, but the top half of my body kept swaying. Anyhow, I tried to make straight for the butt. 'It's about twenty feet away. I must walk straight ahead or I shall miss it.'

"I tried to take a step forward, but I couldn't, as my legs were giving way. 'Oh, to think these are my own pair of legs and I can't do a thing with them!' I felt so vexed. Then these damned convulsions came on. The convulsions are cruel! They are cruel!

"Without my wanting them to, my legs suddenly began to dash in all directions. I couldn't stop it. I ran right past the cigarette end. 'Oh, no! These convulsions! Not again!' In the midst of these thoughts, I began to feel dizzy. I stopped for a moment and looked back. I wanted to go in that direction but my legs wouldn't let me ... I was falling down, my dear! My husband took hold of my back. My body was sticking out backwards. When I fall, I fall backwards as if I were starting back from something. But before I fell the convulsions came on again and suddenly 1 started forwards again. I have never run in such a confused manner—tumbling and jumping even when I used to run at the school sports when I was a schoolgirl. Without my wanting them to, my legs started running away with themselves in the silliest way.

"I ran around in such a way no one could stop me. Everyone stared in surprise. But I was the one who suffered most. Tears flowed down my cheeks. I got out of breath. Suddenly the convulsions stopped and my legs went all stiff. I was able to catch my breath for a moment. I looked around and wondered where the cigarette end was. Gasping, I told my husband I wanted to smoke. With tears in his eyes, he told me that as I wanted it so much, I might smoke. Since then they have allowed me to smoke. But I am allowed to smoke only one-third of a cigarette every day."

POLLUTION DAMAGE:
WHO PAYS?

Editor's Introduction: Pollution of the environment is today a fact of life, in Japan and in America. In both countries, there is growing awareness of the need to take corrective steps. But who is to pay for these steps? Should local or national governments foot the bill? Or should the industrial plants that bear primary responsibility also bear part of the cost? And how do we determine responsibility? What does "responsibility" mean?

In the case of Japan's pollution diseases, how shall the victims be compensated? By whom? Obviously, no amount of money can buy back the health of the woman whose story you have just read. But what are the obligations of industrial enterprises that have wreaked ecological destruction?

The next selection describes a recent law suit against the company considered responsible for the Minamata disease. [43]

IN THE FISHING TOWN OF MINAMATA in southern Japan 20 years ago, cats began dancing in the streets and fell dead, writhing in pain. Dogs and pigs went mad. Crows dropped from the sky.

Then the mysterious malady struck human beings. It destroyed their control over their arms and legs, made them blind and deaf, and killed them. It hit babies in their mothers' wombs and condemned them to live after birth as mental and physical vegetables.

Last week [mid-March, 1973] the storm stirred up by this phenomenon culminated in a court decision that underscored the growing concern about pollution in Japan.

Medical researchers had determined by the late 1950s that the victims had been poisoned by mercury. They traced the mercury to fish and shellfish eaten by the victims. The mercury, in turn, was traced to sludge at the bottom of Minamata Bay dumped by the chemical plant of the Chisso Corporation.

An executive of a chemical firm (right) presents a check for $3.54 million to a lawyer representing the families of 67 persons who died of Minamata disease contracted by eating contaminated fish. Photo from Wide World Photos.

The company denied it was responsible, and some of the victims eventually went to court in 1969. The case ended last week when a district judge ruled that Chisso was at fault and ordered it to pay $3.6 million in damages to 138 persons in 30 families. It was the highest industrial pollution claim yet awarded in Japan. The company accepted the decision and agreed to compensate other victims who had not gone to court.

The Minamata decision was the last of four major court tests here. All ended in favor of the victims. Together, the decisions set a legal precedent holding industrial companies liable for the effects of their pollution and gave new stimulus to demands that Japan be cleaned up.

In a recent published survey, Ui Jun, a chemical engineer at Tokyo University and an acknowledged authority on pollution, says, "We Japanese are living in the most heavily polluted country in the world." He blames it on "the rapid development of the economy, the symbiotic [mutually reinforcing] relationship between political power and industry, a very weak conception of basic human rights, and the degenerate use of science and technology."

> *Editor's Postscript:* The four major cases have established a principle of responsibility without criminal guilt. That is, the companies are liable for damages but not for criminal action.

In 1971, a new law became operative that is designed specifically to make possible the criminal prosecution of industries that endanger human life or health.

But what are the long-range prospects for the Japanese environment? Civil and criminal prosecution can begin to make amends for specific and extreme cases of damage to life and health, but does this action really get at the heart of the problem? Is pollution the result of the "degenerate use of science and technology"? Or is it an inevitable by-product of science and technology?

THE JAPANESE PEOPLE
AND NATURE

Editor's Introduction: Ui Jun's statement that "We Japanese are living in the most heavily polluted country in the world" was not true when he made it and is less true today. Through auto emission standards and other steps (including the export of pollution-producing factories to other countries), Japan has reduced its pollution in significant measure.

How do Japanese people look at nature? That question is impossible to answer today, for there are as many Japanese views of nature as there are American views. But if we look back at traditional Japanese literature, we can find at least a partial answer. [44]

NATURE HAS NOT BEEN OVERLY generous to the Japanese. She has given them an island country with less than 20 percent flat land; the rest, or more than 80 percent, consists of mountains. She has given them an extra helping of natural disasters: volcanoes, earthquakes, typhoons. But in past ages the Japanese have responded more with appreciation of natural bounty than with fear of natural disaster. Among the names for Japan in the earliest myths are "The Land of Luxuriant Reed Plains" and "The Land of Fresh Rice Ears of a Thousand Autumns."

The native Japanese religion, Shinto, included the worship of nature. The sun and moon were considered divine beings, and the Sun Goddess was the most important of all Shinto gods. Even rocks and trees and flowers were considered in some sense divine.

It should not surprise us, then, to find that the Japanese throughout their history have lived close to nature and referred to nature to express their deepest feelings. Consider these three poems, written in the seventh and eighth centuries A.D.*

Manyoshu (Tokyo, 1940), pp. 3, 95, 383. Translations by the Japanese Classics Translation Committee. Reprinted by permission.

Countless are the mountains in Yamato,
But perfect is the heavenly hill of Kagu;
When I climb it and survey my realm,
Over the wide plain the smoke-wreaths rise and rise,
Over the wide lake the gulls are on the wing;
A beautiful land it is, the Land of Yamato!
　　　　　—EMPEROR JŌMEI (593-641)

The mallards call with evening from the reeds
And float with dawn midway on the water;
They sleep with their mates, it is said,
With white wings overlapping and tails asweep
Lest the frost should fall upon them.
As the stream that flows never returns,
And as the wind that blows is never seen,
My wife, of this world, has left me,
Gone I know not whither!
So here, on the sleeves of these clothes
She used to have me wear
I sleep now all alone!
Cranes call flying to the reedy shore;
How desolate I remain
As I sleep alone!
　　　　　　—TAJIHI (eighth century)

I will think of you, love,
On evenings when the gray mist
Rises above the rushes,
And chill sounds the voice
Of the wild ducks crying.
　　　　　　—Poem of a frontier guard

　　By the fourteenth century Japan had become a very different place. In the intervening 600 years, Japan had borrowed almost a whole culture from its Asian neighbor, China. In the tenth and eleventh centuries, there developed around the Emperor's court one of the most refined and exquisite cultures the world has ever seen. In the twelfth and thirteenth centuries, that court culture fell into decline, and a society of warriors, monks, and peasants took its place.

Respect for the power of nature is dramatically illustrated by this famous woodblock print, "The Great Wave at Kanagawa, " executed in 1823-29 by one of Japan's best-known artists, Hokusai. Mt. Fuji is in the background. Source: The Metropolitan Museum of Art, Howard Mansfield Collection, Rogers Fund, 1936.

It was this society that was first attracted to Zen Buddhism and that developed the art of landscape gardening. Japanese landscape artists sought both to reproduce nature and to compel the viewer to stop and reflect. The best known of these gardens is made up primarily of sand and rocks. Each morning a monk rakes the sand into wave patterns to give the impression of a vast sea, in which the rocks appear to be islands. Western architects sometimes seek to create a serene and reflective atmosphere in a cathedral or a chapel in Japan, landscape artists have used different means—gardens—to the same end.

Yoshida Kenkō was a leading figure in the new society of Zen and landscape gardening. The following passages come from a daybook he kept for his own entertainment around the year 1330. Interest in the changing seasons, so evident here, is prevalent in Japanese literature. As this selection indicates, the seasons in Japan are very similar to the seasons in the northeastern United States.

> The changing of the seasons is deeply moving in its every manifestation. People seem to agree that autumn is the best season to appreciate the beauty of things. That may well be true, but the sights of spring are even more exhilarating. The cries of the birds gradually take on a peculiarly

springlike quality, and in the gentle sunlight the bushes begin to sprout along the fences. Then, as spring deepens, mists spread over the landscape and the cherry blossoms seem ready to open, only for steady rains and winds to cause them to scatter precipitously....

Orange blossoms are famous for evoking memories, but the fragrance of plum blossoms above all makes us return to the past and remember nostalgically long-ago events....

In the fifth month [summer], the irises bloom and the rice seedlings are transplanted.... Then, in the sixth month, you can see the whiteness of moonflowers glowing over wretched hovels, and the smoldering of mosquito incense is affecting too....

The celebration of Tanabata [an early autumn festival] is charming. Then, as the nights gradually become cold and the wild geese cry, the under-leaves of the bush clover turn yellow, and men harvest and dry the first crop of rice. So many moving sights come together, in autumn especially.... Winter decay is hardly less beautiful than autumn. Crimson leaves lie scattered on the grass beside the ponds, and how delightful it is on a morning when the frost is very white to see the vapor rise from a garden stream. At the end of the year it is indescribably moving to see everyone hurrying about on errands. There is something forlorn about the waning winter moon, shining cold and clear in the sky. unwatched because it is said to be depressing....*

Between the 1330s (when Yoshida wrote) and the 1600s, Japan again saw great changes. Disunity and fighting yielded to unity and peace. The society of warriors, monks, and peasants was forced to make room for a new and active group of people: merchants and other city dwellers. Commerce and city life became the themes of the age.

The *haiku* is a verse form that developed in this age of bustle. A *haiku* poem is made up of only 17 syllables arranged in three lines of, respectively, 5, 7, and 5 syllables. *Haiku* seem simple, and the form did make it possible for more people to write more poetry. One man is supposed to have written 20,000 *haiku*—in a single day.

Nevertheless, *haiku* are not simple. The ideal *haiku* contains two elements: first, a general setting of the scene or mood or condition; second, a statement of something momentary and startling, a sudden flash of insight.

As the following *haiku,* all by the seventeenth-century poet Bashō, indicate, the world of nature maintained its hold on the Japanese imagination even in a world of city life and commerce.

---

*Essays in Idleness, translated by Donald Keene (New York: Columbia University Press, 1967), pp. 18-20. Reprinted by permission.

Kiyotaki ya	Clear cascades!
Nami ni chiri naki	In the waves immaculate,
Natsu no tsuki	The summer moon.
Chō tori no	To bird and butterfly
Shiranu hana ari	It is unknown, this flower here:
Aki no sora	The autumn sky.
Furuike ya	The ancient pond
Kawazu tobikomu	A frog leaps in
Mizu no oto	The sound of the water.

—BASHŌ*

*Haiku 1 and 3 were translated by Donald Keene; haiku 2 by Harold G. Henderson. Donald Keene, ed., *Anthology of Japanese Literature* (New York: Grove Press, 1955), pp. 38,384; Donald Keene, ed., *Japanese Literature* (London: John Murray, 1953), p. 39. Reprinted by permission.

A TALE
OF WHALES

Editor's Introduction: Nature has figured importantly for most Japanese. Until the twentieth century, most Japanese lived close to nature, as did most Americans. Why, then, do they tolerate the spectacular deterioration of their natural environment? What could be more important to them than the preservation of this environment?

One aspect of the worldwide ecological crisis is the threat to the continued existence of various forms of wildlife. In the 1960s, Americans and other Westerners became increasingly aware that whales were in danger of extinction as a result of overhunting. The issue seems a simple one: unless whales are protected, and soon, they will disappear. However, when the interests of many nations are concerned, no issue is ever simple.

The following essay first appeared as an editorial in a magazine aimed at Western readers. The author's name is not given, but it is safe to assume that he is Japanese. His closing reference to Vietnam is indicative of the outrage many Japanese felt at American actions in Indochina. [45]

IN JUNE 1972, the United Nations sponsored a Conference on the Human Environment in Stockholm, Sweden. This conference adopted a resolution that commercial whaling should be stopped altogether for ten years. The news of this resolution came as a great shock to Japan. It made the headlines of virtually every newspaper in Japan. For Japan has reason to have greater concern for the whale than any other country in the world. Why? Because in Japanese life the whale ranks with the cow and the pig as an important source of protein....

A high official of the Japanese government's Fishery Agency reacted immediately. Japan, he stated, had already agreed to a ban on the catching of any species of whale considered (by competent scientific analysts) to be in danger of extinction. Japan respects the competence of the International Whaling Committee, which has designated four species of whale (including the blue whale) as endangered species. These species the Japanese do not hunt.

However, he went on, the recommendation for a complete ban on whaling was totally unrealistic, idealistic, and lacking in scientific rationale. Such a ban was entirely unacceptable to Japan. The Conference on the Human Environment, he concluded, had no competence to initiate a moratorium on whaling. In a similar vein, the chief industry spokesman made it clear that under no circumstances would Japan consider itself bound by the resolution.

The International Whaling Committee met in London immediately after the Stockholm conference. The Japanese government sent its delegates with firm instructions to stop the ten-year moratorium. At this meeting the United States campaigned for support for the Stockholm resolution. But Japan and the Soviet Union both urged its rejection. In effect, they demanded that catching operations continue.

The American side called for a complete ban on whaling. It made no mention of a ten-year period, and thus it was even more drastic than the Stockholm resolution. The result of the vote: four in favor, six against, four abstaining.

Clearly, the American side had not presented a compelling case.... Still, the International Whaling Committee did act to reduce the number of whales to be caught in 1972. That figure is down one-third from 1971....

Japan and the U.S.S.R. are the only countries in the world that engage in large-scale whaling. The North Atlantic quota for the U.S.S.R. in 1972 was very low: 359 blue-whale units, down from 560 units in 1971. [Blue whales are now protected, but catches continue to be measured in "blue whale units."] Some observers feel that this new quota will bring an end to Russian whaling in the North Atlantic. An industry reduced to a catch of 359 units, they feel, cannot make ends meet.

In Japan's case, the quota for North Pacific whaling fell 30 percent and for Antarctic whaling, 20 percent. Still, operations will continue. Why? Because Japan utilizes all of the whales it catches, including the whale meat. As a result, the Japanese whaling industry has a stronger economic base than the Russian or American and is able to operate even under the new restrictions.

To the Japanese, whale meat is a staple food. There are "whale restaurants" that serve nothing but whale meat—thin sliced whale meat (raw) on rice, fried whale meat, whale steaks. While other nations discard whale meat, Japan consumes 140,000 tons of it each year. This is roughly ten percent of all the meat consumed in Japan. Whale meat has a certain natural popularity in Japan, for it costs about half as much as beef. As a result, popular or not, it is featured in school lunch programs.

Japan also makes use of most other parts of the whale, from snout to tail. Whale bones become buttons, pipes, mahjongg pieces, brooches. The tendons of the whale's head become tennis racquet strings. Whale oil (some 70,000 tons a year) is used in margarine, shortenings, detergents, high-grade alcohol, and cosmetics. Whale products contribute to the seasoning of ham and sausage, and to the manufacture of such medicines as liver oil and insulin. There are literally dozens of uses to which Japan puts the whale.

Altogether, the whaling industry grosses around $100 million annually. That figure is just over 2 percent of Japan's total income from fishing. Since demand exceeds domestic supply, Japan imports whale products. In 1970, Japan imported 17,000 tons of whale products, including 15,000 tons of whale meat....

In all, approximately 8,000 people are directly engaged in whaling. Eight thousand becomes 20,000 if you include all the processors of whale products, and 20,000 swells to 100,000 if you include the families of these workers. The large fishing companies can cushion the shock by diverting their staffs to other jobs, but the small operators will lose their livelihood should whaling be prohibited.

The source of the American pressure for a complete ban on the catching of whales is a fear that otherwise this giant mammal will disappear forever from the oceans of the world. American scientists have recorded the voice of the whale. They have circulated their recording widely as part of their effort to get whaling banned. American conservationists never lose an opportunity in any international forum to plead with the world for the protection of the whale. In Japan, too, voices are speaking up in defense of the whale. The former chancellor of Tokyo University has formed an organization called the "Society for the Protection of the Whale," and Ōe Kenzaburō , a very distinguished author, has published a book entitled *The Day the Whale Became Extinct*—a plea for its protection.

There is no doubt that indiscriminate catching has sadly depleted the world's whale population. And Japan must bear some of the responsibility. In the early years after 1945, when food was very scarce in Japan, whale meat was a crucial source of protein. Hence Japan's fishing companies outdid each other in hunting the whale. In 1960, for example, seven fleets entered the Antarctic waters and caught some 6,000 blue whale units—in 1960 alone! One veteran hunter had caught personally something like 10,000 whales by the time he retired in 1969.

But this postwar activity was not limited to Japan. In 1960 Norway killed some 5,000, Russia 3,000, Great Britain 2,000, and Holland 1,000 blue whale units. As it became evident that whales were decreasing in number and perhaps facing extinction, the International Whaling Committee agreed upon a total world catch for 1963, and quotas for each country were set up. This total world catch was reduced progressively in subsequent years. Moreover, in certain areas and at certain times an absolute prohibition was imposed on taking blue, hump-back, and sperm whales. Great Britain, Holland, and Norway were interested only in whale oil, and these restrictions have caused their whaling industries to cease operations. Today only Japan and the U.S.S.R. still catch whales.

The International Whaling Treaty now totally prohibits the catching of four species: right, gray, blue, and humpback whales. Moreover, by 1971 the total world catch quota had fallen to 2,300, and further special quotas on particular species were in force for 1972.

These restrictions are already severe, and still the United States urges an end to all whaling. To the Japanese whaling industry, the indignation of the Americans seems somehow artificial. After all, only seventy years ago the Americans hunted the Pacific whale without mercy. The Americans seem to think they have a monopoly on concern for the whale, but Japanese representatives point out how mistaken this is. Japan knows better than any other country how grave the loss would be should whales become extinct. Japan can be relied on to observe the terms of the International Whaling Treaty meticulously. Some Japanese com-mentators have noticed an apparent absurdity in the American position: the United States exerts itself to protect whales, and yet at the same time it is killing tens of thousands of human beings in Vietnam....

The plight of the whales has lent drama and poignancy to the ecological movement. It has led increasing numbers of people to realize that irreplaceable natural resources must not be destroyed. In this sense, the plight of the whales has given the Japanese reason to think about the broader problem of marine re-sources as a whole.

SWITCH OFF

Editor's Introduction: The most common form of environmental destruction is pollution of the air. A major cause of air pollution is the automobile.

In Japan, as elsewhere, prosperity has brought a growing demand for private cars. Today more than 75 million cars and trucks throng a highway network that was designed to carry only a fraction of that number. As recently as 1970, that figure was below 20 million. Further, that highway network cannot readily be expanded or improved: the construction of new highways is even more expensive in Japan than in the United States, where the cost is astronomical.

The rapid growth of car owning has had many adverse effects on the environment of Japan. The most obvious is air pollution, and this may well be the most critical. But there are others. Cars make noise. Cars need space to park. (No Japanese city has adequate parking facilities, and few Japanese homes have a garage or a place to put a garage.)

But there seems to be no way, short of special legislation, to keep people from buying private cars, and special legislation would be next to impossible to pass. Japan's auto industry is a major pillar of the economy and therefore has a powerful influence on government policies.

There are a few rays of light in this otherwise gloomy picture. More and more people are beginning to realize that the unlimited use of private cars may mean the death of the city as we know it today. This realization has led municipal authorities in several Japanese cities to declare "no-car days." By prohibiting driving by city residents on these days, these cities have cut traffic and improved the quality of the air.

Regulations imposed by municipal, state, or national officials represent one form of attack on the problem. A second consists of decisions and actions by individual citizens. As the following essay shows, the reaction against cars indicates a growing awareness of ecological crisis and a growing concern with the quality of life. [46]

231

TIME AND TIME AGAIN, car salesmen have called upon me. Time and time again, my friends have done their best to win me over. Nonetheless, I have never become the owner of a motorcar, and I have never in fact even considered becoming one. Some of my friends have gone so far as to call me an anachronistic [outdated] fossil. For me, however, the prospect of being called an anachronism holds no terror at all. In my opinion, the automobile is guilty of twofold sins against mankind; my anti-automotive attitude springs from a desire to avoid these evils.

The first of the crimes committed by the automobile is external and exterior by nature. This includes a variety of offenses, from the most blatant and obvious crime, the killing and maiming of numberless human beings, through pollution of the air by exhaust gases, to the noise of traffic. In Japan, the human casualty rate is showing a particularly marked increase. The number of persons killed annually by the automobile exceeded 10,000 in 1959, 12,000 in 1960 and 13,000 in 1964. Subsequently, even this record was surpassed in 1969 when the number of annual fatalities reached 16,000.

This concrete cloverleaf, impressive as it is, robs the Japanese of scarce fertile land, and the vehicles that use it spread exhaust fumes over the surrounding area—one more price of progress. Photo from the Consulate General of Japan, N.Y.

Such is the extent of the human sacrifice demanded by this material Moloch [a god demanding great sacrifice]—the motorcar. In addition, we must include the destruction of nature as another of the external ills resulting from the automobile, which greedily insists upon the building of innumerable concrete highways and parking lots as its due. It destroys mountains and forests, meadows and farmlands—in a word, nature itself. The very idea of getting "back to nature" even provides an excuse for the odd spectacle of row upon row of motorcars thronging into the heart of the mountains.

The second great evil resulting from the automobile is internal and personal. By this I mean the diabolical transformation which takes place in most drivers the instant that they touch the steering wheel.

When people grasp the controls of a car, they turn into savages. They put on speed and more speed. They attempt to pass other drivers. They blast away on their horns as though they were madmen. With furious glares or curses, they attack the drivers of other cars that may happen to overtake them. At the same time, however, if these very same people happened to be on foot, they would, in all probability, never dream of acting so barbarously. When the thoroughfares are crowded, they grow irritated, and mutter angrily about "the number of cars on

Mass-transit systems are a possible solution to the problems of highway crowding and air pollution. Japan has one of the best rail systems in the world, but it is still not adequate to accommodate all the passengers in comfort. Photo from the United Nations.

The "Bullet", the world's fastest train at 150 mph, races past Mt. Fuji, providing a sharp contrast between the world of technology and the world of nature. Photo from the Japan National Tourist Organization.

the road these days." Never, of course, do they stop to reflect that they themselves are contributing to the problem. When they enter a small by-way hardly wide enough to permit the passage of a single car, they roar through it, scattering terrified pedestrians in all directions and rejoicing all the while over having found a good short cut. They think it no shame to park their cars so as to block entrance to other people's very doorsteps. Thanks to this destructive psychological

influence exerted by cars upon their drivers, more than 16,000 human beings are slaughtered annually. Nevertheless, in spite of the appalling number of dead and wounded, the drivers all too often hide behind a cowardly, quibbling line of reasoning, claiming that they themselves are innocent of the murders. Is it possible that the automobiles are to blame? ... Truly, when drivers drive, they lose all trace of conscience and human feeling.

Or, rather, we must go further and say that this dehumanizing tendency is not limited only to those times when drivers are clutching their levers and steering wheels. To a car owner, his car is as precious as a treasure or a loved one. If anyone else should touch his car, or smudge it, the owner immediately loses his emotional equilibrium. It is not unusual to hear of car-owning schoolteachers who have struck pupils for soiling their cars.

How are we to interpret the emotional make-up of drivers? Can it be that they are making use of noise and speed to rid themselves of daily frustrations? Does becoming the owner of a car give one the delusion of being also the master of a world? Do the intoxicating fumes of petrol and upholstery leather cause drivers to undergo a Jekyll-and-Hyde transformation? Whatever the reason, people driving cars do turn into complete egoists; even into veritable beasts. Surely, there is no one who has not seen the ... struggles for supremacy taking place on the roadways in the course of everyday traffic—small cars lording it over bicycles, large cars over medium-sized vehicles, and dump-trucks over large cars (almost as if to say "I'll smash you if you don't clear out of my way"). For this reason, we cannot hope to solve the problem simply through the invention of the so-called exhaust-free automobile. Even though this may reduce the degree of air pollution, it will not do away with the destructive effect of the automobile upon the human psyche.

When I reflect upon the matter in this way, I deplore the present state of affairs, in which more than twenty million cars are racing about throughout Japan's all too narrow land area. I am therefore in complete accord with the "no-car movement" which is actually being carried out on certain appointed days in the Tokyo suburban town of Hachioji and other cities. I am aware that many people feel that this movement amounts to a form of tyranny, insofar as it is advocated and handed down from above by the heads of city government. But I cannot agree with them, for they are viewing the problem in a form far distorted from its real nature.

If there exist persons who regard the ownership of a car as a symbol of social status, they are probably gullible souls who have believed all the inveiglement [enticements] of car salesmen. If there are people who believe that cars bring freedom to humanity, they are doubtless overly simple-minded, for in actuality cars both confine people and drive them into madness. As for those who truly seek for freedom, they are more likely to abandon automobiles or seek to do away with them....

If all Japan's private cars took to the roads at the same time, there would be four cars per foot of highway. This fact alone indicates that most owners of private cars keep the cars out of use most of the time.

Self-portrait of Japanese teens. Photo by Maeji Akihiro, from *Japan Forum*; used with permission.

At this point, I call to mind my travels through the U.S.A. and the Polynesian islands extending over a two-and-a-half month period in 1969. America is a nation of machines, and I cannot deny that in some respects machines have made the daily lives of its people easier and more convenient. Nevertheless, we must recognize the sad truth that machines have also made puppets of them. Lunar rockets, nuclear weapons, automobiles, computers—is it not true that all these blessings have brought tragedy to the American people? In the so-called uncivilized islands of Polynesia, the moving force of life is found in nature. There the evils created by machines do not exist, and human beings are able to live a life in tune with a peaceful rhythm of their own amid the luxuriance of nature. They are utterly free from the poisonous elixirs of strife, vanity, and deceptive trickery.

> *Editor's Postscript:* The private car boom would be easier to understand if Japan had an underdeveloped system of mass transportation. But this is not the case. Indeed, Japan's train, subway, and bus service is remarkably quick, efficient, and inexpensive. Most spectacular is the high-speed express line between Tokyo and Osaka, completed in

1964. Its trains run at speeds of up to 150 miles per hour, yet there has not been a single collision or derailment. During 1975 this line carried an average of 470,000 passengers per day. The total number of passengers it carried was significantly larger than the entire population of Japan.

This express line is the showpiece of Japan's railroad system. All by itself it averages 150 million passengers a year—more than Japan's total population. A large number of smaller railroads supplement this express line, and buses and subways add a third level. During rush hour at some Tokyo stations, for example, subway trains depart every 30 seconds—from the same platform!

In Japan as elsewhere, the use of private cars reduces the use of public transportation. Decreasing numbers of passengers mean increases in fares and a decline in services, which in turn stimulate the desire for private cars. If our experience in the United States is any indication, this vicious cycle may well be unbreakable.

CLEANING UP
MT. EVEREST

Editor's Introduction: Noguchi Ken, the author of the following excerpt was born in 1973 (in Boston), son of a diplomat. He climbed Mt. Blanc (15,721 feet, France) at age 16; Kilimanjaro (19,340 feet, Tanzania) at 17; Kosciusko (7,310 feet, Australia), Aconcagua (22,834 feet, Argentina), and McKinley (Denali, 20,320 feet, Alaska) at 19; the Vinson Massif (16,860 feet, Antarctica) at 21; Elbrus (18,510 feet, Russia) at 22; and Everest (29,028 feet, on his third try) at 25. [47]

ON MAY 13, 1999, I reached the summit of Mt. Everest, also known by its Tibetan name Chomolungma (Mother Goddess of the Earth). That brought to an end my quest to climb the highest points on the world's seven continents. My next challenge was to return to clean up Everest.

When I first attempted to climb Everest in 1997, the sight that met my eyes on Everest was trash much worse than I had imagined. Moreover, the greater part of the garbage had been left behind by expeditions from various Asian countries, including Japan. Other members of the team remarked on the lack of environmental awareness of Japanese climbers. When team members the next year (an unsuccessful attempt from the Nepalese side) scolded me, I felt like saying, "It may be trash from a Japanese expedition, but I didn't throw it away. It's got nothing to do with me!"

It was at this time that I decided I would first climb this mountain, then form an expedition to return to clean up the mountain. So in 2000, the year after I summitted, I returned to Everest with a team of 32: three Japanese, 25 sherpas, four Tibetans. We cleaned up between base camp and the highest camp (27,000 feet).

At altitudes above 18,000 feet, helicopters cannot function, so we had to carry the trash down ourselves. In 45 days we collected a ton and a half of trash. Because of heavy snow, we had first to dig the stuff out—even at heights close to 26,000 feet! At that height, a person capable of carrying 90 lbs. at sea level can carry only about 45 lbs. This clean-up was more tiring physically and mentally than climbing to the summit the previous year.

I don't wish to criticize previous Japanese expeditions, since much of the garbage on the mountain dates from a time when Japanese were much less aware of environmental problem. In fact, there is relatively little debris from Japanese expeditions after 1995. The pollution of the past will not simply go away, so isn't it a good idea to go back to Everest and clean up the garbage left by our predecessors?

We collected one and half tons of rubbish, but the mountain is still covered with large amounts of debris. I hope to return next year with another, international clean-up expedition. How long will it be before Chomolungma, Mother Goddess of the Earth, returns to her pristine beauty?

> *Editor's Postscript:* How many loads does it take to carry a ton and a half of garbage at 45 lbs. per load? Can you lift 45 lbs. at sea level? What is the highest elevation you have reached, with or without a 45-lb. pack? (The highest mountain in the United States—apart from Alaska's Denali, which is just over 20,000 feet—is under 15,000 feet.)
>
> On May 28, 2007, the Associated Press reported that Noguchi had just returned from his fifth trip to Everest. He estimates he and his helpers have removed a total of 20,000 pounds of garbage in those five trips: "During this year's clean-up expedition, I found that the amount of waste on the mountain has decreased dramatically."
>
> Japan's highest mountain is Fuji (12,388 feet). Some 200,000 climbers a year hike up it. After years of clean-up efforts by the Fuji Club, the paths are largely clear, but around the base? Says one volunteer, "We've found everything from household trash to broken TV sets and other appliances. Sometimes we find hazardous materials like leaky old car batteries." Noguchi, who works with the Fuji Club, says: "Picking it up is not enough—people have to learn not to create so much in the first place."*

---

* Carl Freire [AP], "Mountain of Litter Mars Mount Fuji," *Boston Globe*, June 9, 2007.

VIII
GENDER

WOMEN IN JAPAN:
THE DISTANT PAST

Editor's Introduction: As we have seen, technology and urbanization have had a profound impact on Japan and the Japanese. So have political and military events, such as the Pacific War and its aftermath, the Occupation of Japan. Among the areas in which changes have come is the status of women.

Today more Japanese women go to college than ever before, more pursue careers outside the home, more stay unmarried, or if they do marry, decide against having children. At least since the 1600s, Japan has been a society in which males had the dominant roles. The following selection comes from a textbook for women written in the late 1600s. [48]

IT IS A GIRL'S DESTINY, when she becomes a woman, to go to a new home and there to obey her father-in-law. Consequently, it is even more important for her than for a boy to accept with gratitude the instructions of her own parents. If her own parents, thinking that she is after all a member of the weaker sex, allow her to grow up with an independent mind, she will surely prove to be independent in her husband's house. Thus, she will lose his affection. Further, if her father-in-law is a man of strict principles, she will not be able to live up to them. She will hate and blame her father-in-law, and the result will be that she will be sent away from her husband's house....

In a woman, a virtuous heart is more important than a beautiful face. The heart of an unvirtuous woman is always upset. She will glare wildly around her. She will take her anger out on others. Her words will be harsh and her accents vulgar. When she speaks, it will be to give herself airs, to scold others, to envy others, to be puffed up with pride, to jeer at others, to outdo others. All these things are very much different from the way a woman should be. The only qualities suitable for a woman are gentle obedience, purity, mercy, and quietness....

A woman has no particular lord to serve. She must think of her husband as her lord, and she must serve him reverently. She must not despise him or think little of him. Obedience is the great lifelong duty of a woman. In her dealings with her husband, her facial expressions and her language should be courteous, humble, and yielding. She should never be peevish or obstinate, never rude or arrogant. That should be the first and most important concern of a woman. When her husband issues instructions, she must never disobey them.... A woman should look upon her husband as if he were heaven itself. She should never stop thinking how she may yield to her husband and thus escape the anger of heaven....

The five worst weaknesses of women are disobedience, unhappiness, slander, jealousy, and silliness. It is beyond doubt that seven or eight out of every ten women have these weaknesses. This is why women are inferior to men. A woman should correct these weaknesses by self-inspection and self-criticism.... Women are so stupid that it is important for them always to distrust themselves and to obey their husbands....

Parents! Teach these rules to your daughters from the very beginning. Copy them out from time to time, so they may read and remember them!...

> *Editor's Postscript:* The status of women in Japan was not always low. Until the ninth century A.D., Japan had several women rulers. In the court society of the tenth and eleventh centuries, the leading writers were all women. The first psychological novel in the history of world literature was written by a Japanese woman, Lady Murasaki, in the early eleventh century. And finally, the leading Shinto deity is a woman, the Sun Goddess.

SOME PREFER
NETTLES

Editor's Introduction: The "liberation" of Japanese women is not a purely contemporary development. It began at least as early as the 1920s. The following selection from a novel published in 1929 illustrates this point.

The central figures in the novel are Kaname and Misako. Although they are married, they lead quite separate lives and are almost at the point of divorce. Misako is a "liberated" woman. She has a lover, and she is deeply interested in everything modern.

Kaname, too, is very modern. He encourages Misako to take a lover, and he himself frequently visits Louise, a Eurasian prostitute. However, almost in spite of himself, Kaname feels drawn to the past, represented in the novel by the puppet theatre and by Ohisa, the female companion of Kaname's father-in-law.

All the characters in *Some Prefer Nettles* face a conflict between old and new, between tradition and change. Indeed, this novel is the classic fictional statement of that conflict. The title comes from a Japanese proverb: "Every worm to his taste; some prefer to eat nettles." It may indicate that the author did not expect many readers to share his own preferences.

Many people think of Japan today in terms of this conflict between what is "Japanese" and what is "Western." Yet *Some Prefer Nettles* was written in the 1920s. Today the "modern" and "Western" aspects of life that fascinate Kaname and Misako are second nature to the vast majority of Japanese. [49]

"YOU THINK YOU MIGHT GO, THEN?" Misako asked several times during the morning. Kaname as usual was evasive, however, and Misako found it impossible to make up her own mind.... Misako's father had called from Kyoto the day before and asked if the two of them would join him at the theatre. Misako

A master puppeteer manipulates his puppet from within, using his left hand for the puppet's head and his right hand for the puppet's right hand. Two assistants (not shown here) control the puppet's left hand and legs. Photo from the Japan National Tourist Organization.

had been out, and Kaname had been rash enough to say that they "probably could." As a matter of fact he could not very well have refused....

The old man, now nearly sixty, was in retirement in Kyoto, where he lived the life of the conservative man of taste. While Kaname's own tastes were rather different and he was often enough annoyed at the old man's displays of connoisseurship, still the latter had played the gallant in his youth, it was said, and there remained something open and easy in his manner that Kaname found very attractive. The thought that soon they might no longer be father-in-law and son-in-law gave him considerable regret—in fact, he sometimes told himself ironically, the regret at divorcing his father-in-law might be somewhat stronger than the regret at divorcing his wife—and, though ordinarily such an idea would not have troubled him, he wanted one last chance to demonstrate his sense of filial duty....

"Do you want to see it?" she asked....

"Not especially. I told him I did, though."

"When?"

"When was it, I wonder.... He got so excited about his puppets that I finally nodded back to make him happy."

Misako laughed pleasantly, as she would for the merest acquaintance. "You hardly needed to do that. You've never been that friendly with Father, after all."

"In any case, maybe we ought to stop by for a few minutes."

"Where is the Bunraku Puppet Theater?"

"It's not at the Bunraku. The Bunraku burned down. It's at a place downtown called the Benten."

"That means we sit on the floor? I can't stand it, really I can't. My knees will be agony afterwards."

"There's no avoiding it. That's the sort of place people like your father go. His tastes have got a little beyond me—and after the way he used to love the movies. I read somewhere the other day that men who are too fond of the ladies when they're young generally turn into antique-collectors when they get old. Tea sets and paintings take the place of sex."

"But Father hasn't exactly given up sex. He has Ohisa."

"She's one of the antiques in his collection, exactly like an old doll."

"If we go we'll have her inflicted on us."

"Then let's have her inflicted for an hour or two. Think of it as filial piety." Kaname began to feel that Misako had some very special reason for not wanting to go.

She went briskly over to the chest, however, and took out a kimono for him, carefully folded in a paper cover. "You're wearing a kimono, I suppose."

Kaname was as careful about his clothes as Misako was about hers. A particular kimono required a particular cloak and a particular sash, and each ensemble was planned down even to accessories like the watch and chain, the wallet, the cloak-cord, the cigarette case. Only Misako understood the system well enough to be able to put everything together when he specified the kimono he would wear. Now that she had taken to going out by herself a good deal, she always made sure before she left that his clothes were laid out for him. Indeed, when he thought of it, that was the only function she really discharged as a wife, the only function for which another woman would not do as well....

[Kaname and Misako decide to go to the puppet theater that day. They take a train to Osaka, and then a taxi to the theater.]

"What is playing?" Misako asked.

"Love Suicide," he said, "and something else. I've forgotten."

As if forced to one concession by the long silence, each made his one remark. They gazed rigidly forward as they spoke, the one seeing the line of the other's nose dimly through the corner of the eye.

Misako, who had no idea where the Benten Theater was, had no choice but to follow when they left the cab. Kaname had apparently received instructions from the old man. They went first to a teahouse that catered to theater guests and were guided from there by a kimono-clad maid. Misako felt more and more oppressed as the time approached when she would have to appear before her father and play the part of the wife. She pictured him on his cushion in the pit, his eyes fixed on the stage, a sake [rice-wine] cup raised to his lips, and beside him his mistress, Ohisa. Misako felt tense and uncomfortable with her father, but Ohisa she actively disliked. Ohisa, younger than Misako, was a tranquil, unexcitable Kyoto type, whose conversation, no matter what was said to her, seldom went beyond one amiable sentence. Her lack of spirit went badly with Misako's own Tokyo briskness, but, more than that, the sight of her beside the old man was to Misako insufferable. It made him seem less her father than an old lecher whom she found generally repulsive.

"I'm staying for only one act," she murmured as they stepped inside the door. The heavy, old-fashioned theater samisens [musical instruments, with three strings], whose twanging echo assailed them in the lobby, seemed to stir her to rebellion.

How many years had it been, Kaname wondered, since he had last been to the theater the old leisurely way, escorted by a teahouse maid? As he stepped from his sandals and felt the smooth, cold wood against his stockinged feet, he thought for an instant of a time, long ago—he could have been no more than four or five—when he had gone to a play in Tokyo with his mother. He remembered how he had sat on her lap as they took a rickshaw downtown from their house in the old merchants' quarter, and how afterwards his mother had led him by the hand, padding along in his holiday sandals, as they followed the maid from the teahouse. The sensation as he stepped into the theater, the smooth, cold wood against the soles of his feet, had been exactly the same then. Old-fashioned theaters with their open, strawmatted stalls somehow always seemed cold. And he had worn a kimono that day too....

Ohisa saw them as they came down the passage. "Oh, you're here," she said in her soft Kyoto accent. She carefully piled the lunch boxes at her knee, elaborate goldflecked tiers of them, and moved back to make room for Misako beside the old man. "They've come," she said. He greeted them shortly and turned to concentrate again on the stage....

"You must be uncomfortable. Why don't you stretch your legs a little this way?" Ohisa said solicitously, and busied herself in the narrow little stall making tea, pressing sweets on the others, now and then trying softly to make conversation with Misako, who disdained to look around. The old man held his sake lightly behind him in his outstretched right hand, balanced against the corner of an ashtray, and among her other duties Ohisa had to be sure that it was never allowed to go dry. The cup was one of three decorated in gold on vermilion with scenes from Hiroshige's prints, the old man having recently taken to insisting that "sake must be drunk from wooden lacquerware." Everything—the sake, the sweets, the cups and boxes—had been brought from Kyoto; with just such an assortment of gold-flecked lacquer, one could imagine, court maidens set out long ago to view the cherry blossoms. The old man, so particular to bring his own supplies, was not a guest to make the theater teahouses prosper, and clearly it was an effort for Ohisa to plan such expeditions.

"Won't you have some too?" Ohisa took another cup from a drawer and handed it to Kaname.

"Thank you. I never drink in the daytime.... It is a little chilly, though. Possibly I should have just a swallow."

She leaned to pour for him, and a suggestion of something like cloves seemed to come from her high, upswept hair as it touched against his cheek. He stared down into the cup at the gold-embossed Fuji, now shining through the sake, at the tiny village below it, done in the quick style of the color prints, and at the characters indicating which was the roadside station represented.

"It makes me a little uncomfortable to drink out of anything so elegant."

"Really?" One of the traditional charms of the Kyoto beauty, the discolored teeth, showed itself in Ohisa's laugh. Her two front teeth were as black at the roots as if they had been stained in the old court manner, and farther to the right an eyetooth protruded sharp enough to bite into her lip. There were many who would have seen in such a mouth a winsome artlessness, but in honesty it could not have been called beautiful. Misako was of course being cruel when she pronounced it filthy and barbarous. To Kaname it seemed rather a little sad. That such an unhealthy mouth should be left uncared for suggested something of the woman's ignorance.

"You brought all this from home with you?" he asked Ohisa.

"We did indeed."

"And you'll have to carry all the boxes back? I sympathize with you."

"He says the food at theaters is inedible."

Misako glanced back at them, then quickly turned to the stage again. Kaname had noticed how sharply she pulled herself away when in her efforts to find a comfortable position one of her feet brushed against his knee. He could not help smiling, a little wryly, at the trial it was for them to be put together in such a small space.

"How do you like it?" he asked in a husbandly way, hoping to dispel the mood a little.

"You must have so much excitement," Ohisa put in. "I should think you might like a nice quiet play now and then."

"I've been watching the singers. They're really much more interesting than the puppets," said Misako.

The old man coughed somewhat threateningly. His eyes still fixed on the stage, he groped about his knee for his pipe. The tooled-leather case had slipped under the cushion, however, and he was still feeling blindly for it when Ohisa noticed and retrieved it for him. She filled it, lighted it, and laid it carefully in the palm of his hand. Then, as if it made her want to smoke herself, she reached into her sash, took out an amberred leather case, and pushed her small white hand in under the lid.

There was much to be said for seeing a puppet play with a bottle of sake at one's side and a mistress to wait on one, Kaname thought as the conversation quieted, and, for want of anything more to distract him, he turned his attention to the stage. The first act of *Love Suicide* was drawing to a close. The lovers, Jihei and the geisha Koharu, held the stage, Koharu seated to the right. The sake cup had been rather a large one, and Kaname felt a little heady. Perhaps because of the glittering reflections, the stage seemed a great distance away, and it was all he could do to make out the faces and the costumes. He concentrated on Koharu. Jihei's face had in it something of the dignity of classic dance masks, but his exaggerated clothes hung lifelessly from his shoulders as he moved about the stage, making it a little hard for one as unfamiliar with the puppet theater as Kaname to feel any human warmth in him. Koharu, kneeling with her head bowed, was infinitely more effective. Her clothing too was exaggerated, so that her turned-out skirt fell unnaturally before her knees, but Kaname found that easy to forget. The old man, when he discoursed on the puppet theater, liked to compare Japanese Bunraku puppets with Occidental string puppets. The latter could indeed be very active with their hands and feet, but the fact that they were suspended and worked from above made it impossible to suggest the line of the hips and the movement of the torso. There was in them none of the force and urgency of living flesh, one could find nothing that told of a live, warm human being. The Bunraku puppets, on the other hand, were worked from inside, so that the surge of life was actually present, sensible, under the clothes. Their strongest points perhaps derived from the good use made in them of the Japanese kimono. The same effects would be impossible from puppets in foreign dress, even if the same manipulating techniques were adopted. The Bunraku puppet was therefore unique, inimitable, a medium so skillfully exploited that one would be hard put to find parallels for it anywhere.

Kaname found himself agreeing....

Kaname had seen the Bunraku puppets once ten years before. He had not been impressed—he could in fact remember only that he had been intensely bored. Today he had come solely out of a sense of duty, expecting to be bored again, and he was somewhat astonished that he should almost against his will be drawn so completely into the play. He had grown older, he had to admit. He was no longer in a position to make fun of the old man's dilettantism. Given another ten years, he would find that he had come precisely the same distance over the same road as the old man. There he would be, a mistress like Ohisa at his side, a tooled-leather pipe-case hung at his hip, a tiered lunch box flecked with gold ... but he might not need even ten years. He had always affected a maturity beyond his years, and he would age fast.... He looked at Ohisa. Her face was turned a little so that the line of her cheek showed, round, almost heavy, like that of a court beauty in a picture scroll. He compared her profile with Koharu's. Something about the slow, sleepy expression made him think of the two of them as not unlike each other.... A pair of conflicting emotions pressed themselves on him: old age brought its own pleasures and was not really to be dreaded; and yet that very thought, a symptom of approaching old age, was something he must resist, if only because of the advantage it might give Misako. The reason for their decision to separate, after all, was that they did not want to grow old, that they wanted to be free to live their youth again.

"Thank you very much for the telephone call," Kaname said as the curtain fell and the old man turned half around to face him. "I'm beginning to see some of the good points in all this—I really am."

"You needn't try to please me. I have no professional interest in it," the old man answered, with a touch of the self-satisfaction that comes with age. His shoulders were hunched for the cold, and his neck was buried in a scarf, a piece of silk crepe, softened with age, that had once been meant for a woman. "I don't expect you to enjoy yourself, but it does you no harm to see something like this at least once in your life."

"I'm enjoying myself thoroughly, though. Why do you suppose it is?—I see a great deal I missed before."

"These are almost the last of the great puppeteers. I wonder how it will be when they are gone."

Misako cupped a small compact in the palm of her hand and began powdering her nose. "And so begins the dissertation," the expression on her face seemed to say as she bit back a sardonic smile....

"Really, young people are beyond me. Look at this, for instance—women have simply forgotten how to take care of themselves. What's that thing in your hand?"

"That thing is called a compact."

"A compact. I don't object so much to the fad for compacts, but I do object to the way women take them out in public, no matter who might be watching. It's inelegant, ungraceful—a woman's charm disappears. I had to scold Ohisa about it just the other day."

"A compact is very convenient." Misako turned to get a better light and, taking out a kiss-proof lipstick, solemnly drew a line of crimson across her mouth.

"But that looks so dreadful. In my day a well-bred woman would never have thought of doing such a thing in public."

"Well, everyone does now. I don't see how you're to stop it. I know a woman who is famous for making herself up at the table. Whenever we have lunch together, she takes out her compact and forgets the food. It takes forever to get through a meal. She's an extreme case, of course."

DRIVEN BEYOND
DIGNITY

Editor's Introduction: Some women in Japan today have already achieved spectacular success, particularly in the entertainment world and in sports. The following account describes the rigorous training of a Japanese girls' volleyball team. Consider the qualities that brought success to this group of women athletes and compare them to an American team. [50]

JUST MINUTES OUT OF TOKYO on the 7 A.M. flight, the great white cone of Fujiyama slides majestically past the starboard wing and then dims in the distance as you drum southward toward Osaka. In Osaka barely an hour later, you hire a cab for the drive to the neighboring town of Kaizuka—a two-hour journey to what will prove to be a profoundly shocking experience.

I had come to see the sensational Nichibo Kaizuka women's volleyball team: world champions, winner of 137 consecutive contests since 1960 and the favorite to retain its upstart mastery over the powerful Communist bloc—long the hotbed of world volleyball—at October's Tokyo Olympics.

Widely acclaimed in packed arenas from Warsaw to Tokyo and now hailed as the new idols of Japanese sport, the girls are nicknamed the Kaizuka Amazons. The name does not remotely prepare you for what you find when you drive through the gates of Kaizuka's huge Dai Nippon spinning mill, where the Amazons work and play.

Whisked to a cluttered reception room jammed with souvenirs and trophies, I met the coach, Daimatsu Hirobumi. Daimatsu, 43, is a short, lean, muscular man with a shaggy crew cut over cold features. Talking softly through an interpreter, he told about his team.

His 16 volleyballers are the pick of 1,242 girls employed in the Dai Nippon mill in Kaizuka. They live here with the other girls in the austere company dorms, work in the company office, average $50 per month take-home pay after board.* They rise each weekday at 7, work from 8 until 3:30, change and are in the company gym by 4. There they practice non-stop until midnight, six days a week, 51 weeks a year—barring road time on competitive tours, when things get, if anything, a little tougher. On the seventh day, Sunday, the office is closed, and practice sessions are even longer.

Except for a one-week break around Eastertime, this is the routine year in and year out. Says Coach Daimatsu: "There is time for nothing else. The players know absolutely no other life. They do it because they choose to. The preparation for winning is a personal, individual challenge. It is accepted without question."

Ah, but then, I said to myself, it's only volleyball, played by girls.

So I had lunch, toured this vast, ultramodern textile plant, and then promptly at 4 adjourned to the gymnasium. It is a bleak, chill, poorly lit building heated by three small charcoal pots. The girls are already on the floor. They are big, strong, rangy, averaging around 5 feet 7. Their fingers are heavily taped, and they wear knee and elbow pads. Engaged now in a playful, boisterous scrimmage, they move the ball with an astonishing acrobatic dexterity and slam it across the net with a jarring power, screaming in shrill unison at every "kill."

The scrimmage switches to a warmup drill in which an assistant drives them through a grueling, nonstop half hour of dives, rolls and tumbles. Then Daimatsu takes over. He mounts a platform at center net, flanked by a huge wire basket filled with balls, tended by a girl assistant. The squad queues in separate lines at opposite ends of the gym's rear wall, facing the net.

Daimatsu signals, and in rapid rotation the girls charge toward the net, crisscrossing from their respective corners. With the ball girl feeding him swiftly, silently, Daimatsu swings his fist in a swift, rhythmic motion, slamming the balls first to one side and then the other as the girls come charging in. The balls are aimed deliberately short so that the girls must hurl themselves headlong in a desperate, often futile attempt to retrieve and keep them in the air. They land jarringly on their chests and shoulders, then roll out and recover with a sprawling, judolike somersault.

As each girl recovers, she dashes back to the wall to charge in immediately for the next retrieve, sometimes as many as six times before the next girl comes hurtling in.

---

*This rate of compensation was not grossly inadequate in 1964. Indeed, it placed them in the middle ranges of the Japanese wage scale. Since 1964, wages have risen rapidly, to the point that they are roughly equal to American wages. In purchasing power, Japanese wages are still inferior to American wages.

Children of many ages watch experts demonstrate judo. Baseball is the single most popular sport in Japan, but karate, judo, and other traditional sports have their devotees as well. Photo from the Japan National Tourist Organization.

An hour of this and the girls are sweat-sodden, soiled and gasping with the exertion. After two hours Daimatsu, expressionless, his arm still swinging like a piston, closes the range. He now imparts a vicious spin to the ball. A heavy-set girl lumbers in, overcharges, slams onto her shoulder and grimaces in pain as she hobbles drunkenly back to the wall, where she bends in agony. Daimatsu, his motion unbroken, is now jibing softly.

"If you'd rather be home with your mother, then go. We don't want you here."

Another girl hurtles to the floor, goes sprawling across the court and hits an ankle against an iron bench with a sickening crack. She is sobbing as she limps back to the wall.

"There's a South Korean team in town. If this is too tough for you, maybe you should go and play with them," says Daimatsu.

It is 7 o'clock now and the girls' supper is wheeled in in metal urns: rice, meat and fish. Daimatsu ignores it and quickens the pace. His grim, wild-eyed intensity is frightening. His face is still a mask, but it is strained and beaded with sweat. Now many of the girls are openly sobbing, their faces distorted with the agony

Marriages by Age of Bride, Japan

	1975	1985	1995	1998
Under 20	24,400	21,700	19,400	20,200
20-24	464,600	283.500	238,500	204,300
25-29	271,600	261,600	314,500	326,900
30-34	39,400	56,800	89,100	98,600
35-39	14,100	23,900	25,200	28,900
40-44	7,500	9,300	11,500	10,800
Over 45	7,800	10,700	18,400	19,300

Source: United Nations Statistics Division.

What trends do you see in these figures? What kind of graph would illustrate those trends most dramatically? (1998 is the most recent year for which the UN has these figures.)

of effort and the physical punishment. But they keep staggering in, and the food sits for half an hour before Daimatsu gives a curt signal and the first-team girls— always the first to eat—go to the urns. The others shift to a brisk scrimmage as Daimatsu goes to the sidelines for his own meal, which is served to him by a ball girl. As he dines he is even more chilling to observe, for now one seems to see in him the cool arrogance of a despot.

After ten minutes the first team is back on the floor with Daimatsu, who has left his supper half-eaten. The second stringers now sit down to the rest of the cold food. Minutes later they too are back. At 10 o'clock—they have been practicing six hours now—they switch to what I was told is a drill to "test the spirit as well as the body."

In this drill girls are singled out and subjected to a merciless bombardment aimed purposely, diabolically, well out of reach. This goes on until each lurching, sobbing girl is utterly exhausted, plainly driven to the absolute maximum.

It is now midnight, eight hours gone, and it should be all over, but one girl, the weeping wretch who cracked her ankle, has displeased Daimatsu. She is called out and now defends herself desperately with forearms and elbows as he shells her again and again and yet again from close range.

A Visit to Hooptown

I press my nose against the chain-link fence as loud rap music echoes in the background. The earringed boy in the baggy Chicago Bulls shorts takes the pass and makes his move to the hoop. The chubby kid in the Air Jordans is all over him, but somehow he manages to get the ball in the bucket as they both come crashing to the deck.

Chicago? L.A.? The south Bronx? No, Hooptown, a small piece of urban America nestled in the chic and slightly freaky, but definitely moneyed, section of Tokyo called Harajuku, where Japan's young come to play and spend their yen. But don't expect to see any guns, knives, broken pavement or worn metal backboards in this dolled-up version of schoolyard half-court basketball. After all, this is Japan, land of the eternal spirit of Walt Disney and all things good and clean. So you can bet Hooptown is clean, well managed and, most likely, well behaved. After all, the sign on the wall states in plain English and Japanese, "No foul language" and "No hanging on the rim."

If the Nike, Air Jordan and Force ads wired to the fence don't discredit Hooptown's authenticity, perhaps the colorful Keith Haringesque court surface will. Giant posters of American basketball gods Michael Jordan, Charles Barkley and Scotty Pippen look down on the six Japanese teens haplessly missing shot after shot. Overhead, spectators sit in the plush comfort of the Player's restaurant and take in the action while dining on "Three-point Pizza" and "M.J. Hamburger Steak." Later, after settling their tab with a waitress clad in a skimpy Laker Girls costume, they might stop by the NBA Shop for a souvenir and catch a real game on the shop's monitor.

So, as the hard core fans down near the action at the Hot Dog Court wolf their Dunk Shot Dogs with draft beer chasers, I sit on the sidelines and watch them smirking while the boy in Patrick Ewing sneakers coughs up yet another air ball. O.K., so the level of play isn't up to snuff, but these homeboy wannabees have chipped in about $30 for their hour of court time and they're going to get their money's worth. It's Hooptown, it's Americana, sort of, and it's in Japan.

Source: Thomas Boatman and Mark Darbyshire, *Tradepia International*, no. 55, Summer 1993.

At 9 the next morning, barely eight hours after the girls have staggered back to their dorms, I visited the mill office and, incredibly, they were already at work. Dressed in neat blue smocks, they have been here as usual since 8, demurely fingering the abacus board, filing, answering the telephone. Daimatsu sits nearby at his office manager's desk, engrossed in accounts. That these serene young women are one and the same with the wild-eyed creatures I had seen just a few hours ago brutalizing themselves almost beyond human dignity seemed truly unbelievable.

Not quite all of them are here. It is explained that four are at the mill hospital getting treatment. They are expected back at work by noon and, of course, in the gym at 4, with the others.

The team's captain, tall, graceful Kasai Masae, smiles shyly from her desk. Little stories like hers tell the big one. Two years ago, at age 28, Masae was in love and engaged to a young man from Osaka. She had a choice: marriage and a home, or a continuation of the daily torture under Daimatsu Hirobumi. She chose the latter, for at the 1964 Olympics the glory of Japan will flicker again, and glory is everything.

Perhaps Masae had said it all the previous night when I asked her about the team's chances at the Olympics.

"You must understand," she said gravely. "We have never experienced defeat. We must win."

> *Editor's Postscript:* The Japanese team did win. It took an Olympic gold medal by defeating a powerful Russian team in the finals. No one who witnessed the scene will ever forget it. A few seconds passed before the team members realized that they had indeed achieved their goal, that the human dignity they had sought for so long and with such great determination was in fact theirs. There was a long moment of stunned silence on the floor. Then came tears of joy or relief or release—perhaps a combination of the three. On the sidelines stood Coach Daimatsu, no expression at all visible on his face. During the climactic match he had rarely displayed any emotion, and now he stayed on the sideline, leaving the team to accept the adulation of the crowd.

But Coach Daimatsu was not an ogre without feelings. Nor were the team members Amazons without grace. Daimatsu had arrived at his fearsome coaching technique by a cool analysis of the realities of the situation. As he told a reporter,

> We have to compensate for our disadvantage in height and reach with fast reflexes and leaps forward and to the side. I deliberately throw balls at them just out of their reach, close enough so they will give their maximum effort to reach them, far enough so they will fall to the floor. Sure, they get angry. Sure, they get bruised. But if they improve their reach by just a thousandth of an inch they will save points they might otherwise lose and it is all worth it. So I have to be mean and laugh at them.

Moreover, Daimatsu's sacrifice was almost as great as that of his team. In a revealing comment, he conceded: "This is wearing on me, too. I get home at 2 A.M. and must be up at 7 to get back to work. This is no way to be a family man, and I've almost had enough of being tough."

The team members were already famous, but their success at the Olympics made them national heroes. Within a few years, the team of 1964 was gone. A few members stayed on as the core of a new team, but most of the women resigned and married. The wedding of the team captain, Kasai, was a major social event attended by many prominent figures from Japan's athletic, political, and theatrical worlds. (The Prime Minister himself had acted as go-between in arranging the marriage.) "Driven beyond dignity"? Perhaps.

Birth Rate

In 1998 the Japanese birth rate dropped to the lowest figure ever: the average number of children born to a woman over her lifetime fell to 1.38. 1.38 is well below the rate necessary to maintain the Japanese population in its current numbers, so by the middle of the 21st century, the population is expected to fall from 127,000,000 today to 100,000,000.

Source: *Japan Now*, March 2004.

Question: Suppose there are ten women, and one woman has three children. How many children could there be in the other families to meet the 1.38 figure? Could that average be met in more than one way? If none of the ten women gives birth to more than two children, how many possible combinations could there be?

PRO SOCCER TODAY

Japan's pro soccer league opened for business in May 1993. There were 4,000 tickets for the first match (and the tickets were personalized—the purchaser's name was printed on the ticket). Some 300,000 people sent in applications for tickets. In its first year, League sales totaled over $6 billion. The comparable figure for Japan's professional baseball establishment, in operation for decades, was over $9 billion.

WORKING
WOMEN

Editor's Introduction: In Japan at the turn of the twenty-first century, most Japanese women work or want to work. In the 1980s, 85 percent of women in the 20 to 24 year old group wanted to work, and 70 percent of them did work outside the home. These numbers dropped in the 30 to 34 year old group (to 80 percent and 50 percent respectively), only to climb again after the age of 40 (to over 80 percent and the high 60 percent range, respectively).

What are the consequences of this pattern of working women? For themselves? For their families? For the economy? We can't answer all those questions, but we do have some fascinating interview material dating from the mid-1980s about blue-collar working women. These women worked in a company in Tokyo, under trying conditions. Most notably, the company president felt strongly that there was something wrong about women working. Here is part of a speech he made (via video) to all company employees:

> ...in the background [behind the men in Japan's past], there were always the women, who, with firm hand, maintained the household and brought up the children, encouraging their husbands and sharing their hardships. One could say that men were like bunraku puppets, always on center stage, but there was someone who made the puppets dance. In Japan the men were the puppets who were made to dance, and in the shadows were the wonderful, staunch women.... The postwar recovery [after 1945], which required tremendous strength, is also due to such women....
>
> Nowadays, women have totally changed. The women who had had a wonderful tradition and extraordinary strength have now begun to decline.... They no longer maintain the household. They dislike raising children. This

is what it has come to.... Today, who is going to maintain the household? I think that Japan has already started on the road to ruin, since so few people are alert to this. Unless women awaken and take hold of themselves, more and more good women will be made fools by these new social trends.

Most of the women of these interviews have only the compulsory education, through junior high school. [51]

Ms. Hanami (30 years old, 12 years' experience; recently married but without children): "My husband wishes I'd stay at home, even without kids. He does give his OK, however, since we just barely make living expenses as it is, with our combined salaries. Rent is expensive."

Ms. Nishitani (married, with two children, and pregnant with a third): "He [my husband] probably thinks I don't appreciate him. If on occasion I'm tired and can't do the housework, he doesn't say, 'Do this' or 'Do that.' Even in regard to the children, if I say, 'Boy, am I tired today!' he'll say, 'Shall we eat out?' I think he probably doesn't like it. He probably thinks I have absolutely no appreciation of him. He seems to keep his feelings back."

A young Tokyo office worker.
Photo by by Doug Hurst.

Ms. Usui (31 years old, with two children; she started work at age 15 and holds a supervisory position): "He [my husband] seems to take it OK because we can't make it on his salary alone. At first I promised that it would only be the first three years of our marriage, but we can't live in our present house—because we have two kids, and there's no space. So he's come to terms with it, I think."

Ms. Koga (age 30, with 15 years of experience; married with two children): "It's a given [that I work]. [Does her husband support the idea?] Yes. Because he knows we couldn't make do if I quit. Sometimes I say, 'It's only proper for a man to provide for his wife.' I get lazy and he says, 'Do such and such,' because he doesn't want to do it. In those cases I say, 'OK. OK then. I'll quit work, and you support me.' Then he says, 'Come on now!'"

Ms. Hasegawa (mother of two married daughters and at 52 close to retirement age): "He [my husband] thinks that women turn into loudmouths when they work. Because you get tired—after work. It'd be great if I could listen and do whatever he tells me to, saying 'Yes, yes,' but I go and say, 'But I'm so tired already!' Therefore he probably is somewhat unhappy about it. But since I'm making money for us...he's quiet about it. But when women work, they always get uppity.

[About her children] "Hmmm...they say I yell too much. I get mad. They say if I were taking it easy at home I wouldn't get mad. Naturally, when they make demands on me in spite of the fact that I come home tired out, I end up just saying whatever I feel like off the top of my head."

Ms. Fujii (age 28, two children, thirteen years on the job): [Is her husband supportive?] "Not especially." [Does he complain?] "No, he doesn't. If I say I'm tired or I'm busy, he always says, 'If you're tired, then why don't you quit?' But he's just saying that. He doesn't really mean it. I guess he thinks if I want to work, then it's OK by him.

[Her children] "They don't say anything much. But when they say they don't like going to day care, I say, 'Mother is going to go to work and do her best, so you do your best, too!' and we spur each other on, each going to work or day care. If you work, it becomes an encouragement to them, it seems. If you're just at home lazily looking after the kids, neither mother nor child grows. Because your knowledge is limited—what can one parent teach a child? But at nursery school, many different teachers with varied knowledge teach the children all sorts of things—

Self-portrait of Japanese teens. Photo by Sato Satomi, from *Japan Forum*; used with permission.

more than a parent teaches. So parents aren't quite as good. They end up having a lot of teachers, but I think that's good for the children."

Ms. Ogawa (43 years old, 10 years on the job; married, with two children): "Well, buying a house was why I went to work. So I had to work. The children knew it. The older one was a fifth-grader and the younger was a second-grader. They were pretty understanding and did things around the house for me. So they didn't object to my working. But my older child—that was just about the time he was beginning to make his own judgments and become independent. I think he must have been lonesome for a while. I had him babysit for his younger brother during the summer and winter vacations. I had him take him roller skating...and he had to look after him in Boy Scouts. That was a big burden on the elder child, and after he started junior high, for a while he ran off the track. I guess I didn't give him enough love...I think now he was lonely then. Since I had him take care of the younger one. I haven't actually told him, but I think it was bad of me."

Ms. Kamida (37 years old, with 22 years' experience; married with two children): "If I bring home my troubles when I'm tired, he tells me to quit. In our case, I'm working because I like to, not because there's any special financial difficulty. I want

Self-portrait of Japanese teens. Photo by Tsubono Masako, from *Japan Forum*; used with permission.

to work, so I do, but if I say anything, he says, 'Then quit and be done with it.' So I don't bring that up at home. I don't mention that I'm tired, and I don't bring up my gripes. Therefore, I don't talk about company matters at all...

[The children] "They understand. I do things for them. It wouldn't do for people to talk about them because they have a working mother, so I do my best to wash their clothes. If I had them wear anything dirty they'd be talked about—so I have them wear clean things, and on vacations I take them places, since usually I'm not around."

[Housework] "Sometimes I have them help. The older one is very nice and does anything. She spreads out the bedding for Grandma, and so on. Today she did my hair, see? With the dryer. She's so nice. That's why everyone comments on how gentle they've been brought up to be. Despite my working. After all, they were left to themselves. I guess the kids know that, since their parents are working, they have to be responsible. So I guess they have an independence about them already. They even say I needn't come and watch their classes anymore, since I have to take off time from work."

> *Editor's Postscript:* Does your mother work outside the home? Do your friends' mothers work outside the home? Did your grandmothers? What does your mother think of this? What does your father? What do you? Or is it simply not an issue?

JAPANESE WOMEN
IN THE OLYMPIC MARATHON

EACH NATION CAN enter three qualified representatives in the Olympic marathon. Here are the Japanese women's results for the last four Olympic marathons:

1992, Barcelona, Spain:	2nd—Arimori Yūko, 2:32:49
	7th—Yamashita Sachiko, 2:36:26
1996, Atlanta:	3rd—Arimori Yūko, 2:28:39
2000, Sydney, Australia:	1st—Takahashi Naoko, 2:23:14
	(This is the Olympic record for the women's marathon; in 2004 Takahashi tried out for the Japanese team but didn't make it.)
	7th—Yamaguchi Eri, 2:27:03
2004, Athens:	1st—Noguchi Mizuki, 2:26:20
	5th—Tosa Reiko, 2:28:44
	7th—Sakamoto Naoko, 2:31:43

There have been only six Olympic marathons for women. Joan Benoit-Samuelson, an American, won the first in 1984. Of the 48 top-eight finishes, eight have been by Japanese women, including two top-eight finishes by Arimori Yūko. The other countries with many top-eight finishes are Russia (six), Portugal and Germany (four each), and Ethiopia and Kenya (three); the U. S. has two. Japan is the only nation to have two winners.

To run the marathon in 2 hours and 20 minutes means averaging roughly 5:30 per mile—for 26.2 miles! How fast can you run one mile? 8:00? 7:00? 6:30? 6:00? 5:30? 5:00? Only a handful of U. S. high schoolers, all male, have broken the four-minute barrier.

IX
ASPECTS OF
LIFE TODAY

PARENTS AND
THEIR CHILDREN'S
EDUCATION

Editor's Introduction: In Japan, parents—at least mothers—tend to involve themselves in their children's education, at school and after school. They exchange written comments with schoolteachers almost weekly; they make sure that their children do their homework (in part by providing conditions that encourage the children—a desk, a good light, quiet, and snacks); and they shape their own lives around the after-school activities of their children. These activities have given rise to the phrase "education mama," a put-down of sorts, but at least through elementary school, few children show resentment.

Mori Hiroko, 39 when she was interviewed in the early 1980s, is hardly a typical wife and mother. A skilled piano player, she turned down the chance to become a concert artist in order to stay close to her family. She lived for eight years in New York City. But she is not wildly atypical in her attitudes toward her children's education. She has a 13-year-old daughter, Yuki, and a five-year-old son, Takeo. The *okeiko goto* of which she speaks are after-school lessons—anything from music to swimming. [52]

MANY AMERICANS ARE WONDERING now why the Japanese children have higher IQ scores. It's very, very simple. They do *okeiko goto*. The children are used to studying hard and playing hard, i.e., training, from a very early age. That way their brains work very fast. Both of my children have *okeiko goto*. I take five-year-old Takeo to his hour-long swimming lessons twice a week. Ear-training and piano lessons are also twice a week too. My daughter, Yuki, thirteen, takes piano lessons and ear-training too, plus English lessons. I know that in America children play after school. But Japanese children have afterschool lessons. It's the custom.

DOONESBURY

DOONESBURY copyright © 1986 G.B. Trudeau. Reprinted by permission of Universal Press Syndicate. All rights reserved.

Of course, some mothers don't do this. They are too busy, especially when they have jobs. But if you really want to educate your children, you have to stay home. The mother can't work. It happened to me. I wanted to give concerts, but if I did, I would have had to travel a lot. I had a difficult time deciding. But what if one of my children became sick? Then I'd have to cancel the concert. Besides, my husband wanted me to stay home, too.

Japanese spend a lot of money on education, so we'll never get rich. Our family spends almost one-quarter of our income on the children. My husband doesn't like to spend money on a house or cars, but he will lavish money on the children's education.

Yuki's piano lessons cost $240 a month, her ear-training $86, and English lessons $68. The English lessons aren't so expensive because a relative who lived in the States for ten years teaches her. Takeo's piano lessons cost $50, ear-training $34, and swimming $42.

It's a lot of work to take the children here and there four days a week. For example, I have to drive Takeo to his swimming lessons, change him, and then he wants me to watch him from the gallery. In his swim school, each child advances from level eleven down to level one. At the end of every month, the swim teachers give tests in diving and different swim strokes to determine if the children should change levels. Takeo is level ten now. He has failed to change levels four times now, so it's so discouraging for him. He hates it. Whenever he has to go to the swim school, he always pretends to have a headache, stomachache, or cold. But swimming is good training for him. My husband feels the same way. It builds up a strong body. The lessons are not just for his health alone. Swimming builds up his determination and courage. (When I was a girl, I used to be afraid to dive and my father was so disappointed.) Anyway, once we get into the swimming pool building, he looks so happy. He gives up on his stomachache or whatever. He smiles. He seems to enjoy it.

Do you know I signed him up for swim lessons when he was three and a half years old? (The children can start when they are three years old.) I had to wait one and a half years to get him into this class. You have to sign up early. Now that it's in fashion to go to swim school, there is a waiting list of 200 children.

When everyone goes to *okeiko goto*, no one complains. If all Takeo's friends are busy with lessons, he gives up wanting to play and wants to take his lessons. But if his friends are playing, he doesn't want to go.

So a group of mothers made up an *okeiko goto* list. They know Takeo has lessons on Wednesdays, Thursdays, and Saturdays, and I know which days their boys have lessons. So if Takeo wants to play on one of his lesson days, I just call up a boy who also has lessons that day. Then Takeo gives up wanting to play. We avoid calling the children who are free.

Usually more girls than boys go to *okeiko goto*, especially for music training. Boys often give up music training in the higher grades of primary school because they have to concentrate on their schoolwork. I'd say most children start lessons like these at age three and stop around fifth grade to prepare for the junior high school exams.

Some people say it's vain to continue to take the lessons when other children stop. Some people feel it's vain to take lessons at all. They say, "Let the children play." (I used to have the same opinion, because my parents pushed me too much. I gave up piano for five years.) But I feel that, once the child has the training, he or she can pick up an instrument or whatever again when that child is an adult.

Family outing.
Photo by Doug Hurst.

When I was a girl, I took *okeiko goto*. I used to love ballet lessons. I wanted to be a ballerina, but my father said he didn't want his daughter raising her legs in front of other people. I studied Japanese dancing, too, but I didn't like it too much; the movements were so slow.

When I was five, I started piano once a week. I was still playing at age twenty-two after university when I met my husband. We were taking piano lessons from the same teacher. He loved music, so he wanted to marry a musician.

By this time, I felt my parents had pushed me too much. I wanted to get married so I could stop playing the piano. I was sick of it. I hated music and my piano. So I asked my husband to stop all the music in the house. I wanted to have a baby and become a common housewife. This caused a great misunderstanding between my husband and me. He married me because I was a musician. But whenever I asked him, "Did you marry me because I'm a pianist," he had to answer, "No, I married you because I love you." He was so unhappy. This was the most difficult time of our marriage.

So I became a common housewife doing this and that for four years. Then suddenly I got sick of it. I hated housework. And one day I heard a record as I walked down the street and thought I'd like to play like that.

Then we were transferred to New York. Six months later my husband very timidly handed me an application for Juilliard. "Are you interested?" he said. I answered, "I have a child. I don't have time." But he pointed out, "There are babysitters here in America."

At the time, I was practicing only an hour a day while Yuki took her nap. On weekends my husband took her to the zoo so I could have time to practice. At the entrance exam for Juilliard, I played terribly, but I passed, and thus began five years of study. So I owe my husband a lot.

Of course, I had to find a babysitter, and I was lucky to find a very good Italian-American lady. In Japan, nobody wants to be a babysitter. Parents and children are afraid of babysitters, too. When we came back to Japan, that's what I missed most about America. For three years, I couldn't go to a concert.

Here everyone thinks the mother should stay home until the baby grows up—maybe until the third or fourth grade. Mothers have to give up concerts and parties. Wives are usually not invited to parties anyway, because it's so hard to get a babysitter. (Actually, if we were invited and didn't want to go, not being able to get a babysitter would provide a good excuse.) There is no system of babysitting.

In Japan, men make their own world and women make their own world. Women gather in town during the day to have lunch while the children are in school. You'll only see women in the nice French restaurants at noontime. The women never complain, because everyone also is doing the same thing.

But in New York, couples are always invited to parties. It's only after living in the U.S. where husbands and wives do things together that the Japanese women start to complain.

In America, we lived in Yonkers, and as in Japan, my husband never came home until late. I thought the American husbands were so kind. If I had trouble with some machine or other, my neighbor's husband would rush over to repair it. He had all kinds of tools and could fix anything. I respected him.

And when it snowed, all the American husbands rushed out to shovel before the snow became ice. Only my husband didn't appear. He didn't cut the grass. He didn't rake the leaves either. He was the enemy of the neighborhood. In Japan, those are women's jobs, unless the husbands like to work outdoors. I did them for a while—until I learned I could pay the neighbor's boys to do those things. That's another thing I miss about America.

Self-portrait of Japanese teen. Photo by Kato Akihiro, from *Japan Forum*; used with permission.

I tried to explain to my neighbor that, often when my husband wanted to go home, he'd get a telex from Tokyo (due to the time difference of fourteen hours) that he'd have to answer. She couldn't stand to see Yuki neglected, always left alone with her mother, so she was always saying, "Divorce your husband. Divorce your husband." Even today, she still hates him. Every Christmas she sends us lots of presents: about ten gifts for Yuki (she loves her), four for Takeo, and two for me. Nothing for my husband. He always says, "I guess she still hates me."

In Japan, you don't just divorce your husband. You have to think about the children. Do you realize how much power I have? I could really damage his career—particularly at a big company. They're so conservative. I wouldn't dare destroy a man's future. After a divorce, his chances for a promotion would be much less good. The company reasons that if a man can't manage his own home, how can he manage business affairs?

Right now, my husband and I are discussing whether Takeo should go to public or private school after (private) kindergarten. I want him to go to public school so he'll get to know many different kinds of people: the sons of shop owners and fish market owners—all kinds of classes. My husband feels differently. He wants the children to be with children of the same class and the same intelligence level. This is something we discuss all the time.

In truth, we do have high expectations of Takeo, because his father went to Todai [Tokyo University] and his grandfather went to Todai. So I must protect him. Actually I'll do both. I'll pressure him and protect him. His father will want him to go to Todai. So I must protect him, especially if he doesn't get in. I want him to know that getting into Todai is not the only thing in life.

We had a big discussion about Yuki's education when we returned. My husband wanted her to go to the mission school, a private Catholic school, where only the right people go. I had gone to this school, and I didn't like it. All the children were so snobby. The only thing the teachers do is train the students to be polite. I hated it. But it is good in that they teach English from first grade.

She ended up going to public school. Since her public middle school ends in two more years, she will have to choose soon which high school to aim for. Geidai is a well-known, national music school—very hard to get into. (Yes, I went there.) Toho is a well-known private music school and also very good.

Yuki had the biggest adjustment when we came back from the United States. In America, everybody played after school, so I let her do the same thing. But here all the children go to *okeiko goto* after school, and in the beginning it was torture for her.

At first her level of piano was very low. I had to push her very hard. She had *okeiko goto* five times a week: lessons in piano, ear-training, English, singing, and swimming. We did too much. Maybe we overdid it. But we settled in after a few years. Really it was a new life for us, after eight years in America.

After living in America, I could see many things more clearly in Japan. When you live in a foreign country, you don't necessarily get to know that country, but you do get to know your own country. There's a saying that the frog in the well doesn't know the ocean. He can't see the world very clearly. He believes he's the only one in the world. When I talk to housewives here, I've found that they don't think about the rest of the world at all. They just think about their children. They should know that the world is bigger. Japan is only an island.

CELL PHONES

Editor's Introduction: Cell phones are at least as common in Japan as in the United States. There, too, there is a generational issue: the younger the cohort, the heavier the use. To cite my own case, I don't own a cell phone and have trouble using one (if a friend offers it to me to use); in my survey course at the University of Massachusetts Amherst, I require the students to sign a sheet that includes a promise to turn off cell phones (and pagers and wrist-watch beepers) during class.

Are there cultural factors in the use of cell phones? Or is the technology itself so dominant that it reduces cultural factors to virtual insignificance? The survey of children's views includes questions we might ask ourselves before looking at the Japanese results. [53]

IN JAPAN IN 2003, 44% of males and 45% of females between the ages of ten and nineteen owned cell phones that can take photographs. That figure compares with 26% of the total population. For people in their sixties, the comparable figures are 12% of the males and 7% of the females. A survey of 1998 found that 58% of people in big cities use cell phones, while 41% of people in rural areas do so.

Here are some comments by users:

Girl (junior in high school):
The cell phone really is convenient. It's a voice medium for people who want to talk, a text medium for people who want to write, and a graphic medium for photographs. It accommodates users' tastes.

Boy (junior):
A lifestyle with cell phone is so natural that one without cell phones, or one from which cell phones have been taken away, sounds unreal.

Girl (high school student):

Q. In what sorts of places and situations do you use your phone a lot?

A. *At school, during class. I leave my phone on my desk, and it vibes.*

Q. Your teacher doesn't care?

A. *Well, the teacher pretty much knows. He doesn't do anything about it.*

Q. Really? You can leave it out?

A. *Everyone has them out. Some kids even let their phones ring, and the teacher is like, "Hey, it's ringing..." I think this is just our school.*

Q. Do you take voice calls during class?

A. *No. That would be going too far.*

Q. Oh, so you wouldn't answer. What kinds of exchanges do you have over e-mail during class? Do you send e-mail to people sitting in the same classroom?

A. *Yes, I do that, too.*

Q. What do you say?

A. *"This is boring."*

Q. And you get a reply?

A. *Yes.*

Q. When you write your e-mail, do you hide what you're doing?

A. *Yes. When the teacher is facing the blackboard, I type it in quickly.*

Illustration by Roger Dahl.

17-year-old boy, summer 1998:

Your cell phone can do voice and also send text, right? Do you use text messaging?

Yes, I do.

Which do you use more, voice or text?

I use text more.

Why is that?

I use text for simple things that are not worth a phone call.

How many messages do you send a day?

Well, only about five or six.

20-year-old woman, college student:

What do you think are the situations and places in which cell phones shouldn't be used?

On the train, I try not to make voice calls.

What if you get a call?

I do answer it.

When that happens, do you, like, try to appear apologetic? Maybe cover your mouth with your hand?

Yes.

If people around you started glancing at you, would that bother you?

Hmm. Probably if somebody looked at me, I would stop.

If another passenger is making a voice call, what do you think?

Hmm. If they talk just for a short time in an apologetic way, I think maybe that's okay? But if there is, like, a high school girl talking in a way loud voice, then it pisses me off. I think they should cut it out.

Video Game Consoles

Sony's PlayStation 2 was the most used video game console last month, according to a new tracking system by Nielsen Media Research. The system accounted for 42% of total time spent by console users on video games in June, Nielsen said. Microsoft's Xbox...was second with 17 %.

Source: *Boston Globe Wire Services*, July 27, 2007.

Newspaper comment, 1997:
On a train on my way home from work, a young man, probably a student, is talking loudly and at length on his cell phone. I reprimand him. To my surprise, he says into the phone, "Some weird old guy just said something to me" and continues his conversation.... He was still talking as he got off the train at the next station.

From a survey of children's views (199 boys, 265 girls; 165 5th and 6th graders, 266 junior high school students):

"I think cell phones should not be used on train or bus." Agreed: 84%, with little difference between boys and girls or between 5th-6th graders and students in junior high.

"I feel better if cell phones allow me to make calls at any time." 43% of boys and 54% of girls agreed; 44% of grade-schoolers, 53% of junior high students agreed.

"It makes me happy to think I'll always be getting phone calls." 34% of boys, 54% of girls agreed; 47% of grade-schoolers, 44% of junior high students agreed.

"I feel safer alone at night if I have a cell phone." 29% of boys, 40% of girls agreed; 33% of grade-schoolers, 39% of junior high students agreed.

"Owning a cell phone makes me feel grown up." 35% of boys, 37% of girls agreed; 42% of grade-schoolers, 29% of junior high students agreed.

"I can keep secrets from my parents with a cell phone." 24% of boys, 31% of girls agreed; 18% of grade-schoolers, 29% of junior high students agreed.
"I feel self-conscious having a cell phone." 10% of boys, 7% of girls agreed; 10% of grade-schoolers, 7% of junior high students agreed.

"There's no need to worry about being bullied when I have a cell phone." 3% of boys, 4% of girls agreed; 4% of grade-schoolers, 3% of junior high students agreed.

From a recent U.S. discussion of cell phones:[54]
"Some [experts] theorize that constant use becomes ritualistic physical behavior, even addiction, the absorption of nervous energy, like chomping gum.... Interaction with a device delivering data gives a feeling of validation, inclusion, and desirability. (It's no fun to be the only un-pinged person in the room.)

"It's random reinforcement," James E. Katz, director of the Center for Mobile Computing at Rutgers University, says. "The fact that you don't know when important news will come," he said, "means you will quickly engage in obsessive compulsive behavior." [Another expert] uses the term 'acquired attention deficit disorder'.

"Sometimes the habit is there even when the device isn't. Users talk of phantom urges, like (no kidding) the feeling of a hip vibrating, as if to suggest a belt-hooked BlackBerry is buzzing when, in fact, the person is in the shower."

THE OTARU
HOT SPRINGS CASE
AND
DISCRIMINATION
AGAINST "FOREIGNERS"
IN JAPAN

Editor's Introduction: The author of this essay, Arudou Debito, was born in the United States but moved to Japan in the late 1980s. He is a teacher. His former American name is David Aldwinckle. Aldwinckle requires a multi-syllable transliteration into Japanese (A-ru-do-u-i-n-ku-ru), so he shortened it to Arudou. De-bi-to is phonetic for David.

The issue this essay treats became prominent in the late 1990s. Otaru is a port on Japan's northern island of Hokkaido, so sailors from Russia were the immediate issue. But the assumption that there are clear distinctions between "Japanese" and "foreigners" is widespread in Japan. Arudou has published a book about this experience: *Japanese Only.*

(Many Japanese visit Amherst, Massachusetts, where I live because of ties that are now over a century old. Occasionally, a person on campus will ask a Japanese visitor, "How do I get to the Campus Center?" Astonished, he later asks me, "Can't they see I'm a foreigner?" No, I respond, they can't. In the U.S., citizenship isn't a matter of physical appearance.)

Public baths have been a custom in Japan for centuries. It's cheaper to pay the bath fee than to heat your home bath, and communal baths are an exercise in community living. Japan also has many hot springs. In both baths and hot springs, bathers strip and enter a room with sinks, faucets, and flexible shower hoses. Soaping and rinsing take place before the bathers enter the large sunken communal tub that holds very hot water. The bathers sink in—if they can stand the heat—up to their chins.

For a photo archive on the hot springs issue, see http://www.debito.org/roguesgallery.html. [55]

IN 1993, A HOT SPRING in the city of Otaru decided it had had enough of Russian sailors not following bathhouse rules. The managers put up signs saying "JAPANESE ONLY," and refused entry to all foreigners. Those excluded complained about this situation for years, but Otaru city officials ignored the situation. They admitted that this activity was discrimination, but they maintained they had no power to stop it. After all, discrimination was not specifically illegal in Japan, and they considered it "too early" to legislate against it.

Emboldened, other hot springs around town put up their own "Japanese Only" signs. Then other businesses—bars, restaurants, ramen shacks, even a barber and a sports shop—in other towns followed suit.

In September 1999 we came on the scene. Several multinational families (German, American, and Chinese, all with Japanese spouses) and I dropped by as customers at the original exclusionary hot springs. The managers refused entry only to the Caucasians in our contingent. The reason they gave: "Russian sailors disobey our bathing rules. They drive away our Japanese customers."

"But we are not Russian sailors," we replied. "Also, we have lived here for more than a decade each. We have Japanese families. We know how to take baths."

"Doesn't matter," they retorted. "Refusing only Russians would be blatant discrimination. So we refuse all foreigners equally."

"Including our Chinese friend you just unwittingly let in?" we asked. Quick to admit their "mistake," they tossed her out. So, since they were judging "foreign" by appearance, we asked what would happen to our children. Born and raised here, they are full Japanese citizens. The answer: "Asian-looking kids can come in. But we will have to refuse foreign-looking ones."

Thus racial discrimination was afoot. Managers would admit foreigners who look Japanese but bar Japanese who look foreign. We decided from that moment on to fight this policy. Over the next year we tried every possible way to abolish it. However, press coverage from the case, as well as a concurrent police campaign against an alleged rise in foreign crime, prompted businesses nationwide to adopt their own exclusionary policies. In October 2000 I became a Japanese citizen. Proof of naturalization in hand, I returned to Otaru. Guess what? One hot spring named Yunohana still refused me. Their reason this time: "Even if you're a citizen, you still don't look Japanese. Our customers won't understand. Goodbye."

That made the evidence incontrovertible. There was nothing left but for my friends and me to sue the proprietor for racial discrimination. We also sued the Otaru City Government for turning a blind eye to it for nearly a decade. In 2002 and 2004 the Sapporo lower and high courts handed down the following decisions: Yunohana Hot Springs was to pay each plaintiff $10,000. Its actions not only constituted racial discrimination but also "transcended the boundaries of socially-acceptable rational discrimination," whatever that means. Anyway, we won.

However, we lost against the city of Otaru. Even though the United Nations Convention on Racial Discrimination (a treaty Japan signed in 1995) requires "immediate and effective measures" by all levels of government to eliminate racial discrimination, the courts ruled otherwise: "The treaty says nothing concrete about how legislation is to be created. We interpret this to mean that there is no absolute duty to establish anti-discrimination laws in specific, and the government cannot be held culpable for neglecting to do so."

No other developed country has made so ludicrous an argument to escape these treaty obligations, and thus Japan remains the only developed country with no laws whatsoever against racial discrimination.

The case against the Otaru city government then went up to the Supreme Court, which ruled against us in April 2005. It claimed that this case "did not involve any constitutional issues." We respectfully disagree and will now bring this issue before the United Nations. But while we're waiting, let's think about why the Otaru case became such a major issue. There are three cultural misconceptions in Japan that evoke public sympathy and give license to xenophobes:

1. "Japan is unique." Of course, people apply this to public baths, too. After all, no other country has a bathing culture. That is, if you leave out Italy, Turkey, Germany, Bulgaria, Russia, Britain, and most of Scandinavia...

   Um, okay, maybe not "unique," but Japan is always different. So foreigners, you see, will naturally be ignorant of Japanese customs and inevitably cause trouble when they walk into a Japanese public bath or hot spring. Never mind that there are also ill-mannered Japanese and that foreigners can be taught how to bathe.

2. "Japanese is a difficult language." How many times have we heard, despite copious counter-evidence, that Japanese is impossible for non-natives to learn? After all, Japanese is supposed to be one of the world's toughest tongues. So, since foreigners by definition will not know the rules, hot springs managers who speak only Japanese can't possibly communicate with them.

Never mind that bathhouses around the country post signs with the rules in many languages—foreigners shouldn't be in here anyway, you see, if there's a possibility of trouble.

3. "You can tell foreigners on sight." Wrong. Especially nowadays, with record numbers of international marriages, multicultural children, and when Asian and non-citizens of Japanese ethnicity make up the majority of registered foreigners in Japan. But given the stereotype of "foreigner" as Caucasian teacher of English conversation, many people continue to confuse nationality and race, thus ignoring Japan's current diversity.

This is the situation my friends and I are trying to rectify by promoting the passage of anti-discrimination laws and challenging blatantly discriminatory actions in the courts. Like it or not, laws are the only way to stop the bigots—they exist in every society—from having their way.

X
JAPANESE
AMERICANS

THE GOVERNOR
AND THE JAPANESE
AMERICANS

Editor's Introduction: There are today nearly 1,200,000 Americans of Japanese descent, in whole or in part. Sixty percent were born in the United States and are U.S. citizens; an additional ten percent were born abroad but are now naturalized citizens.

Americans of Japanese descent once formed the second largest bloc of Asian minority groups in the U.S, second only to those of Chinese descent. But today they rank sixth, behind those of Chinese, Filipino, Asian Indian, Vietnamese, and Korean descent. Among Asian minority groups, Americans of Japanese descent have the largest percentage born in the U.S., the largest percentage of homes where only English is spoken, the highest median family income.

However, the road has not been easy. Unlike immigrants from white countries, Japanese Americans were visibly distinct from the majority. Moreover, Japanese Americans or their ancestors came to the U.S. from a country with which the U.S. fought a bitter war (later Asian immigrants, most notably those of Korean, Vietnamese, and Cambodian descent, came to the U.S. in the wake of wars in which they sided with the U.S.). These two factors combined to make the history of Japanese Americans a difficult one.

For all practical purposes, immigration from Japan began around 1890. The Japanese Americans settled mainly in California, and white Californians did not welcome them.

In February 1905, the California legislature passed unanimously a resolution asking Congress to limit Japanese immigration. One passage from that act declared:

> Japanese laborers, by reason of race habits, mode of living, disposition and general characteristics, are undesirable.

... Japanese ... do not buy land [or] build or buy houses.... They contribute nothing to the growth of the state. They add nothing to its wealth, and they are a blight on the prosperity of it and a great and impending danger to its welfare.

In 1906, the San Francisco school board attempted to exclude Japanese American children from the regular public schools, but the intervention of President Theodore Roosevelt (he was worried about Japan's hostile reaction) led the board to relent. In 1913, the California legislature passed a law preventing "aliens ineligible for citizenship"—meaning Chinese and Japanese—from owning land. In 1919 the American Legion and the California Federation of Labor were among the founders of the Oriental Exclusion League.

Finally, in 1924, the U.S. Congress passed an immigration act (the "National Origins Act"), which set up quotas for each nationality. These quotas were based on the census of 1890, before the heavy immigration from eastern and southern Europe had begun. Thus the quotas effectively restricted immigration from these areas. But for China and Japan there was not even a quota!

The following selection is a letter from the Governor of California to the Secretary of State of the United States, written in 1920. At the time, the tone of this letter was not considered particularly harsh or intemperate. [56]

STATE OF CALIFORNIA
GOVERNOR'S OFFICE

Sacramento, June 19, 1929

Hon. Bainbridge Colby,

Secretary of State,

Washington, D. C.

SIR: I have the honor to transmit herewith the official report prepared and filed with me by the State Board of Control of California on the subject of Oriental immigration, population, and land ownership.

Twenty years ago our Japanese population was nominal. Ten years ago the census reports of the United States government showed a Japanese population in California of 41,356. A survey and computation recently made by the Board of Control of the State of California indicates that at the present time this Japanese population has been more than doubled—it amounting now to 87,279....

The Japanese in our midst have indicated a strong trend to land ownership and land control, and by their unquestioned industry and application, and by standards and methods that are widely separated from our occidental standards and methods, both in connection with hours of labor and standards of living, have gradually developed to a control of many of our important agricultural industries. Indeed, at the present time they operate 458,056 acres of the very best lands in California. The increase in acreage control within the last decade, according to these official figures, has been 412.9 percent. In productive values—that is to say, in the market value of crops produced by them—our figures show that as against $6,235,856 worth of produce marketed in 1909, the increase has been to $67,145,730, approximately tenfold.

More significant than these figures, however, is the demonstrated fact that within the last ten years Japanese agricultural labor has developed to such a degree that at the present time between 80 and 90 percent of most of our vegetable and berry products are those of the Japanese farms. Approximately 80 percent of the tomato crop of the state is produced by Japanese; from 80 to 100 percent of the spinach crop; a greater part of our potato and asparagus crops, and so on. So that it is apparent without much more effective restrictions, in a very short time, historically speaking, the Japanese population within our midst will represent a considerable portion of our entire population, and the Japanese control over certain essential food products will be an absolute one.

These Japanese, by very reason of their use of economic standards impossible to our white ideals—that is to say, the employment of their wives and their very children in the arduous toil of the soil—are proving crushing competitors to our white rural populations. The fecundity of the Japanese race far exceeds that of any other people that we have in our midst. They send their children for short periods of time to our white schools, and in many of the country schools of our state the spectacle is presented of having a few white children acquiring their education in classrooms crowded with Japanese. The deep-seated and often outspoken resentment of our white mothers at this situation can only be appreciated by those people who have struggled with similar problems.

It is with great pride that I am able to state that the people of California have borne this situation and seen its developing menace with a patience and self-restraint beyond all praise. California is proud to proclaim to the nation that despite this social situation her people have been guilty of no excesses and no indignities upon the Japanese within our borders. No outrage, no violence, no insult, and no ignominy have been offered to the Japanese people within California.

It is also proper to state that I believe I speak the feelings of our people when I express to you a full recognition of the many admirable qualities of the Japanese people. We assume no arrogant superiority of race or culture over them. Their art, their literature, their philosophy, and, in recent years, their scientific attainments have gained for them a respect from the white peoples in which we, who know them so well, fully share.... We respect the right of the Japanese to their true development and to the attainment of their destiny.

All these matters I am at pains to emphasize so as to convince you, and through you the people of our United States, that this problem of ours is not an insignificant or temporary one. It is not factious. It has no origin in narrow race prejudice or rancor or hostility. It is, however, a solemn problem affecting our entire Occidental civilization. It has nothing to do with any pretensions of race superiority, but has vitally to do with race dissimilarity and unassimilability.

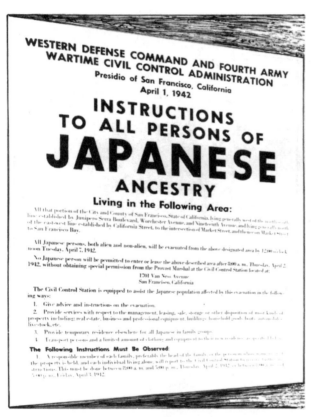

The attitudes represented in the governor's letter led to the forcible removal of all Japanese-Americans from the West Coast after Pearl Harbor. Photo froom the Franklin D. Roosevelt Lirbrary.

But with all this the people of California are determined to repress a developing Japanese community within our midst. They are determined to exhaust every power in their keeping to maintain this state for its own people. This determination is based fundamentally upon the ethnological impossibility of assimilating the Japanese people and the consequential alternative of increasing a population whose very race isolation must be fraught with the gravest consequences.

California stands as an outpost on the western edge of Occidental civilization. Her people are the sons or the followers of the Argonauts who wended their way westward over the plains of the Middle West, the Rocky Mountains, and the desert; and here they set up their homes and planted their flags; and here, without themselves recognizing it at the time, they took the farthest westward step that the white man can take. From our shores roll the waters of the Pacific. From our coast the mind's eye takes its gaze and sees on the other shores of that great ocean the teeming millions of the Orient, with its institutions running their roots into the most venerable antiquity, its own inherited philosophy and standards of life, its own peculiar races and colors.

The Pacific, we feel, is shortly to become one of the most important highways of commerce on this earth. Amity and concord and that interchange of material goods as well as ideas, which such facilities offer, will inevitably take place to the benefit of both continents. But that our white race will readily intermix with the yellow strains of Asia, and that out of this interrelationship shall be born a new composite human being is manifestly impossible. Singularly enough, while historical facts are not always susceptible of scientific demonstration, it is true, if our study serves us, that the blood fusion of the Occident and the Orient has nowhere ever successfully taken place. Whether the cause be but a social sense of repugnance, or whether it be insuperable scientific hindrances, is utterly beside the question....

California harbors no animosity against the Japanese people or their nation. California, however, does not wish the Japanese people to settle within her borders and to develop a Japanese population within her midst. California views with alarm the rapid growth of these people within the last decade in population as well as in land control, and foresees in the not distant future the gravest menace of serious conflict if this development is not immediately and effectively checked. Without disparaging these people of just sensibilities, we cannot look for intermarriage or that social interrelationship which must exist between the citizenry of a contented community.

It may be an exquisite refinement, but we cannot feel contented at our children imbibing their first rudiments of education from the lips of the public school teacher in classrooms crowded with other children of a different race. They do not and will not associate in that relationship prevalent elsewhere in the public schools of this country. We recognize that this attitude is too deep-seated to remove. And we recognize that with this attitude goes the necessity of Japanese isolation and that inevitable feeling which socially a proscribed race always develops.

California wants peace. But California wants to retain this commonwealth for her own peoples where they may grow up and develop their own ideals....

California is making this appeal primarily, of course, for herself, but in doing so she feels that the problem is hers solely because of her geographical position on the Pacific slope. She stands as one of the gateways for Oriental immigration into this country. Her people are the first affected, and unless the race ideals and standards are preserved here at the national gateway the conditions that will follow must soon affect the rest of the continent.

I trust that I have clearly presented the California point of view, and that in any correspondence or negotiations with Japan which may ensue as the result of the accompanying report, or any action which the people of the state of California may take thereon, you will understand that it is based entirely on the principle of race self-preservation and the ethnological impossibility of successfully assimilating this constantly increasing flow of Oriental blood.

I have the honor to remain,

Yours very respectfully,

WM. D. STEPHENS *Governor of California*

REMEMBER
PEARL HARBOR,
AND THEN ...

PART I

Editor's Introduction: Here is one Japanese American's recollection of his own wartime experience. Hiroshi's father was an immigrant, born in Japan. His older brother had returned to Japan for his education. Consequently, Hiroshi's experience was hardly typical of the Japanese American community. In particular, his family is set apart from most Japanese American families by their strong sympathy for Japan. [57]

WORLD WAR II CAME to the Japanese of Guadalupe like a hammer blow. Within hours after the attack on Pearl Harbor clusters of FBI agents had arrived at this small farming town in California's Santa Maria Valley. Swiftly, silently, they sealed off the town, cut telephone lines to Japanese homes and spirited off a score of Japanese leaders. They left as swiftly and as mysteriously as they had come, leaving behind a stunned community.

Hiroshi's father was one of those they had taken away. But it had happened so suddenly, so unexpectedly, that the boy was overcome more by bewilderment than sorrow. As for the war, the very magnitude of the catastrophe gave it a dream-like quality. It was only perhaps four months later, when the sheriff came to their house, that events were reduced to dimensions comprehensible to a nine-year-old boy.

The sheriff, a bluff, bulb-nosed Irishman, was something of a celebrity in Guadalupe. He was acknowledged, even by adults, as the toughest man in town, and his exploits in singlehandedly breaking up barroom brawls had been retold until they had become legendary. The presence of such a personage in their parlor, it seemed to Hiroshi, must mean that extraordinary events were in the offing. Indeed, the sheriff was saying the Japanese would have to leave California

Japanese Americans and their belongings face U.S. troops at one evacuation center. Photo from the War Relocation Authority.

and explaining how the evacuation would be accomplished. Changes, some big, some subtle, followed the sheriff's visit. Strangers came knocking at the door, expressing interest in tools and furniture advertised for sale. Hiroshi, like most Japanese children, now wore cowboy boots. His mother had bought them along with canteens, knapsacks and pith helmets in preparation for whatever wilderness was in store for them. Teachers were more lenient now and apt to overlook lapses in discipline that previously might have brought a sharp whack of a ruler across the wrist. But the children, too, perhaps a bit self-conscious, were better behaved.

Mrs. A., the sixth-grade teacher, even dropped by the house. Her presence in the house was even more alarming than that of the sheriff had been. She was a huge, formidable woman, and next to the principal she was the most feared person in the grammar school. Hiroshi was too young for Mrs. A.'s class, but he had seen her often enough, striding through the school grounds, a yardstick in hand, to break up a fight. The sight of her was enough to make even the innocent quake, and the crowd would quickly part to give her wide passage.

All of Hiroshi's brothers and sisters had gone through Mrs. A.'s class, and at least one of his brothers had felt the sting of her yardstick. So Hiroshi was not prepared for the sight of Mrs. A. tearfully shaking hands with them. And before he could recover from his shock, she descended upon him, swooped him up in her powerful arms and pressed him against her massive bosom.

It seemed to Hiroshi that these were symptoms of catastrophic times. Somehow the world as he knew it had gone askew. The sheriff and Mrs. A. were not strangers. In their own milieu they were as familiar as Mr. Yamada, the grocer. But now they were not staying in their accustomed places, nor were they behaving in their accustomed ways. For Guadalupe was divided into three distinct communities—the white, the Mexican and the Japanese—and the three mixed only in certain places, like the school, and even then to a very limited degree.

The Japanese community was completely self-contained. It had its own shops, farmers' association, women's club, movie theater, gambling hall, restaurants and brothels. For the children there was the Japanese school at the Buddhist church, which they attended every day after regular school was over.

At home and in the Japanese community Hiroshi learned of the divinity of the Emperor. At the American school he learned that George Washington was the father of our country and that Abraham Lincoln freed the slaves. In the newspapers and on the radio he learned that Joe Louis was a credit to his race. In Japanese community meetings he enthusiastically shouted "banzai" [long live!] to the Emperor, and at school daily pledged allegiance to the flag of the United States.

At home he heard again and again how Admiral Togo destroyed the Russian fleet and, like any Japanese schoolboy, knew by heart the inspirational message the Admiral sent to his men before the battle. He was also told that President Roosevelt was a great man, and when he spoke on the radio the family gathered in the living room to listen. The only other time the whole family listened to the radio was when Joe Louis fought.

In the alleys and junk yards of Guadalupe and in the surrounding woods and pastures, the cry of "Hi-yo, Silver!" followed by the staccato of mock gunplay was as common an occurrence as a duel between two silent samurai, leering ... over their wooden swords. It was not uncommon to see a Japanese boy with a six-shooter strapped to his belt on one side and two wooden swords stuck in his belt on the other.

If there was conflict in this reckless mixture of East and West, it went largely unnoticed in the joyful thoughtlessness of childish minds. For the mixture was complete. An after school snack could just as easily be a riceball wrapped in sea-weed as a peanut-butter-and-jam sandwich. And peanuts, hot dogs and ham-burgers were just as great a treat as *sushi* [rice balls, usually with raw fish] and chicken teriyaki.

When Japan attacked Pearl Harbor, Hiroshi's father came home to give the news to the family. He was jubilant. He said all the men gathered at the farmers' association meeting house and cheered. His mother said it was very foolish of them to have done so. Hiroshi didn't understand why the greatest nation in the world would attack the United States, the country with the Declaration of In-dependence, the Constitution, George Washington, Abraham Lincoln, Presi-dent Roosevelt and Joe Louis. He saw the look in his mother's eyes and the furrows in her brow and he knew that all was not well.

Hiroshi's father was arrested by the FBI that very night, and the family was not to see him again until shortly before the end of the war. The family received a solemn letter of farewell a week after his arrest. He had written it from a jail cell, where, fed on bread and water, he had waited, fully expecting to be executed. That he was soon removed to an Army camp where he received good treatment was one of the few pleasant surprises the white man had given him during the 40 years he had been in the United States.

Hiroshi's father was one of many *issei* (first-generation) leaders who were ar-rested and segregated during most of the war. They had never felt any loyalty to the United States, which denied them citizenship, land ownership and the li-cense to engage in most professions. They had professed their loyalty to Japan openly and with bravado, and had contributed heavily over the years to the Japanese war chest from their earnings in the United States. For them it was an act as natural and patriotic as Americans buying defense bonds.

Hiroshi, like most Japanese children, had done his part. He saved aluminum foil from candy bar and cigarette wrappers and rolled them in a ball. When the ball reached the size of a grapefruit, it was sent to Japan to be used for making aircraft.

After the war broke out, however, it seemed just as natural to buy U.S. De-fense stamps, and Hiroshi did so at school and at the post office where a poster showed Hitler saying: "Today Germany, tomorrow the world." Hiroshi's brother, home from the university for the Christmas holidays, would always say it in Ger-man as he passed the poster and only laughed when Hiroshi pleaded with him to stop it. Another poster showed three rats with the faces of Hitler, Mussolini and Tojo. The inclusion of Tojo disturbed him, and he repeatedly asked his mother if Tojo-daijin [cabinet minister] was evil.

As the war progressed, Japanese victories in the Pacific brought fear of sabotage, espionage and fifth-column activity and shrill demands for exclusion of Japanese from the West Coast. The evacuation order came in March of 1942 from Lieutenant General J. L. DeWitt, commander of the Western Defense Command, who echoed what had become the prevailing view, "A Jap is a Jap; it makes no difference whether he's an American or not."

Japanese countered feebly with the whispered epithet, "Nit-wit DeWitt," but made no great protest against the evacuation. Within 90 days 110,000 Japanese—including 70,000 U.S. citizens—living in California, Oregon and Washington, were shipped to concentration camps.

Dr. Seuss and the Internment of Americans
of Japanese Descent

We've already seen two wartime cartoons from the pen of Dr. Seuss. Here is a third. It appeared on February 3, 1942, days before President Franklin Delano Roosevelt ordered the rounding up of Americans of Japanese descent living on the West Coast.

What is Dr. Seuss saying here? Is this cartoon tongue-in-cheek? Or is it straight? Does Dr. Seuss favor "internment" or oppose it? Is he criticizing racism against the Japanese American community or embodying it? Does your argument about this cartoon draw on your interpretation of the two earlier cartoons?

Compare this cartoon with Hiroshi's experience. How do their impacts differ? Why?

Source: Richard H. Minear, *Dr. Seuss Goes To War* (New Press, 1999).

REMEMBER PEARL HARBOR, AND THEN ...

PART II

Editor's Introduction: In the preceding selection, Hiroshi learned of the Japanese attack on Pearl Harbor and saw his father arrested. He also learned of the decision to seize all Japanese Americans on the West Coast and ship them to "relocation centers" well inland.

Here, Hiroshi's story continues as his family travels—under guard—to an "assembly center," from which they ultimately travel to a "relocation center" in Arizona. [58]

THE TRAIN WAS CROWDED AND STUFFY. Huge American M.P.'s sat in the rear of each car. Hiroshi didn't remember much about the trip later on except that when they ate in the dining car, the Negro waiters were surly and the Japanese didn't get the same things as the soldiers. The soldiers got eggs, sunny side up, and ham for breakfast. The Japanese got eggs, too, but they were scrambled and looked like custard; they got no ham.

Their destination was Tulare, California. The race track there had been converted to a temporary camp with hurriedly constructed barracks....

The camp was enclosed with two barbed-wire fences about 10 feet high. Armed sentries patrolled the area between the two fences. Children at first stood by the fence and called out, "Hi!" to the soldiers, but they looked straight ahead and didn't reply. So the children soon didn't pay much attention to them. Towers were constructed along the perimeter of the camp. Each was manned by soldiers armed with a machine gun and searchlight. At night the lights would poke their big yellow beams along the barbed-wire fences.

One boy, about 20 years old, escaped anyway. It was said he did it on a $5 bet. He was caught trying to crawl back into camp after having attended a movie in town. The next morning he came to the mess hall for breakfast handcuffed to a

303

At the relocation camp at Manzanar, California, Japanese Americans celebrate Memorial Day. Photo from the Franklin D. Roosevelt Library.

white man, but he was soon released without further punishment. He was one of the first to volunteer for the Army when Japanese were allowed to do so and was killed in action.

The stay in Tulare was short. As Japanese were shipped to the "assembly centers," such as Tulare, more permanent "relocation centers" were already going up in the wilderness areas in the interior of the country. Hiroshi and his family were destined for a camp in Arizona.

The move to Tulare had had a touch of adventure, but Arizona seemed forbidding. The area, it was said, was infested with rattlesnakes, poisonous lizards, scorpions and centipedes. The three-day train trip, through endless stretches of wasteland, was not reassuring. The last part of the trip was by bus. It was a long ride, sufficiently long to impress upon all their utter isolation. There were no barbed-wire fences around this camp. None was needed.

The family was assigned the number 72-12-A upon their arrival, which meant block 72, barrack 12, compartment A. They were taken there by an Army truck. They had to put handkerchiefs over their mouths and noses as the dust from the unpaved roads swirled into the canvas-topped truck. The camp was still incomplete, and reminded Hiroshi of ghost towns he had seen in Western movies. But unlike the drab, tarpaper barracks of Tulare, the barracks here were made of white plasterboard. They also had red roofs, giving the camp a bright, clean appearance. Everyone was hungry during the first months. Children filched potatoes from the warehouse whenever they got a chance. They would pack them in mud and bake them in the desert. Stealing, if it was from government stores, was not only acceptable, it seemed to be everyone's primary occupation during the first weeks. Adults made nightly raids on government lumber supplies, with which they made furniture, shelves and closets.

Political activity was fierce during the first year of internment. The arrest and removal of *issei* leaders earlier in the war had left the Japanese community politically amorphous [without form]. But as new leadership emerged, the community was polarized into pro-American and pro-Japanese factions. The second generation *nisei* leadership advocated loyalty to the United States and clamored for an opportunity to serve in the Armed Forces. The *kibei* (those educated in Japan) urged renunciation of U.S. citizenship.

The fight was bitter and exploded at times into violence. Saburo Kido, then president of the pro-American Japanese American Citizens League, was ambushed one night by some toughs who beat him so severely that he had to be hospitalized.

Many families were split by the issue. Hiroshi's oldest brother was a *kibei* and a member of the clandestine pro-Japanese organization in camp. Two younger brothers, products of American schools and universities, had cast their lots with the United States, a decision made without hesitation, but not without emotional conflict. The bad feelings generated during this time were to last for the war's duration.

Hiroshi tried not to pay much attention to this conflict, but the issues remained in the back of his mind and troubled him. One morning when he stepped outside his barracks he saw that during the night someone had erected a large Japanese flag atop the butte overlooking the camp. Everybody pointed to it and laughed, for it had the appearance of a schoolboy prank. Hiroshi laughed too, but the sight filled him with foreboding.

It was only a few days later that the government rounded up known hardcore, pro-Japan agitators and placed them in segregated camps. Hiroshi's oldest brother was one of those arrested. He was taken away during the night, quickly and quietly, just as his father had been earlier. The family later learned he was in a camp in Utah.

By February of 1943, *nisei* were allowed to volunteer for military service, and one of Hiroshi's brothers enlisted in the Army, despite the pleadings of his mother. His other brother, after pleading his loyalty to the United States, was allowed to go to St. Louis to work and soon was drafted.

With the departure of the political activists, the camp settled down to a humdrum life. Food supplies by then were sufficient, even abundant, and living quarters were decorated with curtains and furnished with self-made dressers, tables, chairs and other household amenities.

As physical needs were satisfied, the greatest hardship became boredom. Men went foraging in the desert for semi-petrified wood, with which they made various artifacts. Knitting was the chief pastime of women. They were able to order wool from mail order houses, and some of the more skilled women conducted classes. Jobs were available in the mess halls, hospital, school and administrative offices. The skilled workers, such as doctors, dentists and teachers, received $19 a month. The others received $16.

Nisei pledging loyalty to the United States were allowed to leave the camp to find work or to go to college in the East. The camp, thus reduced to mostly old people and children, was cut off from world events, but the realities of war intruded at times. In some quarters gold-star flags hung from crudely fashioned family altars, before which mothers would kneel and present offerings of rice.

The gold-star mothers, however, found some solace not available to others with sons in the Army. For these *issei* women, convinced that Japan would win the war, were caught in a nightmare in which their sons were fighting for a country doomed to defeat. Hiroshi's mother, like most others, turned her effort to the children still in her care. Every day she would save her share of bread from the mess tables, dry it in the sun and store it in paper bags. Food supplies would most likely be cut off when the United States began losing the war, she reasoned.

Hiroshi went to a school staffed by white and *nisei* teachers. His mother tried to instruct him at home in Japanese but could not rekindle her child's interest. She finally gave up with a sigh. For Hiroshi, camp was not unlike summer camp or a vacation trailer court where living is reduced to essentials and the lack of luxuries only adds to the fun. He joined the Cub Scouts, played football and baseball according to the season, and during this three-and-a-half-year stay, he had learned to love the desert wilderness, spotted with sagebrush, prickly mesquites and the trident-shaped saguaro cactuses, standing like sentinels across the landscape.

But the war was coming to an end and the thought of returning to his old home, the memory of which had steadily faded, brought little pleasure. Japanese who had already returned to the West Coast had been greeted with "Japs Keep Out" signs. Vigilante-type groups had fired into Japanese homes. Hiroshi's father was reunited with his family when the war ended, but the family was scattered far apart by then. It was only Hiroshi and his now-aging parents who had the long trip home.

Guadalupe was even more desolate than he remembered it, and considerably smaller. A bowling alley had gone up on Main Street, reflecting the wartime boom, but that seemed to be the extent of the change. It was put up by a Portuguese man who before the war had worked for Hiroshi's father. He had prospered during the war.

Their home was still standing, in woeful condition, but the family, prepared for the worst, was happy to see the house there at all. The community, though reserved, showed no open hostility. Once a husky Mexican boy stopped Hiroshi on the street and said, "You dirty, yellow Jap." But when Hiroshi walked away he was not molested further.

Hiroshi's parents found work as laborers, and white employers who recalled that his father was once one of the biggest farmers in the area, greeted him without condescension. A few *issei* reestablished their farms and businesses, others were scattered throughout the United States living with their children; some had died. It was clear that the Japanese community would never be the same, self-contained society that existed before the war. The war had not only crumbled the Japanese empire, but also the fabric of Japanese life in America.

In Hiroshi's family, as in virtually all Japanese families, the household had passed by now from the first generation to the second, from Japanese to American culture. While there was still Japanese spoken, it was only between Hiroshi's parents and their children. They spoke in halting English with their grandchildren and often needed an interpreter. Before the war, the main language of family life as well as social and business intercourse had been Japanese. Now the language and its attendant culture remained but a minor and moribund adjunct to family life. The final result of the war, ironically, was greater acceptance of the Japanese by the white society and the disintegration of the Japanese community.

Hiroshi's parents accepted the change quietly. When naturalization privileges were extended to Orientals in 1952, they became citizens of the United States. As for Hiroshi, the war had brought to the surface the hidden conflict between East and West. The West had prevailed, and all that is Japanese was to fade farther and farther away until it was irrevocably lost to him and his descendants.

DISAFFECTION

Editor's Introduction: Some 117,000 Japanese Americans were "relocated," like Hiroshi. Of these, 5,000 requested during the war that they be sent to Japan. Who in 1942 would choose life in Japan over life in America? Perhaps those who were not American citizens (they and their small children made up the majority of the returnees), but American citizens? Here is the explanation of one who decided to renounce his American citizenship and return to Japan. [59]

I FEEL THAT I'VE MADE EVERY ATTEMPT to identify myself with this country and its people. But every time I've tried, I've got another boot in the rear.

Why, when I was a kid I went around with Caucasians almost entirely. I'll admit that most of them were pretty nice to me and treated me like anyone else. But even during the time when I was a kid there were incidents that were hard to take. Let me give you an example. I belonged to a Boy Scout troop. Nearly all the members were Caucasians. I and another fellow were the only Japanese. We lived near Vernon and there was a swimming pool there. One time the whole troop was going there for a swim. When we got there they let everybody else in the pool except this other Japanese and me. They said, "You can't swim here, we don't let Japanese in." Naturally we felt pretty raw but I tried to forget about it and say, "It's just a little thing. No use eating your heart out about it."

I got along well with Caucasians in public school. I got along pretty well in high school. But I noticed that after high school most of my Caucasian friends drifted away. The race wall was up and I couldn't make any headway against it. They talk about mingling with other people. You can't mingle with others if you can't live where they live, if you can't go where they go, and if you can't work where they work.

The thing that really woke me up was the work angle. I took in a lot of that stuff about democracy and bettering yourself that they taught me in school. So after I finished high school I enrolled at the Frank Wiggins Trade School. I went in for training in electricity and radio technician. You know, I think the Frank Wiggins Trade School is one of the best in the country. Their plan is to have

Tags identify these American citizens as they travel to an assembly center. Photo from the Bancroft Library, University of California, Berkeley.

their men working part-time getting practical experience while they are going to school. They have very little trouble placing their men. They have all sorts of connections.

So I was working along there, doing as well as or better than most of the students. Only they got part-time jobs and I didn't get any. I didn't think anything of it for the first six months.

After all, I figured that I didn't know much yet and that anyone so inexperienced shouldn't expect too much. But as time went on it just got funny. I knew the head of the place pretty well. He's some kind of a foreigner, a Brazilian, I believe. He had no race prejudice and did his best to help me. Why, I have sat by his desk while he phoned around trying to find a place that would take me on! He'd call up his former students, fellows who owed a lot to him and with whom he had placed many white students, and they turned him down as soon as they heard I was Japanese. I was there two years and a half and I never got a job. I thought to myself, "What the hell am I doing here? What am I spending my money for if it doesn't get me any farther than this?"

Sure, I could have got a job as a gardener or a houseboy or in a vegetable stall. But I had my fill of that and I wanted work in the line I had trained myself for. And it isn't only the money and pride. You are held down in your associations and your social life if you can't get a job in your own line.

Even before the war I was fed up with the way I was treated here. I realized that any white foreigner who came here had a better chance than I had. But I have a Japanese face that I can't change, and as long as I live I'll be discriminated against in this country. Look at the difference in the way they treated the Italians and Germans and what they did to us. You can't tell me that having a Japanese face didn't make a difference. Now they say, "It's all a mistake. We're sorry," and expect us to forget ... and go off and fight in the army. But the thing that gets me is that it wasn't any little group or individual that did it, but the United States Government. If your own government is against you and if citizenship doesn't count, what's the use of hanging around, I say?

I don't expect any easy time in Japan.... I expect a much harder time of it there, at least for the first two years, than I ever had here. But when I get turned down for a job it will be because there isn't a job, and not because I look different from someone else....

It's a funny thing to think about.... Here this government can draft me and send me anywhere to fight. And yet I am not free. I can't go a few miles to Lone Pine to buy myself something. I'm not afraid to die, and I'll fight for any country that treats me right, but I've gone through too much to fall for talk about democracy in this country any more.

WORLD WAR II:
CLOSING THE BOOKS

Editor's Introduction: Although some Japanese Americans returned to Japan, the great majority stayed in the United States and stoically accepted the official nullification of their civil rights and the loss of their homes, property, and businesses. Further, many Japanese Americans played an active part in the American war effort. The famous 442d Regimental Combat Team, which fought in France and Italy and became the most decorated unit in the U.S. Army, was made up almost entirely of volunteers and draftees from the Japanese American community. In many cases, these soldiers fought and died for a country that confined their families in concentration camps.

As a group, the Japanese Americans reacted to the camps with far less hatred, violence, and disaffection than might have been expected. Inevitably, however, the "relocation" experience left its mark. There was enormous financial loss, and compensation for this loss was slow in coming and pitifully inadequate when it came. Here is a news item from 1965: [60]

He was everything an immigrant ought to be—a tall, vital young man, ambitious, hardworking and adventurous. For a while he was a laborer on the railroads, then a sardine fisherman, a laundry operator, an oil driller, finally a farmer. He sent back to the old country for a wife, produced two sons and, in 1927, took a chance on some apparently worthless alkali flats in the San Joaquin Valley. There he created the largest rice-growing, milling and packaging operation in California, and there, fourteen years later, he came to grief. For Keisaburo Koda was the wrong kind of immigrant—a Japanese—in a nation suddenly at war with Japan.

Stringent measures against West Coast Japanese both foreign and native-born went into effect. Koda was forced to stop operating his business, his sons had to leave college and the members of the family, like 110,000 others of Japanese ancestry, were sent to detention camps. Rather than sell his business, Koda placed his mill, factory, and 4,000 acres of land in the hands of a trusted friend.

When the war ended, the Kodas returned to California to find that their trusted friend—who held power of attorney—had sold off the mill, the machinery and 3,000 acres of land—for his own profit. They had 990 acres left, and on these the family buckled down to make a new start. The banks were willing to make loans, there was some old machinery still about and his sons showed the same business acumen as their father. Over the postwar years the family gradually recouped its fortune.

Meanwhile, there was little compensation for the Kodas or any of their fellow sufferers. (The Federal Reserve Bank estimated the property loss of JapaneseAmericans at $400 million.) For those who went to court, the claims dragged on endlessly. Last week, the final one was settled. For a prewar holding worth allegedly $2.4 million, the U.S. Court of Claims awarded 15 percent indemnity ($362,500) to the Koda family—or what remained of it. Keisaburo Koda died in 1960 at the age of 83. His son, William, died in 1961. But Edward, the surviving son, totally unbitter, remembered the statement his father had made to the court in the dismal days shortly after the war. "I have every bit of faith in American democracy," the old man had said. "I have absolute confidence in American justice." Certainly, he was 15 percent right.

THE OLD REMINDERS

Editor's Introduction: In a famous aside during the election campaign of 1968, vice-presidential candidate Spiro Agnew referred to a Japanese American reporter as "the fat Jap." During the Senate Watergate hearings in 1973, the lawyer for two of the witnesses referred to Senator Daniel Inouye (D., Hawaii) as "that little Jap." Said the lawyer shortly thereafter: "That's just the way I speak. I consider it a description of the man—I wouldn't mind being called a little American." Ultimately, the lawyer apologized to Senator Inouye.

Bill Hosokawa, the author of the following selection, is a journalist and historian whose father came to the United States from Japan in 1899 to work as a railroad section-hand. [61]

NOT LONG AGO I was introduced at a cocktail party to a fairly important political figure. Noticing my Japanese features and trying to make conversation, he asked, "Mr. Hosokawa, how long have you been in our country?"

If I had spoken with an accent the question would have been logical. But I am American-born and American-educated and make my living as a writer and editor—in English. Noting his youth, I replied with a smile: "Sir, I think I have been in our country ten or fifteen years longer than you."

He blushed as he realized his *faux pas.* "I'm sorry," he said, "I just wasn't thinking."

How right. He would not have asked a black or a Hispanic how long he had lived in our country. But lurking somewhere in the back of his mind was an old Stereotype—that Orientals are different and couldn't possibly be part of the American melting pot.

More startling is the experience of Utah-born David Ushio, the third generation of his family in that mountain state. Representing the Japanese American Citizens League, a national civic organization, Ushio was seeking a Midwestern Congressman's support for legislation affecting his group when he was asked, "Will you guarantee to me that your country will never bomb Pearl Harbor again?"

Made in Japan.

Every year, Americans salute more and more American flags that weren't made in America. Flags that bear the stars and stripes and little tags reading Made in Japan or Taiwan or Hong Kong.

Those flags aren't the only things with such labels. As low-wage, foreign goods flood the market, American industries shut down. As industries shut down, people lose jobs.

When people lose their jobs, they can't buy the things you make. Chances are if Betsy Ross

(the Philadelphia seamstress who made the first American flag for George Washington) were alive today, she'd be standing in line for her unemployment check.

So help yourself and help us by looking for the union label in everything you buy. You can find our label in women's and children's garments.

This label stands for the creativity of American design, the skill of American workmanship, the importance of American jobs.

Union Label Department, International Ladies' Garment Workers' Union, 22 W. 38th Street, New York, N.Y. 10018

In late 1972, the International Ladies' Garment Workers' Union exhibited this advertisement in New York's subways.

It is preposterous and tragic that a member of Congress—where three Japanese Americans are serving with distinction—should be so ignorant. Still, old misconceptions die hard and it is easy to understand why attorney John J. Wilson, in a moment of pique last week, made angry reference to Senator Daniel K. Inouye of Hawaii as "that little Jap" in connection with the Watergate hearings.

As a person of Wilson's achievement should know, the word "Jap" carries a special bitterness that is not paralleled by Jew or Swede or Turk. "Jap" was shouted as an angry epithet in the West Coast's long and shameful history of persecution against Japanese immigrants and their American-born children....

100 PROTEST GARMENT UNION ADS AS HARMFUL

More than 100 people—Japanese Americans, Chinese-Americans, blacks, Puerto Ricans, and whites—held a demonstration on Broadway outside the International Ladies Garment Workers Union Building yesterday to protest what they said was the union's racist advertising campaign.

Chanting, "Black, brown, yellow, white/working people must unite," they picketed on the sidewalk between 54th and 55th Streets from noon to 2 P.M.

They were protesting an advertisement that shows a large American flag with the words "Made in Japan" under it, and, in smaller letters, the question: "Has your job been exported to Japan yet? If not, it soon will be." Such posters have been displayed in subway trains since the beginning of August.

Source: *New York Times*, October 26, 1972.

The evacuation experience failed to alienate any substantial number of Japanese Americans. Thousands of them volunteered when the Army finally permitted them to enlist. One who did was 18-year-old Dan Inouye of Hawaii where, ironically, the U.S. found it expedient NOT to evacuate the Japanese Americans for reasons of "military necessity."

Inouye went on to win a battlefield commission with the all-Nisei 442d Regimental Combat Team in the European theater. Nine days before the end of the war in Italy, while directing an attack against a German strong point, Inouye lost his right arm. He received the Distinguished Service Cross.

Wilson's angry "that little Jap" epithet must have stirred recollections for Inouye. On his way home to Honolulu in 1945, Capt. Dan Inouye, his empty sleeve pinned to beribboned tunic, was denied a haircut by a San Francisco barber who snarled: "We don't serve Japs here."

Despite Wilson's outburst, most Japanese Americans would agree that their acceptance has been vastly improved since 1941. Thanks to the Nisei military record, their loyalty is unquestioned.

Yet there remains a fear that the old animosities are not far below the surface. In a new time of crisis, as when relations between Washington and Tokyo become strained, many Japanese Americans wonder if once again they will be made the highly visible scapegoats of national frustration and anger. Unwittingly, John Wilson may have reminded us of this possibility.

THE NEW ACTIVISM

Editor's Introduction: It is only in the third and fourth generations of Japanese Americans that radical activism has begun to take root. This development is due in part to America's Asian policy and in part to the rise of "Third World" movements from which the Japanese Americans have taken heart. It is also due to a reaction among younger Japanese Americans against their elders. In the eyes of these young people, many of the older Japanese Americans went too far in accommodating themselves to white society and white values. For these elders, there is a term of derision: "banana"—yellow on the outside, white on the inside.

The author of this poem (meant to be read aloud), Nobuko Joann Miyamoto, is a radical activist and songwriter who works in the Latino and Asian communities of New York City. Although probably too young to have experienced herself the "relocation" years, she draws upon the whole history of the Japanese American community in America. [62]

When I was young
kids used to ask me
what are you?
I'd tell them what my mom told me
I'm an American
chin chin Chinaman
you're a Jap!
flashing hot inside
I'd go home
my mom would say
don't worry
he who walks alone walks faster
people kept asking me
what are you?
and I would always answer
I'm an American

319

they'd say
no, what nationality?
I'm an American
that's where I was born
flashing hot inside
and when I'd tell them what they wanted to know
Japanese....
Oh I've been to Japan

I'd get it over with
so they could catalogue and file me
pigeonhole me
so they'd know just how
to think of me
priding themselves
they could guess the difference
between Japanese and Chinese
they had me wishing I was what I'd
been seeing in movies and on T.V.
on billboards and in magazines

and I tried
while they were making laws in California against us owning land
we were trying to be American
and laws against us intermarrying with white people
we were trying to be American
when they put us in concentration camps
we were trying to be American
our people volunteered to fight against their own country
trying to be American
when they dropped the atom bomb on Hiroshima and Nagasaki
we were still trying
finally we made it
most of our parents
fiercely dedicated to give us
a good education
to give us everything they never had
we made it
now they use us as an example
to the blacks and browns
how we made it
how we overcame.

but there was always
someone asking me
what are you?

now I answer
I'm an Asian
and they say
why do you want to separate yourselves?
now I say
I'm Japanese
and they say
don't you know this is the greatest country in the world?
now I say in America
I'm part of the third world people
and they say
if you don't like it here
why don't you go back?

EPILOGUE

JAPAN HAS NURTURED one of the world's great cultures. Its history is a significant part of world history. In both war and peace, that culture and history have had an impact far beyond the islands which make up Japan. As the last section attests, immigrants from Japan have played an important role in U.S. history (Brazil is a second country where Japanese immigrants have figured large). Japanese businesses—Toyota, for example—play a major role in many countries. Individual Japanese—professional baseball players, for example, but also classical musicians and modern dancers—perform around the world. Japanese architects have transformed world architecture. Japanese students and tourists are an important feature of the world scene. Where would we be today without *karaoke* and *anime*? And don't forget *jūdo* and *karate* and *sushi* and a host of other Japanese exports. Like all industrialized societies, Japan contributes as well to major world problems like pollution and global warming.

The reverse holds true, too. Non-Japanese play a major role in Japan today: businesspeople from the U. S. and Europe and China, *sumō* wrestlers from the U.S. and Mongolia (each country has supplied several recent grand champions), Hollywood actors, musicians, baseball players. There is even a reverse migration from Brazil: Brazilians of Japanese descent emigrating to the land from which their ancestors came.

How do we think about the complexity of today's global community? To be a citizen today of the U.S. or Japan or China: what does it mean? Are there still important differences?

There are at least two major approaches to this issue. They stand in sharp contrast. One emphasizes differences among nations and cultures. It makes statements that begin "Japanese think that..." or "Americans think that..." or "Chinese think that..." It stresses differences among cultures. It looks for the historical origins of difference in climate, religion, language, behavior.

The other approach stresses similarities across cultures in the twenty-first century. The U.S. and Japan are both highly industrialized economies. Those economies impose their own imperatives on each society. Is life in Osaka today all that different from life in Kansas City? Is life in small-town Japan today all that different from life in the small towns of the U.S.? The internet has brought the world closer together. And the common dilemmas of the twenty-first century—global warming, war and peace, the haves and the have-nots (both among nations and within nations)—seem to overshadow the differences among cultures. Who, after all, can complete the sentence, "Americans think that..."? The U.S. is so diverse a culture that the range of opinions and customs is so broad as to frustrate anyone trying to say, "Americans think that...." Though superficially less diverse, Japan too encompasses a wide range of people and practices and thoughts.

Having read of aspects of "Japanese" traditions and behaviors, we may no longer be able to say with confidence, "Japanese think that...." The existing differences between Japan and the U.S. in food and housing and language and customs may seem less significant than the similarities. We have read about Japan and the Japanese. We started by asking who they are, what their experiences have been, what their values are. Along the way we have been asking, too, who we are, what our experiences have been, what our values are. We go in search of "them" and find—perhaps—ourselves.

SOURCES

1. This essay is by Richard H. Minear. The statistics come from various standard sources, including the United Nations Statistics Division, *UN Statistical Yearbook 2006*, and *Europa World Comparative Statistics*.

2. Maynard Parker, *Life Magazine*, ©1967 Time, Inc. Reprinted by permission.

3. Shotaro Ishinomori, *Japan, Inc.: Introduction to Japanese Economics* (*The Comic Book*), translated by Betsey Scheiner (Berkeley: University of California Press, 1988), pp. 3-9. Copyright ©1988 by the Regents of the University of California and the University of California Press. Reproduced by permission.

4. Banana Yoshimoto, *Kitchen*, translated by Megan Backus (New York: Grove, 1988), pp. 3-4, 8-10, 43.

5. Miyabe Miyuki, *All She Was Worth*, translated by Alfred Birnbaum (New York: Houghton-Mifflin, 1996), pp. 101-106.

6. Okuda Hideo, *In the Pool*, translated by Giles Murray (IBC, 2006), pp. 147-149.

7. Richard Minear, adapted from *Japan Report* (June 16, 1979), and *Understanding Japan* (May 1992).

8. Adapted from "Instructions of a Mito Prince to His Retainers," translated by Ernest W. Clement, in *Transactions of the Asiatic Society of Japan*, 26 (1898), pp. 135-36.

9. From W.T. de Bary, ed., *Sources of Japanese Tradition* (New York: Columbia University Press, 1958), pp. 387-88.

10. Tamotsu Iwado, "'Hagakure Bushido' or the Book of the Warrior," *Cultural Nippon*, 7:3 (1939), pp. 38-39, 55, 45.

11. J. Carey Hall, "Teijo's Family Instructions," *Transactions and Proceedings of the Japan Society of London*, 14 (1916), pp. 153, 146.

12. Adapted from Tadatsu Ishiguro, ed., *Ninomiya Sontoku* (Tokyo: Kenkyusha, 1955), pp. 131-32, 146-47, 155-57.

13. Ihara Saikaku, "The Eternal Storehouse of Japan," translated by G. W. Sargent, in Donald Keene, ed., *Anthology of Japanese Literature* (New York: Grove Press, 1955), pp. 357-62. Reprinted by permission.

14. W.T. de Bary, ed., *Sources, op. cit.*, p. 544.

15. From Donald Keene, "Hirata Atsutane and Western Learning," *T'oung Pao*, 42:5 (1954), pp. 374-76.

16. Ibid.

17. From *Select Documents on Japanese Foreign Policy, 1853-1868,* translated and edited by W. G. Beasley and published by Oxford University Press in 1955 for the School of Oriental and African Studies. Reprinted by permission.

18. Fukuzawa Yukichi, "Gakumon no susume," in *Fukuzawa Yukichi zenshū;* III, translated by Richard Minear (Tokyo: Iwanami, 1969), pp. 29-31.

19. From Carmen Blacker, *The Japanese Enlightenment* (Cambridge: Cambridge University Press, 1964), pp. 129-36. Reprinted by permission.

20. Kobayashi Takiji, *The Factory Ship* and *The Absentee Landlord,* edited and translated by Francis T. Motofuji (Seattle: University of Washington Press, 1973), pp. 37-43; xvii-xix. Reprinted by permission of University of Tokyo Press.

21. *Foreign Relations of the United States: Japan 1931-1941*, Vol. II (Washington, D.C.: U.S. Government Printing Office, 1943), pp. 93-94.

22. Richard Kim, *Lost Names* (New York: Praeger, 1970; reproduced by Universe Publishing, 1988), pp. 98-106, 110-15. Excerpts reprinted by permission of Universe.

23. Richard Minear.

24. Nobutaka Ike, ed., *Japan's Decision for War* (Stanford: Stanford University Press, 1967), p. 230.

25. Iichiro Tokutomi, *The Imperial Rescript Declaring War on the United States and British Empire*, translated by Tasaki Hanama (Osaka: Osaka Mainichi, 1942).

26. Adapted from Takeyama Michio, "Ichikō in 1944," in *The Scars of War: Tokyo in World War II,* edited and translated by Richard Minear (Rowman & Littlefield, 2007).

27. Toge Sankichi, "Poems of the Atomic Bomb," in *Hiroshima: Three Witnesses,* edited and translated by Richard Minear (Princeton: Princeton University Press, 1990), p. 281. Reprinted by permission.

28. *Ibid.,* pp. 306-07, 315-16.

29. Kurihara Sadako, *Black Eggs,* edited and translated by Richard Minear (Ann Arbor: Center for Japanese Studies, University of Michigan, 1994), p. 67. This and below selections reprinted by permission. Copyright © 1994. Center for Japanese Studies, University of Michigan.

30. *Ibid.,* pp. 226-27.

31. *Ibid.,* pp. 257-58.

32. Ienaga Saburō, *Japan's Past, Japan's Future: One Historian's Odyssey,* translated by Richard H. Minear (Rowman & Littlefield, 2001), pp. 138-139, 176-177.

33. Ōe Kenzaburō, "The Right to Deny Japan," *Japan Quarterly,* 13:2 (April-June 1966), pp. 226-30. Reprinted by permission.

34. Ishihara Shintarō, *The Japan That Can Say No,* edited and translated by Frank Baldwin (New York: Simon & Schuster, 1991), pp. 42-43, 26-30, 84-85, 87-93, 104-06, 114-16. Copyright © 1989 by Ishihara Shintarō. Reprinted by permission of Sanford J. Greenburger Associates.

35. Kurihara Sadako, *Black Eggs, op. cit.,* pp. 212-13.

36. *Ibid.,* pp. 228-30.

37. *Ibid.,* pp. 259-60.

38. International Society for Educational Information, ed., *Japan in Modern History: Japanese School Textbooks,* 2 vols. (Tokyo: Shobundo, 1996), II: 140-145.

39. International Society for Educational Information, ed., *Japan in Modern History: High School* (Tokyo: Shobundo, 1995), I: 460-463. This translation differs somewhat.

40. Adapted and abridged with permission from Kariya Takehiko et al., "Textbook Authorization: Is It Any Use?" *Japan Echo,* April 2007; the article appeared originally in *Ronza,* January 2007, pp. 102-117.

41. Yamakawa Masao, "The Talisman," translated by Edward Seidensticker, *Life,* 57:2-3 (September 11, 1964), pp. 94-97.

42. Ishimure Michiko, "Pure Land, Poisoned Sea," translated by James Kirkup and Nakano Michio, *Japan Quarterly,* 18:3 (July-September 1971), pp. 299-306. Reprinted by permission.

43. Richard Halloran, "A Case Against Pollution," © 1973 by The New York Times Company. Reprinted by permission.

44. Richard Minear.

45. "A Whale of a Problem," *Japan Quarterly,* 19:4 (October-December 1972), pp. 391-94. Adapted by permission.

46. Sakai Denroku, "Switch Off," *Japan Quarterly,* 19:2 (April-June 1972), pp. 218-20. Reprinted by permission.

47. Adapted with permission from "View Point," *Japan Now,* October 10, 2000.

48. Adapted from Shingoro Takaishi, *Women and Wisdom of Japan,* translated by Basil Hall Chamberlain (London: John Murray, 1914), pp. 33-34, 38-39, 44-46.

49. Tanizaki Junichiro, *Some Prefer Nettles*, translated by Edward Seidensticker (New York: Alfred A. Knopf, Inc., 1955), pp. 3-29. Excerpted and reprinted by permission.

50. Eric Whitehead, "Driven Beyond Dignity," © 1964 Time, Inc. Reprinted by permission from *Sports Illustrated*, March 16, 1964.

51. Glenda S. Roberts, *Staying on the Line: Blue-Collar Women in Contemporary Japan* (Honolulu: University of Hawaii Press, 1994), pp. 160-167.

52. Adapted from Jane Condon, *A Half Step Behind* (New York: Dodd, Mead & Co., 1985), pp. 133-40. Reprinted by permission of Charles E. Tuttle Co., Tokyo.

53. Mizuko Ito, Daisuke Okabe, and Misa Matsuda, eds., *Personal, Portable, Pedestrian: Mobile Phones in Japanese Life* (Cambridge: M.I.T. Press, 2005), pp. 104-05, 269-70, 288-89, 53, 209-10, 214, 288.

54. Matt Richtel, "It Don't Mean a Thing if You Ain't Got That Ping," *New York Times*, April 22, 2007, IV: 5.

55. Adapted with permission and assistance from the author from "Japanese Only: The Otaru Hotspring Case and Discrimination Against 'Foreigners' in Japan," www.Japanfocus.org/176html.

56. Text in E.G. Mears, *Resident Orientals on the Pacific Coast* (Chicago: University of Chicago Press, 1927), pp. 494-504.

57. Gene Oishi, "Remember Pearl Harbor, and Then...," *Los Angeles Times West* magazine, March 12, 1967. Reprinted by permission.

58. *Ibid.*

59. Excerpted from WRA Community Analysis Notes No. 5, November 10, 1944, in *Relocation-Readings* (Pleasantville, New York: Olcott Forward, Inc., 1970), pp. 26-28.

60. *Newsweek*, October 18, 1965. Reprinted by permission.

61. Bill Hosokawa, "The Old Reminders," © 1973 by The New York Times Company. Reprinted by permission.

62. Amy Tachiki, Eddie Wong, and Franklin Odo, eds., *Roots: An Asian American Reader* (Los Angeles: UCLA Asian American Studies Center, 1971), pp. 98-99. Reprinted by permission.

INDEX